BIG LEAGUE BABBLE ON

CONTENTS

ONE

HOW TO PROVOKE THOUSANDS OF RABID SOCCER FANS

(or, as the police run alongside my convertible,
I hear shots ring out and hundreds screaming,
"Death to Gallagher!")

Ahhh, soccer, the "beautiful game." Question: What's the "highlight of the night" in a nil–nil tie with zero shots on goal in a game? Just asking. For decades now I have enraged soccer fans by suggesting it's the stupidest game ever invented. I still believe I may have a point when a team can play a whole game without a shot on goal and still win the league championship. Hello, Seattle Sounders (who beat Toronto FC for the 2016 MLS title without *one shot on net*). Just saying — I *hate* soccer. I know "hate" is a strong word, but it's such a strong hate. I've seen the game on grand scales — World Cup qualifying matches in London and Dublin. And, more importantly, I've played the game. I get it. I made senior varsity soccer in high school. It was a joke. My team at Montreal West H.S. was brutal. Maybe that's why I hate it so much. Honestly, we looked like the Island of Misfit Toys. You didn't, and still don't, have to be fast or big or coordinated or smart to play. Soccer players are usually the guys who couldn't make the cut in other sports. And soccer players are pansies. I yell, laughingly, at my siblings and neighbours who take their kids to soccer games. Let the kid play hockey, baseball, football … come *onnn*! Buy the kid a glove; let him or her play a real sport, I plead …

You see, soccer is the most popular sport simply because it's the least expensive to play. Let's just break that down. All one has to do is look at the economic status of the countries where it's popular to understand that. Hell, if you have five cans and two old boots for goalposts, then you've got a game. Soccer isn't popular because it earned acceptance; soccer is popular because most countries, underdeveloped or otherwise, had no choice but to accept it.

Soccer players openly weep when they trip over another player, as if they've been shot. Hey, here comes the stretcher! Wait, the "magic" sponge will bring them back to life. Miraculous! And "footy" is freaking boring. *Bore*-freaking-*ing*. My standard line on soccer is that the eyes of North American sports fans aren't trained for the sport. We want goals and runs, damn it. Lots of them. Perhaps it's because the first NHL game I ever saw was at the Montreal Forum back in 1972 when the Canadiens beat the L.A. Kings 10–2. I like ten-goal games from flying Frenchmen playing fire-waging hockey. Baseball? Love it. Listen, I saw Bob Gibson of the Cardinals pitch a number of times at Jarry Park in Montreal. The good news is all of his games were under ninety minutes. The bad news is that they ended 1–0 Cardinals. You want a pitching duel, fine. A goaltending duel, great. World Cup soccer? *You* watch it. But where? When I was growing up there was no ABC Monday Night Soccer game on TV. Or an NBC game of the week. All we saw were snippets of the great Pelé scoring for Brazil during the opening montage on *Wide World of Sports*, for goodness sake. Truth be told, if there was a soccer game on, you wouldn't see me tuning in. And what is this with kicking backward? We like our offences moving forward, not backward. Then there's the fact that they're not allowed to use their hands — what the eff? David Letterman and I have a lot in common when it comes to sports. He made a great suggestion for improving NBA basketball, and I've been quoting him on it for twenty years: give both teams one hundred points and let them play the final two minutes. Smart, eh? Dave hates soccer, too. Among his reasons? Here are some from one of his famous top-ten lists:

* Loud horns make it hard to nap through boring parts;
* Bench-clearing brawls not as much fun without bats or sticks;
* Lots of players with umlauts in their names;
* Doesn't have the heart-pounding action of a five-hour baseball game;
* Too much kicking, not enough rasslin'; and look out …
* Too many foreigners.

Ouch. Yet some of these "foreigners" kill people over soccer matches. Hundreds of fans have been killed before, during, and after harmless footy matches. The worst killing was that of Columbian defender Andrés Escobar, who accidentally put the ball in his own net at the 1994 World Cup and became a massive national disappointment. Ten days later, the twenty-seven-year-old Escobar was shot dead in a Columbian disco parking lot in a killing that sparked national outrage. The killers yelled, "Thanks for the own goal!" as they shot him six times. Charming.

I certainly don't want to get killed over a soccer match, but it almost happened. This brings us to the 1994 World Cup final game. I was in Toronto's Little Italy reporting on the championship finale of a sport that I categorically, without question, unequivocally, and beyond any doubt, despise. Well, these observations and more were all contained in my wildly popular Q commentary just before the World Cup final. Not to worry; there aren't any foreigners living in the Greater Toronto Area. Or soccer fans, for that matter. I kid.

Thousands upon thousands of fans gathered at the corner of College and Clinton, a perfect storm of Brazilian/Portuguese and Italian fans waiting for the outcome of this classic footy tilt. Classic, my classical gas. After 120 tedious and goalless minutes — yes, it ended *zero fucking zero* — the match was decided for the first time by a penalty shoot-out. After four rounds, Brazil led 3–2, and Roberto Baggio had to score to keep Italy's hopes alive. He missed by shooting it way over the crossbar, and the Brazilians were crowned champions for the fourth time. That made for a lot of pissed-off Italians. And a lot of drunken Brazilians pouring in from the surrounding neighbourhoods. And there's me, Mr. Soccer himself, on top of the CityTV "live eye" truck broadcasting the results to the football-crazed masses. It wasn't even my regular shift! I was just filling in for the weekend anchor, who'd taken the day off. Remember, hockey fans tried to burn down Vancouver after they lost the Stanley Cup. Hell, my hometown of Montreal attempted the same thing and they *won* the Cup in '93. Some of these Italian fans wanted blood. Well, fee-fi-fo-fum, it turned out they wanted the blood of a soccer-hating Irishman. Me.

The word quickly spread. John "I Hate Soccer" Gallagher was in the area. Now, while we had a terrific security staff at CityTV, nothing was going to stop these yobs if they wanted to get at me, so we alerted Toronto's finest. These fans knew the sportscast was over at 6:30, so they got themselves prepared. The police suggested I lay low in the truck until I had to climb up and begin the sportscast. During this time the yahoos were "fuelling up" with pitchers of beer. We were heavily outnumbered — "we" being two or three monstrous station security men, a half dozen police officers, and little old "wine drinker" me against a crowd of thousands. I had been heckled for most of the day by soccer purists who weren't demonstrating the same eloquence as me with regards to their sport, and they knew when the time was to strike. I did get thousands of cheers as we panned the street, zooming in on raucous Brazilian fans, resplendent in green, yellow, and blue, whose team had just won 1–0, but none were coming from the dozen or so jack-wagons whose hands were filled with the pitchers of cold, delicious beer that they were planning to use as projectiles instead of thirst-quenchers.

Sportscast over, I climbed down the ladder on the side of the truck and braced myself for my first golden shower. No, not that kind. Sorry. Funny thing, though, is these soccer fans should have used their hands more when playing their stupid sport because they were lousy shots. Pitcher after pitcher of beer came heading toward me, but they completely missed, instead soaking the cops and my security guards. *Big* mistake. A melee broke out. One of the City staffers grabbed a guy. Fists and more beer flew. More shoving. The police, who had been doused and were pissed off because of it, intervened. But the cops knew the golden rule in show business: always take care of the talent. And since I was the nearest thing to talent in the area, that meant me. The boys in blue hurriedly got me the hell out of there. Remember, there were thousands of people in the street and more on the way, and the cops had arrived on horses and bikes. There was no ducking into the back of a police car, because there wasn't one in sight.

Another thing — I always drive my way to these live-eye events and park nearby because the technicians and camera crew on the truck have to drag miles of cable and unhook everything and are usually an hour-plus when wrapping up. My car? A 1992 BMW 325i convertible. The roof down, natch. Another mistake. A German car. Germany was the defending champ in 1994. These fans *hated* Germany's soccer team. Add in a couple of world wars and the vibe was not good. So we bounced through the drunken hooligans to my parked car, with some of them still in chase. And, like Batman jumping into the Batmobile, I steeplechased myself into the front seat, started the car, and peeled out. Reminiscent of that scene in the Clint Eastwood movie *In the Line of Fire*, six cops, three on each side, jogged beside the car and ran me out of harm's way and far, far, far from the madding crowd. The soccer douche-waffles were still in chase, shouting, "Death to Gallagher! Death to Gallagher!" Did I hear gunshots, or was that just Guido's '77 Firebird's exhaust backfiring? No matter; I was hammer down, northbound, and out of Little Italy–town. Thank you, 14 Division.

I wondered if any of the cops would have taken a bullet for me. Years later I ran into one of them who remembered the incident well. He said that he in fact *had* taken a bullet for me that fateful day. It was a Coors Light Silver Bullet. Hey now!

TWO

I SHOULD BE
DEAD BY NOW

(or, death by ooga booga or John
Kordic ripping your limbs off)

There's a terrific and underrated film called *Let It Ride* starring one of my all-time favourites, Richard Dreyfuss. He plays Jay Trotter, a dreamer and small-time gambler who receives a hot tip at the racetrack. A woman in the film says to him, "You might be walking around lucky and not even know it." And you know, I've thought about that for years. Sounds like something from a fortune cookie.

Near-death experiences? Gee, where do I start? I once got into a car accident so bad after winning a provincial softball championship that I still have shards of glass from a '75 Volvo in my elbow. A crash so bad it took hours to drag the wreckage out of the tangled brush after sending everyone to hospital.

Have you ever had someone break into your house? It happened to me in a nice neighbourhood in Halifax in the early eighties, on a Sunday night. After being awoken by the break-in, my roommate's bat-wielding boyfriend chased the burglar down the back steps. He used his powerized Willie Mays Louisville Slugger and batted 1.000 on his head. Funny, I've never slept well on a Sunday night since.

* * *

This is spooky. One afternoon in 1973, my dad dropped me off at a theatre on Saint Catherine Street in Montreal to take in *Battle for the Planet of the Apes* (easily the worst film of the franchise). I planned to take the subway home afterward. A good-looking gentleman in his late twenties struck up a conversation with me on my way home. We talked about stuff like the Canadiens' Stanley Cup parade, which I'd attended, on that very street a few weeks before. Harmless chatter. While film of the Habs victory over the Blackhawks was rare, this "nice" man told me he actually had footage of the Canadiens' Cup victory on 8mm that he could play for me on a screen back at his apartment. "Neato!" Well, trying to be polite as possible, I told him I had to decline. He persisted as he "walked" me to the Guy Street subway. He even paid for my ticket and escorted me down to the platform. What a nice man, making sure I got home safe. Right. He kept telling me how cool this footage of the Stanley Cup playoffs was and that

I would really enjoy it. He even, coincidentally, got off at Atwater subway stop, where my bus home — the famous 162 — was waiting. It didn't dawn on me what his intentions might be until he put his hand on my arm as I went up the stairs from the train. I quickly pulled my arm away. I'll never know if he had a chloroform-soaked handkerchief in his coat pocket, but I wasn't going to hang around to find out. As he lunged at me one last time, I kicked our perverted friend in the chuckies and ran for the bus. I told my family over dinner when I got home, and they were aghast. They told me that, although I'd completely done the right thing, I was one lucky young eleven-year-old.

* * *

The clock had already struck midnight on New Year's. My friend and I had just left a party in Notre Dame de Grâce, which can be a tough 'hood in Montreal. He lived a block away from Walkley Avenue, which has had a bad reputation for decades in my hometown, what with street gangs and murders. The old expression still stands: "Run, don't Walkley." We were walking on Sherbrooke waiting for a bus or a cab that never came. We were just kids, and we were being silly, trying to wave down cars and being loud. Not good for two a.m. on any night, let alone New Year's Eve. We saw some guy across the street walking with his girlfriend and yelled something at them. I'm not sure what it was, but it *wasn't* "Happy New Year." Minutes later, after the guy had escorted his girlfriend home, I saw him crossing the street toward us. Out of nowhere, this guy just started kicking and punching the two of us. We got a couple of shots in, but he floored me and started pounding on my friend Jim. Did he have a knife? *Screw this,* I thought, and I ran back to where the party had been and crashed there. Let that be a lesson to you: When confronted by an assailant, you don't have to outrun the attacker; you just have to outrun your friend. Works for bear attacks, too.

This was another close one. It was the mid-1990s. I was driving a Molson Indy Corvette Stingray, and my girlfriend and I were hammer down, westbound to Windsor-town, where she'd grown up. We decided to join some of her friends in their BMW to go across the river to Detroit for dinner at a lovely seafood bistro in Grosse Pointe. On the way, we had to go through a somewhat shady area of Detroit. At a stoplight, we saw a guy on crutches obviously struggling as he tried to cross the street. He even fell in front of our car — several times, mind you — while flailing and waving at us to help. The guy driving the car said to us, "Don't get out of this vehicle." The man continued to lie there and scream in pain for two or three red lights, pleading for us to help him. And all that time we hardly noticed the two cars that had pulled up on either side of us. We were waiting for someone, anyone, to get out and help the poor soul. Of course, I was told later it's all part of a scam. Here's the trick: The thugs wait for an unwitting motorist to get out and help the crippled man. Once out of the car, it's a gun to the temple, and kiss that Bimmer, and perhaps all of us, goodbye. Our Windsor/Detroit friend said it happened all the time. Well, I'm just glad I kept my ass in the car, or else it would have been a "Saturday Night Special" that didn't end well. I could hear the cocking of the unseen gun's hammer for hours in my head.

* * *

How about your affable author being killed by a flying truck tire while driving on Highway 401? I know that "almost" only counts in horseshoes, hand grenades, and the back seat at a drive-in, but ... I'm driving back from my morning show in the westbound lane on a gorgeous sunny day with the roof down on my BMW 325i when here comes this big, black bouncy thing headed right toward my windshield. If you've seen pictures or news footage of tires hitting cars, it's almost always instant death. Yeah, this wheel came loose from an eastbound truck, bounced over the concrete median, and had me in its sights. It would have been a direct hit. I swerved out of the way into another lane (thank goodness it was 10:30 a.m. and traffic was light), but it still skimmed inches over my head (remember, the roof was down) and I saw it bounce down the highway in my rear-view mirror. I called the OPP to ask if anyone got hit. Thankfully, no one did. Not that day, anyway. I told the officer who I was, and he said, "Gallagher, it happens all of the time, and all or most of the trucks in question are big rigs from Quebec!" He said, "The highways and streets in some cities in that province are in such bad shape that the potholes loosen the lug nuts on the wheels and off they fly." He was right: 127 incidents of detached wheels were reported on Ontario roads in 2015. It was even worse in 1997, when 215 runaway truck tires were documented. Man. That was one close shave and a haircut. Two bits?

* * *

In the eighties, doing a few lines — or, in my circles, mountains — of cocaine was ultra cool. We called them "Peruvian chit-chat flakes." Hey, if Clooney, Elton, Bowie, Oprah, sports stars Maradona and Martina Hingis, and baseball Hall of Famers Paul Molitor and Tim Raines (to name two) used it, well, at least I was in good company. Full disclosure: I did enough blow to kill a Shetland pony over the years, but it's been close to twenty years since I snorted any. I'll also admit that cocaine is a terrible drug. Vastly overrated. From nosebleeds to talking about yourself incessantly for hours while hanging out in the toilet, it's just not as cool as it seems. Don't forget hemorrhaging thousands of dollars out of your bank account and shrinking your dick to the size of an elevator button. I've seen it destroy families, cost people their homes, and cause heart attacks. I had my fun with it. Understatement of the century! But it's not worth it.

Back then cocaine made me feel invincible. Like I could conquer the world. That's why I did the stuff. I was just completely confident, and sometimes overconfident. The more you take, the more you want. Cocaine was my "on" switch.

Using coke is a lot like candy: better in moderation. I just took the stuff on weekends, but I took a lot of the stuff. Now, enjoying the party lifestyle is perfectly acceptable. After all, everyone needs a break from the nine-to-five grind. And with coke, "grind" was the operative word. But I learned that the key is self-control. I should have thought of that one long, long weekend in the late 1980s.

One Friday night, I finished my sportscast at six o'clock, so, done for the week, I decided to join a friend (a.k.a. the unofficial Q107 cocaine dealer) at a cocktail party on the Danforth. And, as was the custom on a non–"school night," we decided to get into the Peruvian marching powder quite early. We went well into the evening and the early morning hours, and it was clear that the blizzard was not going to stop anytime soon. Keep in mind there was no sleep, and not a morsel of food was consumed. He kept digging into his own stash, and we continued on all through Saturday morning. After watching *Pee-wee's Playhouse* stoned on the stuff, like a lot of my friends did ("Mekka lekka hi, mekka hiney ho!"), we snorted and drank outside in the sun, and all through the night and into Sunday morning. And drink? Coke has an annoying habit of sobering people up, causing a vicious circle. The more cocaine you have, the more sober you feel, the more you can drink. It was just cocaine and booze, without any sleep or food, until mid-afternoon on Sunday some forty-four hours later. At that point my friend/dealer left my house in East York, and I ordered the largest pizza available in the city. Yeah, that's it: go close to three days doing cocaine, eat a heavily laden sausage-and-pepperoni pizza with extra cheese, and then pull a Len Bias. (Bias was selected by the Boston Celtics as the second-overall pick in the 1986 NBA draft. He died two days after the draft from a cocaine overdose.) Now, I know of people, like my friend the successful contractor and rock 'n' roll impresario Rockin' Robin Campbell, who have allegedly done the coke-and-cocktail mix with no sleep or food for over a week, so my excursion was a blip on a radar screen, but still. Either way, I should be dead by now.

❖ ❖ ❖

How about this one? I was hosting a Grey Cup pre-game party at St. Lawrence Market in 1989. Word came in from Toronto's finest that there were fans in from Hamilton who wanted to harm me in several ways. The Ti-Cats were playing in the annual classic the following afternoon. Earlier that day, I had been unmercifully booed by pockets of fans when I was onboard the Q107 float during the Grey Cup parade up Yonge Street. I hate the CFL because it was, and still is, a bush league and a sub-standard product. Perhaps it's just my disdain for football in general. CFL, NFL, college football — it doesn't matter. This is a game with less than eleven minutes of actual action in the three-hours-plus it takes to watch it. Let's face it: football can be a lot of sizzle and sometimes not a lot of steak. From time to time I have unabashedly slammed the game of football, especially the CFL, and these people knew it. After all, it was the late-1980s, and the league was floundering, at least in Toronto. This is a city that loves winners, and the Argos hadn't won squat since 1983.

THREE

HOW DRINKING WITH JOHN GALLAGHER SAVED MARK WAHLBERG'S LIFE

(or, as the maître d' sits my girlfriend and me down
at Spago, I see Gene Kelly to the left of me, James Earl
Jones to the right, and Tony Curtis waving from the bar)

ere's a slice of my own personal philosophy when it comes to meeting movie and TV stars. I've always known that if I were to meet actors and actresses who were famous when I was growing up, I would have trouble communicating with them. I'd be star-struck. We tend to forget that they're just human beings. Imagine it from the star's perspective. What do they want from fans? The answer is: nothing more than a "Nice to meet you; have fun at the film festival." When I met Brad Pitt, it was all of, "Hi, how long are you in town? So, you're from Oklahoma, huh? Did you really break your hand filming *Se7en*? Do you mind a photo …?" And, wrap. Less than a minute. But sometimes it's just the opposite. The talented, sassy, and accommodating (she's Canadian, after all) Catherine O'Hara (*SCTV*, *Beetlejuice*, *Home Alone*) spent what seemed like hours with me at a pre-fundraiser party I emceed in the Muskokas. We had a blast re-enacting scenes from some of the wonderful films she's starred in: *Waiting for Guffman*, *Best in Show*, *A Mighty Wind*, and *For Your Consideration*.

The wrong seven. With Brad Pitt and Kimberlee Fabian at the *Seven Years in Tibet* (unfortunately not *Se7en*) gala at TIFF in 1997.

I've interviewed and had lengthy conversations with the best of the best in television, sports, music, pop culture, and the like, but I have to tell you, when it comes down to meeting movie stars, I turn to jelly. During the Toronto International Film Festival (TIFF), hundreds of the world's biggest movie stars flood the city. In the early years of the festival, you'd be able to rub elbows with the Hollywood hierarchy who headed north for those two weeks in September. If there was a party, I'd always try to crash it. After that, the objective was to get beyond the velvet rope and into the VIP section. It helps if the bouncers recognize you. You get easy access that way. That was the case during the 1997 TIFF gala, featuring a so-so movie that debuted at the fest called *Seven Years in Tibet*. It wasn't the movie that was important. It was the star of the film, who was standing a few feet away. Brad Pitt was just on the verge of superstardom. He was one of the most influential and powerful people in the American entertainment industry and an international heartthrob, and at the time he was busting out with starring roles in *A River Runs Through It*, the brilliant thriller *Se7en*, and the vastly underrated *Sleepers*. My girlfriend at the time swooned in his presence. And although photos were a no-no in the VIP section, that did not stop me from getting snap happy with Mr. Pitt. Actually, the best shot was taken by my good friend Amy Gilmour, hockey god Doug Gilmour's wife. Brad was an absolute gem. A real mensch. But you never want to take up too much of a superstar's time. I spent most of that party drinking with Canadian screen legend Gordon Pinsent.

* * *

One movie that premiered at TIFF was *Clay Pigeons*, in 1998, starring Joaquin Phoenix, Vince Vaughn, and Janeane Garofalo. The post-premiere cast party was held at Montana's on John Street. From the photo I took with the cast, it appeared as if Mr. Vaughn hadn't slept in days. Janeane and I mostly talked about her work on *The Larry Sanders Show*, one of the greatest television programs known to man. As for Phoenix, this was before his epic film *Gladiator*, or his best-actor Oscar nomination for *Walk the Line*, or even before his famous meltdown on *The Late Show with David Letterman*.

That didn't stop me from making him cry. It's true. It was completely unintentional, mind you. I told Joaquin about the time his older brother

River attended TIFF, in 1991, promoting *My Own Private Idaho*. I'd met River at a post-premiere gala at a club where I hosted Saturday-night events, called Barracuda (formerly the Copa, where I once saw the legendary Ray Charles perform and Ronnie Wood of the Stones fall off the stage repeatedly while swigging a bottle of Jack Daniels and trying to play guitar). I noticed Phoenix and his friend were clumsily attempting to stuff several bottles of beer into their jacket pockets to take back to their suite at the Four Seasons, which was a block away. I told them I could sneak what they wanted and more past security. After all, I had connections. This was my town and, thankfully for them, my bar. Joaquin laughed and said, "Yeah, that's something that River used to do at bars back in L.A." I didn't tell him about the strung-out state that his older brother was in that evening we met or, God forbid, mention River's overdosing outside Johnny Depp's club The Viper Room (a little hole-in-the-wall club I've

10cc was wrong. Big boys *do* cry. I'm about to make Joaquin Phoenix cry something awful at the premiere after-party for the equally awful film *Clay Pigeons* in 1998. With Vince Vaughn, who looks like he hasn't slept in weeks, and Janeane Garofalo. (Photo credit: John Fraser)

been to on the Sunset Strip in L.A.). If you had switched on any TV or radio station a few hours after River's death, you would have heard Joaquin's anguished 911 call being played repeatedly. Small wonder that he now freezes out anyone who trespasses on his memories if River ever comes up in interviews. With him and I, we were just two guys talking at a bar toasting an amazing actor.

I expressed my admiration for River, whose films, although he had done only a handful, for some reason I had seen most of, starting with his career breakthrough, *Stand By Me*, which would have a huge impact on me for years. Also, *Indiana Jones and the Last Crusade*, *I Love You to Death*, and even the obscure *Explorers* and *Dogfight*, a film to which he brought Joaquin, who was fifteen, on set the whole time. The two were obviously extremely close. As Joaquin and I talked some more about River over more cocktails, I saw him start to tear up and then cry. I remember giving him a quick embrace before he was shuffled off among his co-stars. At the time it dawned on me that River Phoenix had died

Sneaking beers out of the Barracuda nightclub with giggly twenty-one-year-old River Phoenix at the *My Own Private Idaho* premiere in 1991.

on Halloween night, 1993. He had been twenty-three years old. On the night I brought Joaquin Phoenix to tears in 1998, he, too, was twenty-three years old.

* * *

Bistro 990 was the place to be during the fest, conveniently located across the street from TIFF's official hotel at the time, the Sutton Place. Mike Myers and I got shnockered there one night. Mike and I went back years and years. During my Q107 days, then–station GM Don Shafer wisely signed up all of his on-air announcers to partake in Second City acting courses, which is the smartest thing a young broadcaster can enroll in. I mean, these are classes that "masters of funny" John Candy, Gilda Radner, Dan Aykroyd, Martin Short, Eugene Levy, and, later in Chicago, Tina Fey, Steve Carrell, Stephen Colbert, Amy Poehler, and dozens of other world-class alumni took to jumpstart their careers. The courses taught us to keep moving forward as actors, to never drop the ball, and to never say "no." You learned to take bigger risks, make more mistakes — and laugh about it.

Co-host and dear friend Jane Brown and I would almost always attend together, then go for drinks and watch the star-studded group of Second City players perform after class. The standout of that particular ensemble was one Mike Myers, who was perfecting an enthusiastic and sardonic long-haired metalhead from Scarborough named Wayne Campbell. Mike would sometimes drop by our classes to help out the instructors, all Second City veterans themselves. Years later, when we met up at Bistro 990, Mike remembered those days and, well, he was a Maple Leafs fanatic and wouldn't miss my nightly sportscasts on City. It broke his heart when he found out I was a Canadiens fan.

On another occasion, *The Usual Suspects* star Gabriel Byrne, the terrific Irish actor, got awfully flirty with my date for the evening, who he said reminded him of his ex-wife, actress Ellen Barkin. Frankly I didn't see the resemblance at all, but if you get a chance to sit down with the man who was shot by Keyser Söze, one of film's greatest villains, you do it. Heck, he could have thought she looked like Ernest Borgnine, as long as he stuck around for a few more drinks.

After another Canadiens win over the Leafs, Mike Myers and I ponder, Dr. Evil-like, why the Habs dynasty continues to this day. Or, at least, that day.

Another fine Irish actor, Colm Meaney, was also a regular during one TIFF. Mind you, we did not talk about his role in *Star Trek: The Next Generation*. I despised that series. No sir, it was his work in the wonderful film *The Commitments*, as Jimmy Rabbitte, Sr. and another hardly heard-of Irish film titled *The Snapper*. But the most memorable night at Bistro 990 was sitting for several hours on the patio with Golden Globe–winner (for the fabulous *In Bruges*) Colin Farrell, the hard-partying Irishman and Hollywood A-lister. Farrell's history of beer, women, and sex tapes distinguished him as a likeable, if sometimes wayward, character. Women? This guy dated Angelina Jolie and Demi Moore. Even singer Britney Spears. Britney Spears?! He was with a mate of his sitting at the next table and started up a conversation with my girlfriend Chick and me. Several rounds later, along with some good "craic," the evening ended with Colin writing his Dublin home phone number on Chick's arm as he and his best pally from Ireland stumbled off into the night. I didn't know where until I saw him the next morning on the cover of the *Toronto Sun*. The paparazzi had caught him coming out of one of the city's finest strip clubs, the Brass Rail, with a big smile on his face.

With Colin Farrell at Bistro 990 in 2002, minutes before he wrote his Dublin phone number on my girlfriend's arm.

* * *

Then there was the second week of June in 1994. I brought my new girl-friend to L.A. and Las Vegas for two weeks, and what an eventful fortnight! First of all, staying at Le Parc Hotel in West Hollywood, we were not far from where O.J. Simpson "allegedly" (yeah right) killed his ex-wife, Nicole Brown Simpson, and waiter Ronald Goldman. It was on a Sunday night, and to be there when it happened and then see the city entranced by the slow-speed white-Ford-Bronco chase days later was incredible. What timing, eh? We witnessed the beginning of the "Trial of the Century"! That was June twelfth. June fifteenth just so happened to be the gala opening for the smash hit film *The Lion King* in Los Angeles. Now, *the* place to see and be seen in Hollywood twenty or so years ago was Spago on the Sunset Strip. This was the original Spago — celebrity chef Wolfgang Puck's first restaurant, and one of most famous spots in the world. It was also virtually synonymous with star-watching.

Spago attracted almost everyone who was anyone in Hollywood, from producers to politicians to major movie stars. Regulars included people who didn't need last names attached to them, like Jack, Oprah, Warren, Goldie, Kurt, Dudley, Michael J., Whoopi, and Clint. It was nearly impossible to get a table there, especially for some schmuck from Toronto. I also loved the place because it was right next door to the famous Tower Records store on the Strip, where I would spend hours and hours buying new CDs and LPs. The first time I dined at Spago, I was seated in the backroom, nicknamed "Siberia," where they sat the unfamous normals. The washrooms were in the "front" room, where you'd go just to get a glimpse of the A-listers. There was no one of notoriety there that first evening. But on this night, we were seated in the front room, where half the cast of *The Lion King* was sitting. Before we were even seated at our table near that "in" crowd, though, we were sitting at a little bar at the front of Spago with one of the greatest actors of our time, Tony Curtis.

Curtis was a major womanizer but had impeccable taste when it came to the ladies, and it showed that night. He'd married one of America's sweethearts — Janet Leigh — and had a torrid affair with Marilyn Monroe. Tony was a single man at that point and was out on the prowl. And he had his eyes directly on my stunning nineteen-year-old girlfriend. He showed absolutely no shame as he ran his hands up and down the Betsey Johnson dress I had bought her on Melrose earlier that day. Suave, good readership, suave. But you know, it didn't seem creepy, even though he was over fifty years her senior. It was just Tony being Tony. And as any good-looking Jewish boy from the Bronx in the entertainment business is, he was insanely funny. And charming. I kept buying him cocktails hoping that I could stall the maître d' from seating us because we were having so much fun with "Stony." Vodka and Diet Coke, of all things, was Tony's choice of poison, or "Vodka Diet,"

With the always "minty fresh" Tony Curtis and my girlfriend at Spago in L.A. in 1994. As you can see, freshly flossed, she's thrilled to be there.

as he called them. We were with Tony for quite a while, and he gladly posed for several photos with us before we were told our table was ready.

Our table was sandwiched between James Earl Jones and a group of his friends on one side, and the incomparable Gene Kelly and his wife Patricia on the other. We were in utter shock. Just gobsmacked. Before I could even order a drink or read the menu, I, of course, did the thing that any patron of Spago should *not* do: I took out my $19 throwaway camera and asked them both to pose for photographs. Of course, they were delighted, but the maître d' was not. After a few quick shots and small talk, most of it with James about Toronto, I sat down and ordered an insanely expensive bottle of wine to "call off the dogs" — the staff who were glaring at me. Truth be told, James actually seemed thrilled I'd made an effort to say hi to the surrounding tables, because he had never met Gene, and they had a spirited little chat while I stood there beaming.

Oh yeah, the maître d'. He expressed his disapproval of my behaviour, saying he had already sent our waiter home because he'd let this happen on his watch. On the outside I was nodding and politely apologizing, while briefly explaining that because Mr. Curtis had obliged us with several photos at the bar, we'd thought it was okay in the main room. But on the inside I was just thinking, "This is going to look awesome on my mantel back home!" James Earl Jones, Tony Curtis, and Gene Kelly. Wow. I did not, by the way, ask another star of *The Lion King*, Matthew Broderick, who was seated nearby, for a photo. I would have literally been sent to Siberia. The real one. With a swift kick.

Sadly Gene would have a serious stroke less than a month after we met him. He died a couple of years later in 1996. As for Tony, the strangest thing happened. I got a call from my girlfriend weeks after we got back, and she said, "Are you watching Tony Curtis on A&E?" I turned it on and, no word of a lie, he says to this interviewer, "I was talking to this kid [that would be me] and his girlfriend at a bar the other night — some sportscaster from Toronto — and I told him that if he didn't start taking care of himself — boozing and chasing women — he's going to end up like me, old and single." Tony would eventually meet his own statuesque beauty in 1998, Jill Vandenberg Curtis, who

James Earl Jones and I re-enacting his *Field Of Dreams* dialogue (which we both know by rote) at Spago in L.A., 1994. "Baseball reminds us of all that once was good and that could be again. Oh, people will come. People will most definitely come."

he married and who stayed with him until his death at the age of eighty-five in 2010. I had a Vodka Diet in his honour.

* * *

You're probably wondering by now how I helped save Mark Wahlberg's life. Would it surprise you if I said it involved copious amounts of booze? It happened on the eve of one of the most horrific and unforgettable tragedies in our lifetime: September 11, 2001. The 2001 TIFF was in full swing. That Monday night, the Royal Ontario Museum was host to a huge star-studded gala event. It was the final social occasion of TIFF that year. After what transpired the next morning, everything stopped, and for good reason. I spent most of the night talking with the wonderfully talented David Paymer, who's been in dozens of terrific films and was nominated for an Oscar for his performance in *Mr. Saturday Night*. Personally I loved the film, but critics were "meh." Mind you, Paymer was sensational. When I asked him who he lost the Oscar to in 1992, he told me Gene Hackman. "That hack!" I replied. William H. Macy was also there, as were *Taxi Driver* and *Pulp Fiction* star Harvey Keitel and the legendary hell-raising Irishman Richard Harris. They were having a cigarette in the smoking section of the ROM, and as I approached them for a light, the two shot me a look that said "Fuck off" all over it. I quickly thought twice about interrupting *that* conversation.

Which brings us to Mark Wahlberg. The man has since become one of the biggest box-office draws in the world. I guess it started with a simple beer at the ROM that night, the one that Mark is holding in a photo that long-time Toronto photographer Tom Sandler took the night of the pub crawl. Tom would put that shot on display years later during a gala cocktail party at Casa Loma in Toronto featuring all of his best TIFF work. That beer. There were others. Several others. After we left the ROM, Gallagher/Wahlberg sightings were popping up all over Toronto. On the ten-year anniversary of 9/11, Facebook friends posted a number of recollections with me as part of Wahlberg's entourage. (Fun fact: The HBO hit show *Entourage* is, in fact, mainly based on Mark Wahlberg's rise in Hollywood.) With sixty-five bars approved by the Alcohol and

Gaming Commission of Ontario to stay open until four a.m. for the full run of the festival, there were a lot to choose from.

By the time our bar-hopping was done, it was well into the night. Peter Howell of the *Toronto Star* wrote that Wahlberg "had originally booked to fly from hometown Boston to Los Angeles the following morning." Yes, but that was before meeting me. "But for that impulse," Howell wrote, "he'd have been on one of the two L.A.-bound Boston jets crashed by the 9/11 hijackers. 'We chartered a plane to Toronto and we had a lot

As Mark Wahlberg and I "fuel up" into the wee hours of 9/11/2001, his ill-fated American Airlines Flight 11, from Boston to Los Angeles (which he missed), was fuelling up as well. (Photo credit: Tom Sandler)

of fun that night drinking Canadian beer, which is much stronger than U.S. beer. I woke up in the morning ... and people were calling and beating on my door. It was hard to wake up that morning. But then there was the shock of seeing the television.'" Later Wahlberg regrettably said events may have turned out differently had he been on one of the planes that had crashed on 9/11. In an interview with *Men's Journal* magazine, he said, "If I was on that plane with my kids, it wouldn't have went down like it did. There would have been a lot of blood in that first-class cabin and then me saying, 'Okay, we're going to land somewhere safely, don't worry.'" Yikes! He later apologized after incurring the wrath of critics and one victim's widow: "To speculate about such a situation is ridiculous to begin with, and to suggest I would have done anything differently than the passengers on that plane was irresponsible. I deeply apologize to the families of the victims that my answer came off as insensitive, it was certainly not my intention." Still, that near-brush with death still haunts his dreams. Wahlberg recalled what might have been had he and his buddies been on that flight: "We certainly would have tried to do something to fight. I've had probably over fifty dreams about it."

As for me, I had dozens of answering machine messages from people who were watching the carnage unfold live on television. After every beep it was, "Are you watching this? Oh my God!" Since my shift started at CityTV at four p.m., I, like the hungover Mr. Wahlberg, slept through it all. I watched in horror as I saw what had unfolded on TV, hours after the fact. I do distinctly remember driving to the station that day and looking over the dashboard of my Bimmer trying to spot planes that weren't there that could crash into the CN Tower. At City, the newsroom was abuzz. Like nothing I've ever seen before or since in broadcasting. I did a story on the last time an entire schedule of sporting events had been postponed or cancelled as a result of such a tragedy. It was in November of 1963, when John F. Kennedy was shot. I wore an American flag shirt, like the one the Abbie Hoffman character wore in *Forrest Gump*, on air that night. Hundreds of people wanted to know where I got it and how to purchase one. Unfortunately, Melrose Avenue in L.A. was the answer. Station owner Moses Znaimer picked up the tab as the entire newsroom went out for drinks afterwards. All told, 2,996 succumbed in the attacks. The effects of that day will linger forever for me.

٭ ٭ ٭

Some celebs I've met and spent hours with are just camera shy and politely tell me, "No photos tonight. Are you cool with that?" That's been John Cusack's line every time I've met him. Ditto Philip Seymour Hoffman and Jack Black. The same with Wesley Snipes. Even Art Garfunkel, who I said hi to as we were about to board a jet, was not up for a photograph. Art Garfunkel, the Andrew Ridgeley (opposite George Michael of Wham!) of his time? And then he sat in front of me on the flight and I couldn't see the film because of his huge and hilarious hair! "Hey! Down in front!"

I understand not wanting to take photos with fans every two minutes. But that's different from being a tosser about your fame. Bruce Willis is one of Hollywood's notorious douche nozzles and allegedly one of the most

If you would've told me when I was five that I would actually meet Al Lewis, a.k.a. Grandpa Munster, I would've crawled into the top of my chest of drawers like Eddie Munster. Here we are at the Toronto Planet Hollywood opening in 1996.

difficult actors to work with. Here's an example: According to Deathandtaxesmag.com, director Kevin Smith said that working with Willis on the set of *Cop Out* was nothing short of "soul crushing." Willis, notorious for giving reporters hell come promotion time, wouldn't even pose for a photo of him next to a poster at one *Cop Out*–related event. Smith gladly shared his antipathy with cast and crew members at the release party: "I want to thank everyone who worked on the film," he said, "except for Bruce Willis, who is a fucking dick." The night of the opening of his ill-fated Planet Hollywood restaurant, I was drinking and mixing with fun, upbeat, and jovial types like Sylvester Stallone, Tom Arnold, and "Grandpa Munster" Al Lewis, and even spent several minutes chatting up Willis's then-wife Demi Moore. Maybe *that's* what turned him off. At every attempt to get close for a photo, Willis kept waving me off. When I got closer and asked again, he snapped, "I don't think so. I saw you earlier with my wife." Okey-dokey, doggy daddy.

In line at the "Hell Cineplex" for the *St. Elmo's Fire* marathon — a film so bad, it plays in Hades twenty-four hours a day — with Demi Moore, who at the time of this photo (1996) was the highest paid actress in film history.

FOUR

HEY, WANNA GO TO THE PLAYBOY MIDSUMMER NIGHT'S DREAM PARTY AT HUGH HEFNER'S MANSION?

(or, as I lean in to light David Bowie's cigarette …)

My love for Le Parc Hotel in Los Angeles is enormous. Heck, one fateful afternoon, as I pulled in on my fiftieth birthday (on April 5) with my then-girlfriend, Emily, who was twenty-three at the time, Stevie Wonder was getting into his limo. We stopped for a chat and photos and he told me of his affection for those lucky enough to be born under the Aries sign.

My favourite moment at Le Parc was when WWE wrestler Chyna arranged a surprise birthday party for me. I first met Chyna at Gino Empry's place at 130 Carlton Street in Toronto. Gino was an eccentric, flamboyant press agent to the stars (Frank Sinatra, Tony Bennett, et cetera) and always invited me to his lavish parties. Gino had a great relationship with *Playboy* models, who he handled (carefully), and Chyna was one of them. She later appeared on *The Gallagher Show* on TSN and also on my Sunday night talk show on CP24 numerous times. Whenever she had a *Playboy* magazine layout to promote (she was on the cover of two of the bestselling *Playboy*s in history) or a book (a *New York Times* bestseller, in which, by the way, she paid an

Not a bad way to spend your fiftieth birthday. With Stevie Wonder and Emily Victory in Hollywood, California.

enormous compliment to yours truly), I had her on. And for some reason we just hit it off. And became fast friends. And with all of the flirting and sexual tension on air (if you could have bottled the sexual tension between us, we could have solved the energy crisis), people started to talk. In fact, CityTV entertainment reporter George Lagogianes did a story on the six o'clock news suggesting that the two of us were, in fact, dating. We weren't. That would have been a colossal mistake due to the fact that she *was* going out with WWF world champ Triple H. Uh, that would have ended badly … for one of us. But the phone calls and the emails continued, and when she learned that I was coming to L.A., she arranged a big party in my room at the hotel. Chyna, the "Ninth Wonder of the World" (André the Giant was already billed as the eighth), with all of her Los Angeles gal pals popping champagne in my honour. To quote Mel Brooks in *History of the World, Part 1*, "It's good to be the king." I was hoping she would ask what I wanted for my birthday, but the party was good enough. If I had gotten drunk enough, I was going to put my face between her forty-inch fake breasts and give her the "motorboat," but

WWF star and *Playboy* magazine cover girl Chyna throwing a surprise birthday party for me in Los Angeles in 2002.

why ruin things? I was already way ahead of the game. Mind you, as the night wore on and we went clubbing at Chyna's favourite spots in L.A., where she was a superstar. When I returned to Hollywood four months later, she did have an idea for a belated birthday gift for me. She would take me to the annual *Playboy* Midsummer Night's Dream Party at Hugh Hefner's Playboy Mansion the next night. Now *that's* a birthday present. Sadly, my girlfriend and I were flying that day. I considered changing the flights, since that was an invitation of a lifetime, but I honestly didn't want to strand my girl alone on a Saturday night. But still, I thought long and hard about it.

The wrestler Sable, another bestselling *Playboy* cover girl, also became a good friend over the years, and she once invited me for dinner at the 360 restaurant atop the CN Tower. Just the two of us. We got a few looks from passersby that night, I can tell you. I had Chyna and Sable, along with another stunner, Debra McMichael, on *The Gallagher Show* in 1998, and it ended in some serious fireworks. Chyna and Sable got into a finger-pointing cat fight during the end of the show, Chyna suggesting she would break then–WWF Women's Champion Sable into pieces (she would have), and Sable accusing Chyna of being hopped up on steroids (weren't they all?). It made for great television and huge ratings, but the real fun started when they got into a *real* scrap while getting into their limo afterwards on Mercer Street outside Gretzky's. That one was not staged, and it was nasty. Cat fight! Meow!

※ ※ ※

Over the years, I would meet up with my share of big-name wrestlers. I was a big fan as a kid, watching rasslers named Haystack and Fargo and Vachon. And when André the Giant fought Don Leo Jonathan in Montreal in the early seventies, it was front-page news. But that was nothing compared to what happened in the 1980s and the start of Hulkamania. I hadn't watched wrestling for years, but when NBC started pre-empting *Saturday Night Live* with the WWF's Saturday Night's Main Event in 1985, I had to take notice. And when Toronto played host to WrestleMania 6 on April 1, 1990, in front of 67,678 — then a record for SkyDome — I giddily attended, along with Q107 co-host Brother Jake Edwards. This was the night of the "The Ultimate Challenge," the main-event match that saw Hulk Hogan lose to The

Ultimate Warrior. The event reminded me of Super Bowl week, with parties and gala events, and we had passes and invites to them all. The thing about professional wrestlers is that they're always "on." For instance, I remember one afternoon trying to interview baseball Hall of Famer Nolan Ryan of the Texas Rangers before a Blue Jays game. Thing is, it wasn't Ryan's day to pitch, or even to talk, as it turned out. With my microphone in his face, he spent an entire two minutes or so spitting sunflower seeds on to the ground with his head facing the Astroturf. Never looking up. And some of my nights trying to squeeze an interview out of a Toronto Raptor after his team had lost by thirty-eight points to the Lakers were a struggle, to say the least. With

"Look out for the turnbuckle, John." Hulk Hogan promoting the Ultimate Challenge, where he would lose his WWF World Heavyweight Champion title to the Ultimate Warrior (WWF Intercontinental Heavyweight Champion) on April 1, 1990.

wrestlers, though, they're always in the moment, and with WrestleMania being the big event of the year, they're eager to please and sell their "sport." Everybody was there. Randy "Macho Man" Savage was a classic interview. Just so over the top. And the funny thing is, afterwards he'd give you this little wink as if to say, "Listen, man, I know I sound and look totally ridiculous and completely full of shite, but hey, if you saw what they're paying for this act … well."

"Rowdy" Roddy Piper was hilarious, too. He used to date Bro Jake's wife Loris back in Winnipeg! And as for "game day" and the rasslin' match itself? Why, is that Mary Tyler Moore sitting ringside? Yes, it was. I know; don't ask. Is that Steve Allen and gossip columnist Rona Barrett? Uh huh. (Steve sang with the Russian wrestling duo "The Bolsheviks" backstage, and when they started to sing the Russian national anthem, he chimed in with "I get no kick from Ukraine!" It's a line I've stolen and still use to this day.) And Robert Goulet singing a rendition of "O Canada" before the show? Yes. What a silly way to make a living, huh? For them, and for me.

Truth be told, I hated having wrestlers on *The Gallagher Show*. I mean, it was all just a gimmick, right? They weren't really athletes, were they? But the ratings didn't lie. TSN's *RAW* program on Monday night had huge numbers, and reluctantly, we had to book these yahoos. And again, the ratings were through the roof when they appeared. One night we had Ken Shamrock, one of the biggest stars in the history of UFC mixed martial arts, on the show. Shamrock, named the World's Most Dangerous Man by ABC News, had turned to the WWE for some more big paydays and was in town promoting a big scrap. I worked out with him at a gym before the show for a fun segment to be aired later that night. A finer specimen of a human body I had not seen since Montreal Expo Andre Dawson, but Dawson "The Hawk" wasn't going to rip your spine out. During our bit for the show, I was bobbing and weaving and pounding away at his chiselled six-pack like a heavy bag at a gym and inadvertently caught him right on the chin with my skull. I heard "crack" and also heard some "ooohs" from my camera crew and show producers. Shamrock's face turned white. Stunned, I had two choices: run, which was my first instinct, and the proper one, or just keep punching for the good of the show and television ratings and see what happened. Mistake. Shamrock put me in a sleeper-hold headlock and turned me upside down with my legs dangling over his shoulder as I cried — no, make that screamed — for help. Before I passed out, and I was getting there, he let me down. He did buy me several drinks at Gretzky's after the show. It's a good thing the man was a pussycat on the inside. You didn't want to piss him off, though, and I'd come close!

There were other stunts with wrestlers over the years. Like the time the late Jimmy "Superfly" Snuka flew from the top of a wrestling ring and landed on me with his signature Superfly Splash live on CityPulse at six. Two hundred and thirty-five pounds and over six feet of flying Fiji power slammed me to the mat. That was after he performed the Death Valley Driver, where he tossed me off his shoulders, flipping me onto the mat on my back. I'll tell you something, though — the mat has a lot of bounce to it. He slammed me so hard, I didn't wake up until we were in court. Kidding. Actually, I had him right where I wanted him. It was like the time I sparred for three rounds with former heavyweight boxing champion Mike Weaver in an exhibition. I had him worried in the second round. He thought he'd killed me. Hey-yo! Goodnight everybody!

The return of the Thin White Duke. Backstage at the CNE in Toronto during David Bowie's "Sound and Vision" tour on July 4, 1990, sixteen years after I witnessed his comeback at the Montreal Forum in June 1974.

But, honestly, my biggest brush with greatness, and my biggest thrill, was the night I finally got to meet David Bowie. I was at SkyDome for a Blue Jays game in a box with a large group of people, including the dean of Canadian television anchors, Lloyd Robertson, who for some reason was dressed in a one-piece beige safari outfit, but I digress. A limo driver was delivering some celebs to our box. The driver recognized me and knew I was a huge Bowie fan and said, "Guess who I just dropped off at the BamBoo [a swanky watering hole on Queen Street with a fantastic roof deck]? David Fucking Bowie. Want a lift over? He's still there." So off we went, and sure enough, there was the Thin White Duke (or was it Ziggy or Halloween Jack?) cracking up a small group of hangers-on. You've heard stories about Bowie being the coolest man on the planet. Well, I'm here to tell you they're true. Man, he looked incredibly suave, dashingly handsome, and he was the coolest man I've seen smoke a cigarette since French actor Jean-Paul Belmondo. The cigarette that I'd just lit for him, beating everybody else to the punch. And one thing you should know about Bowie: he was insanely quick. Very funny. Full of conviviality. Myself, I was speechless, naturally. I saw the legendary comedian Denis Leary on TV recently tell the story of the time he was booked on the same late-night talk show as Bowie in 1992. He went out to have a smoke, and there he was. Leary was the same as me. Tongue-tied. It was like he wasn't even human, you know? The love and adulation I've had for this man. I could make up a terrific story about how David and I hit it off and drank merrily into the night and "pushed on" till the break of dawn like Stevie Nicks and me, but I won't. That wouldn't be doing my short acquaintance with my hero any justice. No, instead, it was a quick handshake and a little small talk and then back to the Jays game. But my god, it was the coolest ten minutes of my life.

I saw Bowie again before his concert the next night at the CNE. Labatt's had set up an exclusive meet-and-greet with David and contest-winning listeners from my station, Q107, and rival CFNY. It was very clear to the Bowie people: three photos would be taken. Not one more. One with David and thirty-odd winners from Q, another with David and the group from CFNY, and one with just Bowie and me. My chat with David was a little more rarified since I had him one on one. We talked about our meeting the night before at the BamBoo, and he asked, "Oh yes, you were with Art, weren't you?" Never heard of the guy, but I thought I'd just go with it. "Yes, Art. Absolutely." I would see David again a few years later when he was with the group Tin Machine, a much-maligned and underrated band that included two of comedian Soupy Sales's sons. Soupy Fucking Sales? Really? We chatted briefly in the basement of a small club in Toronto he was playing that night. He signed my blown-up photos from the CNE show, and I got out of there just as my car was being jacked up by a tow truck operator on Yonge Street. That was an expensive autograph. But worth it. Years later my high school friends from Montreal West and Loyola contacted me, writing, "So, you finally met your hero Davie Bowie, huh?" Yes, indeed. You know, if you're ever sad about David's untimely passing, just remember the world is 4.543 billion years old and you somehow managed to exist at the same time as David Bowie. How true.

FIVE

KARMA. I HATE THAT BITCH.

(or, as I'm being pulled from the Caribbean Sea, a woman on the beach says, "Abner, I think that's the man who does the sports for CityTV. Is he dead?")

You've heard the expression "Karma is a bitch"? Well, it's true. She lives. She breathes. She can be relentless. I've met her more than a few times. I hate that bitch, Karma.

I made my television debut in the fall of 1990. All I needed was, "Aren't you that guy on TV?" from a stranger and the game was on. I met this attractive, smart, fun-loving woman twirling her hair with her fingers, followed up by a few giggles and then laughter big enough to have her head snapping back, and we were off to the races. We played googly eyes over drinks, soon phone numbers were being exchanged, and before you knew it, it was go time. Hey, come for the night and stay for the weekend, I say! Being on TV is a huge advantage when meeting women. If a girl out with her friends is being picked up by a stranger, her friends might be inclined to run interference — "You don't know him" or "You're not going home with him." With me, it's cool, because if anything bad ever happened, it's not like I'd be hard to identify. I must tell you that the thrill of getting a woman home and upstairs for some intimacy is my all-time favourite sport. And the art of seduction, the thrill of the kill, if you must, is just that: a sport. This type of game can be thrilling and rejuvenating, and the longer it goes on, the more exciting it gets. The little looks and glances. The comments and innuendoes. The sexual overtures. It's all very intoxicating. Yes, sex is the prize, but the chase can be so much fun, especially when played by two evenly matched contestants. There's a scene in a silly little movie called *Hall Pass* where Owen Wilson and Jason Sudeikis are discussing "the arch": "You know when you're taking a girl's panties off for the first time, and you're wondering if she's going to stop you, but then she gives you that little pelvic arch-thrust that tells you that the struggle's over, everything's going to be okay?"

So, because of my newfound status, I was getting new and exciting dates at an alarming rate. That's a good thing. Unless you're already dating someone. Then it's bad. At the time of my "TV boy" debut, I had just started dating Lindy, who was living with her parents and working in Mississauga. Not too far away, but far enough. And you know what they say about what happens when the cat's away. Which brings us to, well, let's call her "Bitsy Von Muffling," who was a large-breasted, gorgeous girl I met at a radio station remote at a sporting goods store. I've never seen a body like hers. Just a stunner. This girl could break you in half — with both halves smiling. She lived just a few blocks away: Advantage Bitsy. I couldn't wait to see this young lady in a bikini on a beach. That was mistake number one. Mistake number two was taking Bitsy to Cancun. It's true what they say about not really knowing a person until you've travelled with them. Well, this was never more true than in Mexico in December of 1990. The whole thing was a mistake.

Our vacation got off to an alarming start. We fought over something so ridiculous I can't even remember what it was, and this was before we had even got out of the airport! The bickering continued at the hotel, and we barely spoke for five days. To top things off, it rained every day. Non-stop. Full torrential waterworks. We spent our time taking separate cabs into town and trying to hide from each other at Señor Frogs. That was the worst vacation I'd ever been on, and I thought, "I'll never cheat on Lindy again. Just get me back home!" Finally it was day six, our final full day in the not-so-sunny south. But the clouds dispersed, and, miraculously, so did our dour and sour mood. Off to the beach we went on a windy, choppy, but incredibly sunny day. Six days in, and this was our first time on the beach, let alone our first time smiling. Not knowing that the beach was unsupervised, I decided to take a little dip into the waves. I did see a red flag on the beach, but I figured that meant "Volleyball at noon — sign up with Raoul the pool boy." Big mistake. And that would be mistake number three. While I did see Bitsy's large breasts bouncing in the waves beside me, they were soon in my rear-view mirror. A huge wave had swept me out about five feet from her. And another one. And another one, and soon there *was* a volleyball game, in the Gulf of Mexico, with the waves using me as a ball. The water just sucked me out several feet at a time. It was impossible to swim through, and I've never been a very good swimmer. Down I would go, and then I would bob up for air several feet further out. They would later explain that Hurricane Gilbert, the most intense tropical cyclone ever recorded in Mexico's history, had ripped apart the surf in Cancun during a nine-day stretch in 1988, and the riptides and undercurrents were deadly. I heard that the wife of the president of TSN's French affiliate, RDS, died on the same stretch of beach in a rip current accident. Well, they never tell you that, do they? Bad for tourism, huh? I'm thinking, "This is *not* what it said in the brochure!"

As I screamed "help" through mouthfuls of water, the ever-so-fit Jewish-Canadian Princess tried to come to my rescue, but I was too far out for her to make any attempt. But I'll give her this: the chick had a pair of lungs on her. No pun intended. When it looked obvious that I was not going to miraculously drift in to the sunny surf any time soon, she started screaming for help. With no lifeguards with boats, I was in a big heap of trouble. I panicked, which was a stupid thing to do. Not knowing the right procedure, I swam toward the waves and not parallel to them, which was even dumber. Rescuers did come. Six of them, in fact. The first five had a hold of me and were trying to pull me in but knew that if I was going down, they were sure to follow. The looks on the faces of a couple of them were of sheer terror. A few even apologized that they had to leave me wailing and bobbing in the water because they, too, were losing strength battling the undercurrent and the huge waves. "Sorry man, but I'm going to go under, too," one man said. This was bad. Real bad. I would joke about this later, but I will tell you, with my hand to God, that I did see "the light." You know the one I'm talking about. The light. The tunnel. Friends later told me, "It's just your brain freaking out and trying to calm you down."

I'm flailing in the water. I'm waiting for a miracle. And one comes. At this moment, I'm between the angels singing and the devil's fire. It was the angels who sang. And here came my angel. I would get his name, but forgot it — I had other things on my mind, like *not dying* — but I do know he was vacationing from Atlanta. Atlantis would have been more appropriate, considering how far out and under the sea I was.

If lifeguarding were an Olympic sport, this guy would have won the gold medal. At this point I was in full panic mode, kicking and screaming. I remember my rescuer was ripped, and he had his big right arm under my chin in a headlock position and was yelling at me, "Don't fucking fight me on this or I'll leave you out here like those other guys! Relax!" What choice did I have? Drifting in and out of consciousness? Well, pull me to safety he did, swimming parallel to the ten-foot waves and *not* into them. He got me to an area where half a dozen people, including Bitsy, dragged me out. I was a mess. My stomach was stretched out to ridiculous proportions from swallowing gallons of salt water. It was gushing out of my mouth like a water hose. I was near unconsciousness as they performed CPR on me, but I do remember this: some guy was filming all of this with one of those oversized nineties video cameras, and Bitsy slapped it right out of his face with an enthusiastic "Fuck off!" Mind you, I would have loved to have seen that footage. The YouTube views would have hit the millions and I'd have been a star on *Inside Edition*. Bitsy would tell me later that she heard an older couple behind her during the mayhem say, "Abner, I think that's the man who does the sports for CityTV ... and he doesn't look so good. Is he dead?"

It turns out I wasn't good at all. I had to spend a week in a Cancun hospital and be escorted around in a wheelchair after suffering from pneumonia, an enlarged heart, and singed lungs from all of the salt water I had ingested. In my oh-so-delicate convalescing state, I called my co-host at Q107, Brother Jake Edwards, and left a message on his answering machine describing my situation. I was told later that Jake and company played that message dozens of times on the air, laughing hysterically in the background. So much for compassion. Would you believe the only time I would have sex in Mexico was in the hospital bed with Bitsy? Repeatedly, mind you. She was on top. She had to be; I was strapped to an intravenous drip. While I was there, I called the travel agency and demanded my money back after six straight days of rain and one day of near death. They refused. So, with one final "Fuck you" to not-so-sunny Mexico, I wrote them a cheque for the hundreds of dollars in medical fees. It was from a bank account that had been closed for months.

At least Bitsy finally warmed up to me. Imagine going through all that and still not getting laid?

SIX

I HOPE I DIE AT THE AGE OF NINETY-NINE IN BED AFTER BEING SHOT IN THE BACK OF THE HEAD BY A JEALOUS BOYFRIEND

(or, I forget the question, but "sex" is definitely the answer)

et me just begin this chapter by saying this on behalf of all men: Ladies, we are lost without you. Truly. Maybe it's because, of the hundreds of women I've dated, and even the skirts I've chased, most of them are still my best friends. Perhaps it's because I come from a family with four sisters and a mother I adore. I don't know. What is it exactly? I love women. The way they look, the way they talk, the way they think, the way they feel.

Plus, women are smarter than men. And funnier. Mind you, they don't fight fair, can be conniving little witches with a "b" in front, and are probably going to keep guys like me around just for the sperm like the Amazons do, but still.

Having written that, I've always agreed with the terrific line from comedian Dennis Miller, who said, "Nobody is more interested in your own orgasms than you, and no one is less interested in them than everyone else." But, here goes.

Everyone has a number. You know, a "number." For instance, Hollywood biographer Peter Biskind did the math in a 2010 book and

Most of them are still my best friends, including wonderful Lindy Robinson, who I've known for four decades. Backstage with a Blue Man at the Luxor in Las Vegas, 1998.

estimated actor Warren Beatty has slept with 12,775 women in his life. It's a figure that I find ridiculous, myself. Not the amount of women, mind you; just the fact that he had it right down to the final 775. What did he do, follow Beatty around and watch the women go in and out of his house to get that final tally? Mind you, the list of his reported romantic pairings — including Natalie Wood, Barbra Streisand, Carly Simon, Madonna, Joni Mitchell, Goldie Hawn, Julie Christie, and even Marilyn Monroe (although Beatty insists he just took a long walk with Monroe) — is legendary.

KISS frontman Gene Simmons, who I've met, says he's had sex with close to five thousand women and has the Polaroid photos to prove it. Coffee table book, anyone? (While holding on to this book with your left hand, pick up your iPhone and say, "Siri, show me John Gallagher interviews Gene Simmons on YouTube." There. You're welcome…. And welcome back. Let's continue.) Not to be outdone, I had the pleasure of interviewing NBA legend Wilt "The Stilt" Chamberlain in our Q107 studios. He was promoting his plans to bring NBA basketball to Toronto in the late eighties. The Q studio where we conducted the interview was a tiny, closet-like room with a pair of lounge chairs. Wilt's seven-foot-one frame was cramped in so tight that his knees were at the same level as my head. Well, Wilt was a monster on the court and is the only player to have ever scored one hundred points in an NBA game, but he's possibly even better known for claiming to have "been" with twenty thousand women.

According to some people who know math, for Chamberlain's claim to be true, he would have had to have sex with 1.14 women every day from the time he was fifteen until he died. Factoring in things like sleep and his job, it has him doing the horizontal mambo with a different woman every three and a half hours. Unless … I wonder how they account for threesomes? Maybe Wilt was into efficiency that way. But twenty thousand?

Chamberlain faced a lot of criticism for his lifestyle over the years and seemed to feel like he had to constantly explain why he'd slept with enough women to populate a small city, but I'm pretty sure "because he could" just about covers it. I didn't bring it up during our interview.

* * *

Well, a lot of ladies are instantly attracted to rock stars (natch), athletes, actors, and TV types. I've taken advantage of every opportunity my bit of fame afforded me ... and not in the creepy hyper-lecherous Tommy Lee/Gene Simmons/Vince Neil/Courtney Love way. Now, after throwing those names into the mix, I'm not suggesting you wash your hands before continuing to read this chapter, and I don't want to come off looking or sounding sleazy. A scoundrel yes, icky, no — but I will say, unequivocally, that I got into TV and radio to meet women. It's because I knew early that I kinda, somewhat had a shot at the big leagues.

Enter Sheila Danaher: *the* hottest girl in grade seven. My friends and I would always see her and her older boyfriend kissing at the hockey rink or in his car! I guess he graduated from high school — he was three years older — and went off to university. Soon after, Sheila "fixed" a game of spin the bottle on a Friday night, made her move, and started to make out with me. Who can forget their first French kiss? Cinnamon gum will never ever taste the same again. On Monday morning, I was a hero. The starting quarterback. She wanted me to be her new boyfriend, but I had no idea how to do it ... and what to do with "it." British author Nick Hornby, who wrote the novel *High Fidelity*, which was turned into a hit film, absolutely nailed it, pertaining to girls at that age, with: "One moment they weren't there, not in any form that interested us, anyway, and the next you couldn't miss them; they were everywhere, all over the place. One moment you wanted to clonk them on the head and the next you wanted to ... actually, we didn't know what we wanted next, but it was something, something. And they quite clearly had breasts." That's as far as I got: touching Sheila's breast. Just one. Once. I was dumbfounded. I was "in like Flynn," but I had no idea about anything. She dropped me like third-period algebra a week later. It was the same case with Swedish-born Lillian Nillson a year or so later. I got the nerve to ask her out and she said yes. But it was just before Christmas break in junior high and, like a moron, I didn't get her phone number. You might know that feeling, when you were girl (or boy) crazy at that age. The butterflies were so intense that I couldn't eat and could hardly sleep just thinking about her. I rode my bike outside her house in the snow hoping she would notice me. Yeah, that will do it. After the two-week break, she said she'd lost interest.

From then on I always thought, screw it, if they said yes to a date even once, I'll continue punching out of my weight class. I was a middleweight at best, but I was going to pursue the heavyweight champs. My first loves — my great white buffaloes — had gotten away. Not any more. Well, I found out quite early that I had to step it up.

* * *

I will say that a night out on the town with John Gallagher can be summed up this way: every trip is an adventure, and not necessarily a good one.

No — of course it's a good one.

As you know, the sexual revolution began in North America in the 1960s with the advent of the birth control pill and a general loosening of attitudes. A lot of loosening. Of belts, bras, garter belts — if that's your thing — et cetera. This was before the spectre of AIDS, coming on the heels of other sexually transmitted diseases that brought the revolution to a halt. Thankfully, I got in while the gettin' was good.

I must tell you, as a pup I was somewhat of a sex fiend. But, boys, weren't we all at one point in time? I loved visiting friends whose fathers collected *Playboy* magazines. From memory I would draw nudie pictures of women, until I was caught and chastised by my parents. I was eight. At variety stores I would insert *Penthouse* magazines into the middle of *Sports Illustrated* and dream about the women on the pages.

Around this time, while in grade seven in Côte Saint-Luc in Montreal, my friends and I lip synced to the Jackson Five at the school variety show. I, the lone white kid in the group, played Michael. I know. Who knew that Michael would grow up to be the lone white kid in the Jackson Five? My ten-year-old "brothers" had soul. We had all the dance moves down, along with the loud *Partridge Family* paisley shirts, platform boots, and the now-classic hippie suede fringed vests. And we sang "I Want You Back" and "Mama's Pearl." None of this "ABC" shite for our fans! To prepare ourselves, me and two other members of the fake five were invited by our very attractive English teacher and "choreographer" to rehearse at her house after school. Now, you often read stories about teachers having sex with their students and going to jail, and some even marrying them when they get out of the clink. This is not one of those stories. But after a few trips to her place for juice boxes and chips, when she stripped down to her bra and panties for a harmless little tickle fight and started to wrestle us, it was as close to "going over the line" as you're going to get. I recently saw a story about an eleven-year-old who broke down and cried when a porn movie popped up on his computer at a school in Toronto. The parents are considering suing. Meh. When I was his age, I was getting my hands on any *Playboy* magazine under any of my friends' fathers' beds that I could, drawing nudie pictures, and wrestling a gorgeous, half-naked thirty-year-old English teacher while rolling around on the plush carpet of her apartment. And loving it. Mind you, nothing came of it. There were no emotions to follow through on. I mean, it was hard to have an erection at the age of ten. Maybe she just liked the Jackson Five. Maybe I was seven years too early.

In high school I was dating one of the local beauty queens. Absolutely one of the most gorgeous girls you could ever set your eyes on. And I was absolutely in love with her. Now, being that she was a virgin, it took months and months of trying to convince her to have sex with me. I'm sure her mother, who I adored, kept telling her, "Do you know what a penis is? *Stay away from it!*"

Eventually she agreed. Maybe "relented" is a better word. It was exhausting. To paraphrase Billy Joel, "Come on, come on, come on, Celica, don't make me wait!" In reality, first-time sex is just like the first kiss. It's instinctive and personal. And clumsy. But after that, we were totally connected and on a new level with each other. All of the sexual tension was gone, and we just wanted more "rolls in ze hay"! We would have sex almost nightly at her place or mine (backrooms, the alley, the trusty woods?) and pretty well daily at noon behind the top row of the high school theatre. The smirks we would exchange in the hallways later those afternoons were priceless. I've been positive only ONCE in my life. It was the first time I ever had sex and I was POSITIVE that I was going to do that again.

Do you know what? I was the disco champion in high school. What jock sports-type would ever admit to that? But yeah, I won the title "laying down the boogie" to Chic's "Everybody Dance." That was the thing in the seventies. Women went to discos. I'm a rock music fanatic, but disco wasn't as ridiculous a genre of music as people made it out to be. But if all the good looking ladies were line dancing and riding bulls in country and western bars, I'd learn how to line dance. Wait. Check that. I'd never learn how to line dance. I loathe country and western music. In fact, I call it "country and western" because it pisses true country fans off. I remember an ex-girlfriend who would shop for country music CDs on Amazon, and the site suggested that customers who bought this product also bought a .38 pistol so they could blow their brains out!

Another way to attempt to attract women: be really good at Frisbee. In fact, win the New Brunswick Freestyle Frisbee title. The Maritimes are home to the greatest beaches in the world: Parlee Beach in Shediac, New Brunswick, and Brackley Beach in P.E.I. Girls in bikinis watch boys catch Frisbees behind their backs five feet in the air. Cue the ooh's and aah's. The moral of the story: to paraphrase the classic Marlboro cigarette adds: Go to where the flavour is, go to vagina country. LOL.

The eighties were — well, in the words of Eddie Murphy, who's around the same age as me — "the fuck years for me … I'm in my sexual prime, I fuck now! … This is when you do your best fucking." Eddie also said in the movie *Delirious* that women were throwing themselves at him "like frisbees" — well, not to sound too crass, but we did our best to catch as much as we could. My first radio gig (along with TV sports) was at CHSJ in Saint John, N.B. I was still a teenager. It just so happened that I was sleeping with the all-night jock, Deanna Nason, who within a few months of my first job got me to Halifax to do mornings at the CHUM-owned CJCH/C100. She got a huge promotion to the Maritimes' biggest and best city and called me when the morning co-host spot there opened up.

While Deanna and I would end our May-December relationship soon after, there were thousands of gorgeous women in the city available to quickly take her place. These ladies poured into town to attend Dalhousie, St. Mary's, and Mount Saint Vincent universities. I didn't go to college or university, but I did live close to Dal and SMU and got a "hands-on" feel for university life. And university women. They were really something. College and university girls don't know how good they have it. They live alone, with no parental supervision and almost no responsibility. They have crazy amounts of free time and are in close proximity to the opposite sex all day, every day. Even guys like me, who weren't even going to their school. There was an added feature to these bright, attractive young women, and it was this: Maritime girls are easy. There. I said it. I'm glad.

There were some nights (mind you, they were rare, but they did occur) when you could meet a nice, willing young lady at a bar or club early in evening — at, say, nine or ten o'clock — take her home and have sex, and then go back to another bar and do it all over again. And if you're counting the notches in your belt when it comes to how many women you've been with, as some men do, that's a lot of knocking boots. A university town like Halifax was just brimming with local "talent." For those students who found sunlight a burden and wanted to live to see four a.m. on Argyle Street, there was plenty of action just walking distance from the campuses — legendary pubs, bars, and nightclubs that still thrive today. After all, for many students, the day is just something to sleep through until dusk. The same could be said for morning sportscasters, whose working days end at nine a.m. Plus, at the time I was in an Olands Export Ale TV ad (punch "Olands Exports John Gallagher" into YouTube) that was running on all of the local channels. Yahtzee!

✦✦✦

All of that skirt chasing has continued throughout my career — after moving to Toronto in 1986, and in the thirty-plus years since. As it turns out, I like my women with a whole lotta pretty ... and a whole lotta crazy. There are two words for most of the women I've "dated": Koo Koo. Ninety-nine percent of them I have really liked, even adored, even loved, but with some of them, there have been some nutty misadventures in my love life.

In a fit of rage, and after several arguments that day, I once threw a fresh martini in a girlfriend's face before storming out of Gallagher's Steakhouse at New York-New York casino in Vegas, only to have her do the exact same thing at the Beatles Revolution Lounge at the Mirage an hour later. It gets better. After we left Las Vegas the next morning, I was pissed off that she had to snort all of the cocaine that she had bought during our stay before takeoff. Again, I don't do the stuff. Anymore. But I reminded her about customs and drug-sniffing dogs, et cetera, and she just "hoovered" it all up her nose. I was still mad about the night before, and now she was coked out, so "just get me home." Now, it happened to be my birthday, and on the Air Canada flight, the head of the cabin crew (who I mentioned my birthday to and who recognized me) bumped me up to first class. Me.

Not my date. As per my instructions. When said flight attendant escorted me to seat 1A, my soon-to-be-ex-girlfriend asked, "You're not leaving me here in steerage, are you?" To which I responded, "Leaving you in steerage? Damn, girl, I'm leaving you forever." And when the entire plane sang "Happy Birthday" to me, I could almost see her seething in seat 38B. For the next four hours and forty-four minutes. Funny thing, when I got off the air the next day at AM740, she was sitting on the hood of my car in the parking lot. Chicks, man.

There was once a fellow TV sportscaster who was, in his eyes, my stiff competitor. And we didn't see eye to eye. Hey, I don't have any competition. Just opposition. What did I do? I met a beautiful woman one night who just happened to be his sister. A lawyer. Very tall and gorgeous. Yes, I wanted to shimmy up her like a little island boy looking for coconuts. And I did. I would have loved to see the sportscaster's face at the Sunday family dinner when little sister told him what she'd done last night. I also dated a woman who kept breaking and entering at my house, calling it "the five-finger discount." She snuck into my place one night when I was on air at CityTV and played music so loud the police came by after the neighbours complained about the noise. And I dated a nymphomaniac who liked to have sex up to ten times a night while her cat just looked at us from a chair in her bedroom. Staring.

I had a "series of accommodations" with the receptionist at the radio station in Halifax. She had called in sick for a few days, so I went to see her. She had ink-stained blue hands, and no matter how hard she tried, she couldn't wash the ink off. Huh? Yes, she had tried to steal the station's money from a bag with a dye-pack device that had exploded when she'd tried to open it. (These devices explode, staining the stolen money a bright blue or red colour, alerting everyone to the fact that the money being passed to them is stolen.) It was the last time I or anyone from the station would see her. Crazy! Just recently I dated a woman who, after our break up, would send Facebook messages to women I was photographed with, "friend" them, then call them to tell them about how I broke her heart. Honey, call 1-800-GETOVERIT.

***

Again, I've done enough "blow" to kill a small village so naturally, yes, I've snorted cocaine off the inside of a woman's naked thighs. (Too cliché.) I've also had a threesome. (Double cliché.) Once. Honestly, it was too much trouble trying to convince the two women, who were roommates, to be naked in the same bed together. My contention is that one at a time is a lot more "hassle-free." Here's one: I once dated a girl who wouldn't have sex or even climax without the *Blade Runner* movie soundtrack playing on the stereo in her bedroom. Ahhh ... taxi!

Do you want to talk about dedication? I broke up with a woman I was madly in love with. In an attempt to win me back, Celeste Howarth had the Montreal Canadiens logo tattooed on her hip. Now while we did reconcile, unfortunately the love faded. But the tattoo lives on in red, flesh, and blue. Thank goodness they were actually her initials.

✦✦✦

Tattoo You! GF Celeste and then–Montreal Canadiens Shane Corson at his annual golf tournament in Muskoka, Ontario, 1996.

I've never been part of the mile-high club, or does fellatio under the covers on a red eye from L.A. to Toronto count? Would you count making love on a train? Wait. That's the four-foot-high club. Okay, how about being in the line of succession to the British throne? It almost happened. Well, for my unborn child, anyway. In the mid-eighties I was visiting my mom and some friends in Rothesay (a bedroom community outside Saint John — the city that fun forgot — New Brunswick). I met an English nanny named Sarah who was in her early twenties and in Canada for her first job. Being a nanny is a noble profession, but this wasn't your normal nanny, no sir. Her name was Sarah Spencer, and she told me she was a cousin of Lady Diana Spencer's. She even had photos of her and Diana in her purse and proudly showed me the Spencer shield. After getting to know Sarah a lot better, I suggested we grab a six pack and go watch some television at my mom's place down the street, where I was staying. She happily agreed. Well, one thing led to another, and soon we were doing the "mommy and daddy dance" under my mother's favourite quilt on a couch in the basement. As she was a beautiful and funny British gal with an accent that drove me batty, we kept in touch through phone calls after I left to go to Halifax. We made plans to see each other again, but during our conversation she lamented that she was "late." As in late by two weeks for her period. Hoo boy. Well, as it was too early for either of us to have children, that pretty much sucked all the fun out of this tête-à-tête. So, always the gentleman — take note, boys — I made arrangements to drive her to Bangor, Maine, to have the "procedure" done. But, breaking news! The day before we were going to make the trip, she let me know that her time of the month had arrived. So our little Baby Spencer was not to be and would not be in line for the big throne in London. I looked it up. The last person in the line of succession is Karin Vogel from Germany, who is approximately 4,973rd in line to the throne. Our son or daughter would have been in that string of royal possibilities somewhere. Little King John Jr. Ah, what might have been.

Still with the royals, I pulled off a huge scam in Halifax on the night of June 15, 1983, at a dinner hosted by Prime Minister Pierre Trudeau at the Hotel Nova Scotian. Di and Prince Charles were in town on their first visit to Canada. I wasn't going to miss this event. This was before the malice-at-the-palace days, and the two were the biggest celebrities on the planet from the publicity surrounding their 1981 wedding and the birth of their son, William. Since I had worked that same room while on a waiting list for broadcasting school years earlier, I had kept my old-school monkey-suit uniform for just such an occasion. Just for a goof, I wanted to see how close I could get to them. The security was insanely tight, but with my connections, I managed to get up behind the head table, and I placed a plate of those little butter slabs, on ice of course, between the prince and princess, slightly touching Princess Di's hand with my pinky finger in the process. Completely on purpose, and just like Hannibal Lecter did to Agent Starling in *Silence of the Lambs*, but a little less creepy. I got the strangest look from the head of security, who noticed me and probably thought, "This guy is *not* on my list! Blimey." It made for a great story the next morning on CJCH/C100.

***

I dated a stripper once. Hey, speaking of noble professions, you gotta do what you gotta do. Only this striking figure didn't want to tell me what she did for a living. She told me she worked at a bar late Thursday, Friday, and Saturday nights. I suggested I come in one night and she could serve me free drinks. "No," I was told, "my boss wouldn't be into that." A little suspicious, I walked into the place where she worked. Hello! Do you remember that great scene in the brilliant *Carlito's Way* when Carlito (Al Pacino) sees his girlfriend Gail (Penelope Ann Miller) on stage swinging on a pole? That happened to me. Hey, I always say there's no shame in chasing after a woman with an ass like a twenty-year-old stripper and someone whose breasts were so hard I could bounce a quarter off them and get back two dimes and a nickel. I did.

***

This COULD have been a huge feather in my cap. I was infatuated with Angela Dohrmann, who played Jerry Seinfeld's girlfriend Donna Chang in the *Seinfeld* episode "The Chinese Woman." At the time she was a VJ for MuchMusic. I was denied when I asked her for a date. The nerve, huh? Same with two-time Canadian gold-medal-winning hockey player, the stunning Cassie Campbell-Pascall. We have a standard "bit" every time we see each other. It goes: "Cassie how many times have I asked you out over the years and you've said no?" Cassie always responds "Every time, John. Every time." Now I did, over a span of a few years, go out with one of Canada's top female sportscasters who, as of this writing, is still on the air from coast to coast. She's married now and will remain anonymous. When she asked me if she'd be in this book she said, "You're not telling anybody that we used to — you know — in your new book are you?" "Anybody?" I said, "I'm telling EVERYONE!" I kid. How about a Raptor girl from the NBA's Toronto Raptors Dance Pak? I even signed off my morning show once, as a joke because I knew Raptor Girl was listening, with, "This is John Gallagher. So long, *arrivederci*. I'll send you a thought today as I lie in my stretch limo having sex with the Raptor cheerleader of my choice. And that thought will be 'Thank God I'm me.'"

✦✦✦

I sent this next story to the *très* popular *Toronto Star* Saturday Life section. Dating Diaries is a funny little column and is extremely addictive. Each week someone goes on a date with a person they met online, then describes the date and rates it out of ten. I'd noticed a theme in these columns. Often the person writing the column rates the date low and says that the other person talked about themselves the entire time. No second date. This story is not one of those. Twenty years ago I would have considered mailing this into *Penthouse Forum*.

After a few months of me being single, some of my ex-girlfriends demanded that I start online dating. I balked. Repeatedly. Tinder was for one-night-stands and weekend hook-ups, correct? And I'm a relatively well-known TV "on air" type, right? I couldn't be exposed to this, could I? Plus, comedienne Amy Schumer recently announced that anyone who's ever been on TV or film is not allowed on dating sites. And that was that. But, I thought, since Amy refuses to return my calls, there could be something more to this. Then I watched the Showtime drama *The Affair* and noticed that Maura Tierney's character (who's about the same age as I am) went on Tinder and met all kinds of shiny, happy people. Still, I enjoy meeting single eligible bachelorettes the old-fashioned way: at bars and cocktail parties. I asked a bunch of my guy friends, and not only were they all signed up, but they were also "cashing in" on a regular basis. I realized that I was extremely late to the party on this one. So I entered the world of online dating via Tinder and Bumble. If you haven't heard of Bumble, it works the same as Tinder: swipe right if you find someone who meets your criteria attractive; swipe left if that's a big nope. If you get a match, the difference is it's up to the woman to make the next move.

Now, prior to signing up, I had a lot of questions: What are people doing on here? Is anyone normal? What do these women really want? To scope, swipe, match, fall in love, and get married in the mountains? I found some humorous tips from *The Everygirl* columnist Lyndsay Rush, including, "If you didn't know you had a type: you do. Hence the quick-fire way you can absolutely *hate* or love someone's face"; "There is no smooth way to start a conversation with a total stranger with whom the only thing you have in common is the belief that you both are not ugly"; "A clever one liner goes a *long* way"; "Having attractive friends makes you seem more attractive"; and "Everyone loves travelling! And working out! And trying new things! And food!" She also points out that if the main photo is of two guys (or, in my case, girls), the one whose profile it is will *always* be the less cute one, and she advises that if someone is less than a mile away, you should put your phone down slowly and run for your life. Makes me think I could be one swipe away from ending up with some stage-five clinger who lives a block away and knocks on my door at all hours, just because she had a cheeky tagline and a photo of her in a Montreal Canadiens sweater in her profile pic.

On my end, I feared that women would recognize my face and think, "Wow, has he ever gotten desperate." But here's the interesting twist. Many women who I've met and dated on these sites have told me that my picture and profile took all of the guess work out of meeting up with me. Many women actually seek out more details about their potential dates to screen for criminal offences or court appearance, for instance. They told me that they look at my profile and say, "Oh, John Gallagher, the TV guy. He's legit." That's the way it's been for decades, though.

Back to my date. Let's call her "Charlie." You know, "kinda young, kinda now, Charlie. Kinda free, kinda wow, Charlie!" We went through the usual process: emailing for a while, followed by some funny phone calls and humorous texts. We set up a date for drinks at a popular downtown Toronto bar on a Saturday night, where she and some friends were gathering for a birthday party. Strength in numbers, right? Oh, and I would find out later that the birthday was hers. Charlie was an out and out knockout. She was a Bay Street player. Wealthy. Never married. No kids. Coming off a long-term relationship that hadn't panned out. I loved her playfulness and silliness on the phone and the night we met. It was looking like the start of, well, something. All evening it was just a single, double, triple, "Here comes Gallagher around third base and they're waving him in" kinda night. Everything was aces. She looked as good as she did in her photos. And, I'm here to tell you, that's a relief.

Charlie had long black hair and was curvy in all the right places. And like me, she was currently "between assignments" in the dating world. The whole gang and I hit it off immediately. The bottle-service vodka at their corner table was flowing quite nicely, and Charlie and I were definitely clicking. I'm sure the $300 bottles of Grey Goose were helping immensely. Our conversation wasn't sexual in nature, it was very lighthearted and fun, but the sexual chemistry was building. After a couple of passionate snogs and harmless embraces on the dance floor, Charlie asked if I'd like to join her in the stretch limo she had rented for the occasion for an after-hours birthday party at her place with all of her friends, along with some who were meeting her there later. Small catch: "There" just happened to be in Bolton, which is fifty-odd kilometres from downtown Toronto. She assured me that I could stay the night since she had a huge house and lots of room. She also promised me that she'd get me home safely the next day. Okay, I quickly weighed the pros and cons. Limo? Stocked bar? Charlie and her gorgeous friends? Extremely good possibility of some extracurricular activity? Check, check, check, and check, so we piled into the limousine and it was hammer down, northbound for Bolton-town. "Release the hounds" and let the silliness ensue, I say.

Oh, and it did. The hour or so drive was hilarious, with your correspondent holding court and Charlie with five or six of her friends — all women — popping bottles of champagne. The ladies were asking me about all of the famous people I've met, the sporting events and concerts that I've covered, and so on. I'm the king of the name drop, you see, and the ladies were quite enthralled. And drunk. Perhaps, also, it was the fact that they all lived way northwest of the city and had a big TV sportscaster in the back of their limo heading home to show off to all of their friends. I swear to you that I've been to après-ski house parties in the 705 area of Ontario with people who have demanded I show them my driver's licence to confirm that I was who I said I was. "What is John Gallagher doing in Calabogie, Ontario? You're not really him, right?" Now, besides Charlie and I making googly eyes with each other during the drive north, I noticed an insanely attractive young woman in the corner of the stretch who was smiling for the entire drive but not saying much. We'll call her "Willow." The party in Bolton was next door to Charlie's, at her best friend's place. She took me on a quick tour of her place, and while there was lots of amorous canoodling in her bedroom, Charlie suggested that there was lots of time for that later and that we should get back to the party. This was turning into a fabulous night. The party was an expensive, elaborate, raucous affair, with dozens of people spilling in and out of the place. About an hour after getting there, I headed upstairs in search of a washroom. While looking for the little sportscasters' room, I inadvertently walked into a room that had no lights on. Just a cigarette that glowed in the dark. Someone had to be on the other end of that dart.

After a moment, I heard, "Hi, come on in." That was pretty well the first time I'd heard Willow say anything. She asked me to sit down next to her on a chair in the bedroom, and within seconds she started to kiss me. This woman, this friend of Charlie's with her bright eyes, silky long hair, and a smile that could start a revolution, was a knock-out. She then got up, closed the door, smiled, got down on her knees, and looked straight up at me. I asked how a young lady as attractive as her didn't have a boyfriend. She said she had one, but he was "open" to things like this. Like "*this*"? Basically, you know what happens next. As she was pulling my trousers down, I stumbled to the door to try to look for a lock. There wasn't one. *Who doesn't have a lock on their bedroom door?* I lamented to myself. I mean, what if my prearranged date happened to walk in?

Moments later, guess who walked in looking for me? It could have been any of the dozens of people at the party, but no. Doesn't anybody knock anymore?! I was so busted. But since it was so spontaneous and "this" was just happening, I *so* didn't care. Well, kind of. I also figured that the possibility of spending the night at Charlie's place after my malfeasance was remote. I was right. Charlie didn't seem happy after I zipped up and joined her downstairs. After a few minutes of rather uncomfortable awkwardness, I suggested that I order a cab and head home. She didn't object. I think word of my little tryst with Willow must have spread, because I soon felt a chill begin to fill the room. There wasn't really anything appropriate to say to Charlie, Willow, or any of Charlie's best-wishing birthday friends as I slipped out and into the night. I'd just count my blessings — and there were many on that memorable night — and swallow the $80 cab fare and head south back to the "6."

Just then, and this is no lie, I saw a pickup truck with — is that a gun rack? (it was Bolton, after all) — fly up the driveway, driven by a man who jumped out and ran into the house. *Willow's boyfriend?* I wondered. I was safe in my cab and on my way home with a smile bright enough to light up the city skyline that glowed in the distance. But mostly I just felt this "You have *got* to be kidding" and "I can't make this stuff up" feeling while thinking, *this could only happen to a guy like me.* I hope I die at the age of ninety-nine in bed after being shot in the back of the head by a jealous boyfriend. Yeah, ninety-nine. Not forty-nine.

✣ ✣ ✣

These days, it's the mystery of women that sustains me. My number? I'll never tell. But I will say this: If my number were home runs, I'd be the all-time MLB leader. More than Ruth, Aaron, and even Bonds. But not by much. I don't want to brag! Hey, at times I've felt like I'm at Universal Studios. I've had a free pass and I've gone on every ride. So, the question remains: Is it better to love or be loved? Well, I guess it depends on how tired you are.

Let me finish with this thought: Anyone in film, music, the media, what have you, who tells you their story of wanting to impart some greater knowledge to humanity is not really telling the truth. The reason

I, personally, got into television and radio, as I've mentioned, was to get women. And lots of them. And their daughters, too. Good God, my dear friends, radio and TV types who were instantly recognizable had "followers" decades before I came along. Respected journalists — faces you'd easily identify, who I worked alongside at CityTV — used to rampage through the Toronto streets after their newscasts as the notorious "Hard To Swallow Boys." I know, but it was the Ron-Burgundy-and-gang seventies and early eighties. Add this to the fact that station owner Moses Znaimer hired beautiful (some talented, some not so much) women who all wanted to be on the air — whether they were receptionists, floor directors, or newswriters — to work at CityTV. They were all gorgeous, and a lot of them made it to the other side of the camera, but they were in every corner of 299 Queen Street West. And a lot of

A quiet, normal life. Just a regular day at Le Château de Chardonnay with GF Kimberlee Fabian in 1997.

them were available for drinks after the show at the hundreds of bars in Toronto's entertainment district, where CityTV was situated. Another fun fact: A recent *Business Insider* survey indicated that 54 percent of respondents had sex with a coworker. Nearly 85 percent believe they should be allowed to have sex with a colleague, and 64 percent said that they'd at least attempted a hook-up by hitting on a coworker. Welcome to CityTV, everywhere.

SEVEN

LET'S TALK ABOUT CHICKS, MAN

(or, when your dreams get destroyed,
get some new dreams)

thought of this the day I turned fifty years old, after my "silly rich" and gorgeous twenty-three-year-old girlfriend ordered a bottle of Veuve champagne at the pool of the Standard Hotel in L.A.: *Mmm, I think I'm probably going to "Clooney" it for the rest of my life.* That was then. Of course, George went ahead and ruined everything for single men everywhere when he married Amal Alamuddin and had kids. First of all, I think marriage and family are probably the best things you could possibly have in life. I've been close. Very close. I had a common-law marriage with a woman that lasted for nine years, so that has to count for something, right? That worked out fine. In fact, a *Men's Health* article mentioned one study that followed 2,737 people for six years and found that "in comparison to married couples and singles, cohabiters reported higher levels of happiness and confidence." But the question remains: Why am I single and childless? It's just too risky. The divorce rate is too high. Households headed by married adults are now in the minority. Jobs in the broadcasting business are scarce. A large percentage of well-educated women don't want kids or want them later in life. There are fatherless kids all over the place. Look at NBA baller Shawn Kemp, "The Reign Man," who has seven kids with six women. According to rumours, it might actually be eleven with nine women. As Complex.com quipped, those are some "near double-doubles on and off the court." You'd think he'd learn to keep it in his pants or something. One slip-up with a woman and your life could be ruined. Once, a friend of mine told me that his girlfriend dialed 911 during an argument. A chill ran down my spine. It is painfully simple to ruin someone's life with one phone call these days. I have a great career and my own home, so there's no way I am betting all that on the flip of a coin. I can't even fathom how families with children handle divorce. It's the most soul-crushing thing in life for all involved. I know. I've seen it first hand.

A lovely woman I was dating was going through a rather tumultuous time with her soon-to-be-ex-husband during their divorce proceedings. One night she called him regarding a small matter involving a quarter of a million or so dollars he was supposed to deposit into her bank account (nothing "major") and put him on speakerphone. I've never heard such childishness. This is a man whose highlight of the day was coming home and telling his wife about the different toppings he'd had on his Subway sandwich at lunch. This was before sitting down to a bass fishing marathon on the Outdoors Network. If you think I'm making this up, I'm not. After she (rightfully) accused him of cheating on her with her best friend and neighbour, his comeback on the phone was, "Oh yeah, what about the time I paid for your pottery class? How come you never give me any credit for that?" And when she asked, "What have I ever done to you?" he answered, "Like that time you woke up in the middle of the night and drank up all the milk. And then I got up to have my Corn Flakes and there was none left!" "What?!" she yelled. "You cheated on me!" He ended with, "Oh, so I'm a cheater, but you can just drink up all the milk!" I tried not to laugh in the background. This was also a man who, after their house was finally sold, removed the large marble island (which he had built) in the middle of the kitchen the very morning the new family was moving in. A failed marriage can bring out the absolute worst in people. This petty little shitheel was exhibit A.

Bottom line: Marriage is buying a house for someone you hate.

EIGHT

SPORTSCASTING: TURNING YOUR PASSION INTO A PROFESSION

(or, cigars with Howard Cosell, drinks with Bob Costas, an afternoon with Danny Gallivan, and something fishy about Marv Albert that night at the Gardens)

As a teenager, I was up for a late-night position as a summer fill-in at one of the local rock radio stations. This, of course, thrilled my sisters, who knew they'd get to call in and request their favourite songs. I didn't get the gig, but months later I did land the job of morning sportscaster at the same station. Jackie and Judy were less jubilant because it's not as if I'm getting a lot of requests for audio clips of Montreal Expo Gary Carter. The thing is, I've always wanted to be a sportscaster. You may not have met me, but you know me. Or at least my type. The hyperactive, annoying kid on the playground who does the "play by play" of a road hockey game, *while* he's playing in it. Emcee of the talent show. Big roles in the school plays, which were so good, we turned pro. (Heck, I was the Shoemaker in *The Shoemaker and the Elves* in grade two.) Dorky, I know, but I was varsity *everything* in sports at school, so things evened out. But girls still love the long ball and the slapshot and sports, which brings us to …

As a teen I used to caddy for some of the local TV sportscasters and their wives on summer weekends at a nearby golf course. I looked at those long, tanned legs and just knew I had to be a sportscaster. The wives had long, tanned legs, too. (Hey-yo!) My high school English teacher suggested that I look into broadcasting, and through his connections he got me a gig at a local radio station at the age of fifteen. I would sneak into the TV newsroom from time to time, and it was love at first sight. The hypnotic, staccato music of the teletype machine and the adrenaline of anchors, reporters, cameramen, and writers preparing for the upcoming newscast were downright intoxicating. I read the *Toronto Sun*'s Bill Lankhof's final column, and just like in the first paper he worked at, for me, my first TV newsroom was "filled with cigarette smoke, urgent voices, the clickity-clack of typewriters, editors yelling for copy boys, rooms stoked with human electricity and energy unlike any other occupation." It did not resemble Mary Tyler Moore's WJM-TV in Minneapolis. But I just wanted to be "in there," you know? I remember on one of my first nights at CityTV, the evening of the Ontario general election of 1990 on September 6, I just kept plunking ice into Colin Vaughan and Gord Martineau's whisky glasses, feeling that I was contributing. Hey, I was a rookie. More ice, "probie"!

Growing up in Montreal, my go-to stations were CBC and CFCF TV, mainly because the sports department employed the legend that is Dick Irvin Jr. along with Brian McFarlane, "Big" Jim Bay, Dave Reynolds, and Ron Reusch, all of whom I would get to know one way or the other over the years. Let's start with Mr. Reusch, by far the least talented of the bunch. While most TV sportscasters were good-looking men with deep voices, and, again, long, tanned legs, Reusch was a little man with a terrible complexion. Ron's history with me and the entire Gallagher family started on my sister Jackie's birthday at Jarry Park in late June 1972. (I would think it wasn't much of a birthday gift for eleven-year-old Jackie. A baseball game? Had anyone ever heard of Malibu Barbie?) Now, for those of you not old enough to remember Parc Jarry, it was a little bandbox of a stadium. It was called rinky-dink, but in a most charming way. And I adored the place. For the most part the Expos were lousy in the Jarry years, but it was home. The ballpark seated just 28,456. There was a little press box just above the seats behind home plate.

On this beautiful Sunday afternoon, the Expos were host to the Phillies in a battle of two teams fighting to stay out of the National League's East division basement. As there was no concession stand for reporters covering the game, the media had to line up with us regular Joes for pop, hot dogs, or, as was the case that day with sportscaster Ron Reusch, beer. A whole tray. I know this because I pointed him out to my father as Ron tried to carry — unsuccessfully, as it would turn out — five or six brewskies up the stairs to the press box. Whether Ron had had a few in him already that day I don't know, but he stumbled big-time on his way up the stairs, and half a dozen cold beers cascaded down onto the unsuspecting Gallagher family. It was a direct hit, with most of it landing on my father. Reusch, seeing the evil of his ways, said nothing (we may have heard a girly little shriek) and ran up the stairs and into the press box for cover. A huge groan came up from the fans around us, and my father, drenched in barley and malt, jumped up and gave chase. Frank Gallagher was a pretty big guy at a little over six feet, and he was the kind of man you didn't want to piss off. The Nazis turned out to be no match for him in World War II. With this astonished look on his face, not to mention several beers dripping off of his Sunday-go-to-meeting attire, "FJ" was on the hunt. He flew up the stairs in pursuit of Mr. Reusch, who had the instincts to quickly slam the press box door and lock it behind him. I looked up in awe as Dad pounded on the door, demanding to have a little "chat" with the suds-spilling culprit. After several attempts to get in and at "Mr. CFCF Sports," he yelled though the door, "Just apologize! Just come out and apologize, that's all I ask!" Now, I'm sure with his wife and half of his kids, including me, just a few feet away, Dad wasn't going to ruin a festive family outing by trouncing a local sportscaster, but what's right is right. A pair of comely usherettes — beautiful women in short, short, short blue uniformed dresses (no grouchy old men, like at Fenway or Yankee Stadium, in fun-loving Montreal, please) — brought us some paper towels to dry off with, and, thankfully, all was forgotten. A round of drinks for my dad from Ron upstairs would have been appropriate, but no.

On a personal note, after several cases of road rage during my lifetime, I eventually subscribed to the FIDO philosophy of driving: Forget. It. Drive. On. I'm glad my father had the wherewithal to do the same thing that day, although I secretly wished that he had waited by the press parking lot afterwards and trounced the little troll. Ron Reusch was a subpar sportscaster and, as it turned out, a coward and a schmuck. I actually ran into Ron outside the Molson Centre after a Canadiens playoff game recently and asked him about that fateful day. He said he didn't remember the incident at all and shrugged me off as if I were some fan. Putz. Also, I smelled beer on his breath. Perhaps the same scent from the summer of '72? After all, he was wearing the same sports jacket.

Before we get to the "Dick and Danny" show (Irvin and Gallivan), let me tell you about another so-called legend of the seventies Montreal sports scene. Say hello to "Big" Jim Bay, who I had the unfortunate displeasure of briefly working with in 1981 while I was with CJCH/C100 in Halifax. Our CHUM station affiliate was CKGM/CHOM in Montreal, two stations I grew up idolizing as a kid. I was covering the '81 NLCS between the Expos and the L.A. Dodgers. The deciding game five on Sunday was a rainout, so my morning team back in Halifax wanted me to stay in Montreal and broadcast my sportscast live on the Monday. Bad, because it was another day to try to track down a fast-selling Youppi (the Expos mascot) doll for $45 at Olympic Stadium for my girlfriend, but great because I would get to see how a big-city radio station morning show — one of the best in North America — and a station I grew up listening to worked "up close." Let me first say this: through my years as a broadcaster, I have never once said no to a high school or university student or intern who has asked for an interview to help them with their career. All I ask is that they bring a recording device. There's nothing worse than having someone trying to slowly write down every word when you're on a roll and have to stop and start every few seconds. I've always been willing to help fellow journalists. It's called professional courtesy. Just something you do. Not so much for "Big" Jim Bay, though. He had neither the time nor even the politeness to help me out that Monday morning. No photocopying of the morning sports briefs from the Broadcast News service. No helping me edit my audio clips from the NLCS. Nothing. I got all of my information from the *Montreal Gazette* newspaper and wrote my sportscast out with pen and paper. Not to mention that this boorish, washed-up former TV star was out and out rude because I was in his way in an already cramped little newsroom. I promised myself right then and there that, if given the opportunity, I would never treat a colleague that way. And I never have. Epilogue: "Big" Jim Bay is an asshole to the nth degree. I feel better now. Do you?

* * *

The first time I met fellow Foster Hewitt award–winner Dick Irvin Jr. was at a Canadiens-Bruins game on the day after my birthday on April 6, 1974. At the "old" Montreal Forum, you could actually buy seats that were next to the gondola where Dick and Danny Gallivan broadcasted their games. And they didn't try to hit on your girlfriend and harass her at work. (Wait, what? Read on.) Now, to almost every hockey fan across the country, these two men were pure gold. Whether you were a Habs fan or not, Dick and Danny were "it." Also part of the crew on this night was Brian McFarlane, who I just happened to pass high atop the Forum ice between periods. Of course, being a cocky young lad with aspirations of a broadcast career, I stopped Mr. McFarlane and told him just that. Plus the fact that I loved his powder-blue *Hockey Night in Canada* jacket. "Can I have it when the show is over?" I might have asked. Well, Brian seemed tickled by my exuberance and asked me if I would like to meet the broadcast team. Mmm ... let me think. While I didn't get the chance to shake Danny's hand — I think he was out having a smoke — meeting Dick was a thrill. They had me sit down in their little booth and put the headset on. We chatted briefly until the Forum siren sounded to signal the start of the next period, and I happily shuffled off back to my seat. Classic.

Speaking of Danny Gallivan, I did have the pleasure of finally meeting him years later at his apartment on Nun's Island, just minutes from downtown Montreal. My cousin Bill Curran lived in the same complex as Danny and one day slipped a note under his door asking him to call us. Bill explained to Danny (who had been sports director at CJCH radio in Halifax starting in 1946) that the young man who was filling his shoes at the same station some thirty-five years later was staying in the building. Danny was delighted to reminisce about his glory days in broadcasting and to just talk about sports in general, and he happily invited us both to his place. We talked for hours. A lot of it had to do with his flair for calling games. His vocabulary included words like "cannonading" and "scintillating," and, after a save, pucks tended to get caught in a goalie's "paraphernalia." I used these expressions on the schoolyard when I was nine

If you want to blame anybody for my sportscasting career, look no further than these guys: with Dick Irvin Jr. and Brian McFarlane in 1998 in Innerkip, Ontario.

when one of *my* saves foiled a "glorious scoring opportunity." Don't forget the "spinarama," the "dipsy-doodle," or when a player would come out of their own zone "rather gingerly." Danny told me during the interview that when a McGill University professor wrote to him protesting that there was no such word as "cannonading," Gallivan wrote back, "There is now." Perfect. In fact, the *Canadian Oxford Dictionary* includes an entry for spinarama. He loved that.

* * *

I've had good and bad experiences with some of the top sportscasters in the world on other occasions. That's if you fit Howard Cosell, Bob Costas, Marv Albert, and Chris "Boomer" Berman into that category, and who doesn't? Let's start with Howard "Tell It Like It Is" Cosell. When you're given his book *Cosell* for Christmas as a pre-teen, you may fall into the "big fan" category. My goodness, the afternoons I would spend listening to Howard call the blow-by-blow fights involving Muhammad Ali on *Wide World of Sports*. The Muhammad Ali–Oscar Bonavena fight in 1970 particularly stands out. Howard was in Toronto doing some press junket that landed him at the Four Seasons Hotel. All of the on-air bigwigs were there, including CFTO's Pat Marsden. I've always liked Pat, and we became friends over the years, but I must tell you, he was not in fine form that evening. Always the "hooch hound," Pat was literally and physically falling all over the great Howard all evening. A tad embarrassing, but Howard was enjoying the open bar aspect of the night's festivities as well, so he was rolling with it. I had five minutes with him. I tried not to stare at his hairpiece. I must say, though, hand to God, that he had the worst breath I have ever had the displeasure of encountering in my life. When he talked, it drifted my way, smelling of a two-week-old tuna salad sandwich from the Carnegie Deli left on a plate to rot. He lit up a cigar before our interview for good measure. You get the idea. I was throwing him softballs and he was hitting them out of the park. Great stuff. Before I wrapped, I knew that he had an upcoming cameo appearance on the TV series *Moonlighting*, starring the ego that ate Hollywood, Bruce Willis, and I asked him about it. Howard briefly talked about his role, and I asked him to embellish on that. "Embellish on that?! Young man, without me, the nature of *any* telecast would be entirely altered. I'll have a palpable impact on the show, giving it a sense of moment. If that sounds like ego, what can I say? I'm telling it like it is. I don't need to 'embellish' on anything!" My steel microphone started to wilt. He gave me a wink, knowing he was sending me pearls. We shook hands. Then Marsden threw up on him. Just kidding. Pat did hand me a cigar, and we lit one up with not-so-humble Howard.

Speaking of the late Mr. Marsden, I have to tell you, he was a piece of work. It's been written that "nobody who ever bellied up to a microphone lived larger, laughed louder, played harder, or enjoyed life more than Marsden." What a life Pat lead. He allegedly once stiffed a Nevada casino over a gambling debt and lived to laugh about it. It's true. In 1981, he managed to borrow $30,000 from the owners of the Dunes in Las Vegas and signed a series of markers when his money ran out. He then left three cheques, two of them postdated. Back in Toronto, he stopped payment on the latter pair. The casino owners took him to an Ontario district court — and lost. The judge said that Nevada's gambling laws and demand for payment were "unenforceable in Ontario." The balls on that guy. I remember when it happened, and I thought, "That's good enough to get *both* legs broken." But he went back to Las Vegas for a boxing match fifteen years later with John Derringer. Pat told John, "Remember my name is Jimmy while we're down here. *Not* Pat. If anybody asks, its Jimmy!" Pat was even bailed out of jail by Brian Mulroney. Colleague Fergie Olver remembered, for the *Toronto Sun*, "He was the only guy who was thrown in jail in Regina on a Friday night, and then went to Montreal, where he was thrown in jail again, and the former prime minister, Mulroney, bailed him out." One night while Andy Frost and I were over at the house of Gary Slaight, general manager of CFRB and Standard Radio at the time and Pat's boss (and my former employer), we had to hide the last bottle of rum from Pat just so we could get him into a cab. I've never seen a man try to suck the last few drops out of a liquor bottle like that. It was as if he was making love to it, and I don't mean that in a Fatty Arbuckle way. (Gary Slaight was the man who hired me out of Halifax, changing my life forever, and for that, I'm forever grateful. He was a brilliant but, at times, eccentric general manager to say the least. On some days you wouldn't know if you were still going to be employed at the end of your shift. It was a prerequisite to go to legendary Q hangout Rock 'N' Roll Heaven for parties on Thursdays, which was difficult if, like me, you had to do the morning show the next day. But Gary would come in at nine sharp the next morning, make sure everyone from the night before was there, and then go home for a long nap. And this is a true story: he once kicked a comedian out of the Q107 studio while he was on the air because he didn't think he was funny. The comedian was none other than David Letterman.)

Still, Pat had that bombastic style and impish grin that made him a staple in the sportscasting field for decades on channel 8, CFTO, (now CTV) in Toronto. That is, until one day he reached over CFTO news director Ted Stuebing's desk, pulled him over, and punched him. That was Pat. Mmm, wouldn't I have liked to have done that with *my* boss, CityTV news director Stephen Hurlbut. Hurlbut, who should have been cast in the film *Horrible Bosses*, had a direct involvement in my relationship with Pat. In 1996, Bob Mackowycz Sr., my old program director at Q, offered me a six-figure contract to do the morning show with Derringer and Mike Richards on the FAN 590. The plan was to replace the FAN's morning sportscaster Ken Daniels and have me co-host the show. Hurlbut and I, who quite frankly out and out hated each other, had exchanged emails and had conversations about me joining the FAN's morning team. After all, from 1990 to 1995 I'd hosted the Q Morning Zoo and still had no trouble anchoring CityPulse Sports at eleven every night of the week. I waited weeks and weeks. Mackowycz needed an answer for his bosses. I even sent CityTV president Ron Waters and Hurlbut bottles of wine in their hotel rooms while they were attending CRTC meetings in Ottawa. The bottles were sent with notes that read, "Dear Ron [or Steve], let's try this FAN 590 morning show experiment for six months. If you feel it's a hindrance to my performance on City, we'll call it off." Hurlbut, nick-named "Hurlabuse" by dozens of good people under his command, had assured me that he would pitch the FAN 590 proposal to Ron and Moses Znaimer. He lied. Ron told me afterwards that he was startled by the wine I sent him and even the news regarding the FAN's offer. Hurlbut also sent me a snarky scribbled note upon his return that read, "What were you thinking trying to win us over with cheap white wine in our hotel rooms? The answer is *fucking no!*" I still have that charming note … and the contract from the FAN. I will say this: while several on-air CityTV staff kowtowed and kissed Hurlbut's ass to keep on his good side, I went nose to nose with him, poking him in the chest (much to the chagrin of middle management — including my sports director, who witnessed these "bursts") because I knew I was tight with much higher-ups, such as Mr. Znaimer and vice-president and general manager of CityTV, Stephen Tapp. Funny; after Znaimer and Tapp left City within a few months of each other in 2004, I was gone, too. Back at the FAN 590, they gave the job to somebody else for a reported $300,000. That somebody else was Pat Marsden. We'll give the last line on Pat to Fergie Olver: "He lived his life the way he wanted.... He'd light up a room. He loved a good argument, a joke, a story, his family. We should all be so lucky to live the life he lived."

Fergie Olver was the on-field reporter for the Blue Jays for fifteen years starting in 1981. A nice enough guy, Fergie was a true-blue homer when it came to his beloved blue birds of happiness. He also ended up costing me a nice little chunk of change over the years. It was all beyond comparison with Fergie's Jays. Win or lose, with Fergie, Exhibition Stadium, and later SkyDome, had impossibly perfect conditions, where everyone was happy and nothing went wrong. Yes, butterflies, rainbows, unicorns, and, oh yes, crisp $50 U.S. bills. Fergie always carried a roll of $50 bills in his pocket before venturing down to the field for pre-game interviews. Now, we local reporters would get our scrum or one-on-one interviews before and after games, but ten minutes or so prior to the first pitch, only personnel of the official broadcaster of the game could be on the field. That would be Fergie. And the Jays players loved him, because after a quick interview, he would slide them a fiddy. George Bell and his teammates called it "cake." Do ninety seconds with Fergie and you have your cab fare home after a night on the town.

Now, no player ever asked me for any money until the day I *really needed* a player. It was during the 1992 World Series in Atlanta. I was on the field broadcasting live back to Toronto for this momentous occasion: the first World Series game involving a non-American team in the Fall Classic. It was 6:20 p.m. and most of the starting lineup was in the clubhouse, while some of the backup players were taking ground balls behind me as my cameraman and I set up behind third base. I heard in my earpiece, "Don't just stand there, get a player!" One of them was light hitting shortstop Manny Lee. I had some time to fill, but since the stars were off limits and not on the field, I had to grab who was available. If my good friends Kelly Gruber, Robbie Alomar, or any of the star players had been out there, they probably would have done it as a favour. Before I went on, I asked Manny if he could do a quick interview. He looked at me and asked, "Do you have some cake?" He wanted a handout. A $50 handout. I mean, Manny's 1993 salary was a million bucks on the nose, and he wanted $50 from me? Yes, he did. He wasn't even a great interviewee, but I needed something to run, so under the circumstances, I reached into my wallet and handed him his "cake," and we did a quick thirty seconds. The same thing happened the next year at the ALCS in Chicago, when career backup Darnell Coles of the Jays asked for some cake before the Jays–White Sox opener at Comiskey Park. At least Coles *only* made $500k that season. "Here, take it!" There went *another* $50 I'd never see again. You can't really ask for a receipt from these guys either. Damn you, Fergie Olver!

* * *

In Canada, there's no bigger name in sports broadcasting than Don Cherry, a.k.a. Grapes. Don Cherry fun fact: When Cherry gives you his phone number on the back of a card or napkin, he always writes "XXX" instead of his name so if someone steals your wallet they won't have his number. Now, the former coach of the Bruins (and one forgettable season in Colorado) and I have been thick as thieves since the mid-1980s. I was the voice talent for his *Rock 'Em Sock 'Em* video series for ten years before, as he informed me one day, I "out-priced" myself. So Don Cherry replaces John Gallagher on the series voiceover work with none other than … you guessed it, Don Cherry. He was a weekly guest on the Q Morning Zoo, and when he didn't want to do it, we would have his lovely wife Rose (who sadly passed away in 1997) come on. I loved that woman. Pure spunk. Don and I always made time to meet up at one of his now-defunct Grapevine restaurants.

One of my favourite Don Cherry stories started in Montreal, when he and co-host Ron MacLean went on a morning walk on Saint Catherine Street in full disguise with sunglasses and hoodies pulled up over their heads. The two spotted me and my girlfriend, who were in town for a

Habs game, window shopping. The GF? I liked to call her the "incredible shrinking woman" because she kept lying about her age. So, instead of being twenty, like she originally told me, she kept changing her age — first to nineteen, then eighteen. At his bar the next week, Cherry asked me about the beautiful woman that he and Ron had met in Montreal. Then he said, "She looked a little young for you. How old is she?" When I told him, he said, "Eighteen? I don't know how you do it, Spike!" (Spike is a nickname Grapes and members of the Q-Zoo have called me for decades.) Besides his bits on Q107, I would use him frequently for stories on CityTV. I would also call up "Uncle Don" when I needed advice. When I told him that local investors and I wanted to open up a sports bar called Gallagher's and that they had asked for a $30,000 fee upfront, Grapes said, "No, no, no, no! Don't give them anything. They build it and call it Gallagher's and give *you* 15 percent annually. That's the way it works." (I also asked friend and bar owner Doug Gilmour for advice, and he told me the same thing.) I finally passed on it when it came down to the name and the design. It's still open. It's called Safari, and it's right at the end of my street.

Laughing with Don Cherry, Tie Domi, and then-heavyweight champion Lennox Lewis after the champ said, "I'll hit you so hard, when you wake up that suit will be back in style!"

Years later I had Don on my TV show on CP24. I told him a story that made him turn white. I used to hang out and "cocktail" with former Bruin Dick Redmond. Dick played for the Bruins when Don was their head coach. In 1979, the Bruins and Canadiens faced off in the semi-finals. The series was widely regarded as the de facto Cup final because the winner was expected to defeat the winner of the other semi-final between the Islanders and Rangers. Something incredible happened in the waning minutes of the third period in the decisive Game 7. With the Bruins leading 4–3, Coach Cherry's team took an infamous penalty for having too many men on the ice. Heck, from my perspective watching on TV, it looked like the Bruins had an entire marching band on the ice. Habs Hall of Famer Guy Lafleur scored on the ensuing power play, which sent the game into overtime. Montreal would, naturally, score, sending the Bruins and Don packing. Well, as Dick Redmond explained to me, it was entirely Cherry's fault. He said that as the game was winding down, Grapes started showboating for the television cameras. He was really hamming it up on the bench, gesturing wildly. According to Dick, had Cherry been more focused on his job, the team wouldn't have blundered their way to defeat. Dick alleged that Don Cherry cost Boston a Stanley Cup championship because of his arrogance and love for the TV camera. I didn't mean it to be a "gotcha" question, but it was. I told Don that story, on the air and he just melted, asking, "Redmond actually told you that?" And he started to seethe. And you know how Don Cherry looks when he gets angry. He, of course, denied it and mumbled something about "that SOB." But I'll never forget the look on his face as it went from white to red.

* * *

In 1988 I was part of Q107's spring training team in Dunedin, Florida. The boss, Don Shafer, took the staff to a big dinner at one of the top restaurants in Tampa. The legend Bob Costas was just finishing up his *Costas Coast to Coast* radio show in the lobby. He was gracious enough to give me and my colleagues over an hour of interviews and photo ops. Bob was friendly and courteous, just like he is on air. He also turned out to be a lot funnier than I thought he'd be. A year later, Blue Jay fans would boo Bob during the 1989 ALCS for an innocent observation that had been taken out of context. In the ninth inning of Game 1, he said, "Elvis has a better chance of coming back than the Jays." It was 7–3 A's, with hall-of-fame closer Dennis Eckersley on the mound. I laughed when he said it, not only because it was dead on, but because it was funny. When the series shifted to Toronto for Game 3, banners hanging all over SkyDome declared that the Blue Jays — and Elvis — were still very much alive. Elvis's hits were even played between innings. Costas became a target for angry fans. "Nuts to Bob Costas" (N.B.C. — get it?) was a headline in the *Toronto Sun*. Bob said, "All I said was, 'Elvis has a better chance of coming back than the Jays' — in the ninth inning of Game 1. Not in the series. I didn't say anything about the series." Bob was right all along. The A's easily knocked off the Jays in five games. I was at the game when Jose Canseco hit a monster home run into the fifth deck of SkyDome. Nobody had ever seen *that* before The ball flew just under five hundred feet and absolutely stunned the home crowd. Another future Blue Jay, Rickey Henderson, hit .400, with one double, one triple, two

Here I am making the greatest sportscaster of our generation, Bob Costas, squirm in 1988 as my producer Dave Barker tries not to giggle in the background. Who says "be careful not to meet your heroes"?

home runs, and eight runs scored. He drove in five runs, walked seven times, and stole eight bases. Elvis and the Jays were indeed dead, but Rickey and the Athletics were very much alive and on their way to winning the World Series. As usual, Bob was right.

⁑ ⁑ ⁑

My Marv Albert encounter was a little bizarre. I was at Madison Square Garden for the first time taking in a Rangers–Winnipeg Jets game while visiting Manhattan in the early eighties. All you have to do is send in a media request with your station call letters and you're in. I was in the press box and encountered the NBC legend and late-night collaborator with David Letterman. I enthusiastically introduced myself. Now, if I'd had the gift of foresight, I would've understood the creepy vibe I got from Marv. It turns out there was something rather kinky underneath one of the most ridiculous hairpieces in the game. Marv was later arrested and charged with forced sodomy and assault after it was revealed that he'd thrown a female companion onto his hotel room bed, bit her fifteen to twenty times, and then forced her to perform oral sex on him. On the night in question, Albert called a hotel employee up to his room to "help him send a fax." She arrived and found Albert wearing women's underwear and a garter belt and, umm … fully aroused. She escaped by knocking Marv's toupee off his head and running out of the room. Wow. Of course, I didn't know about Albert's proclivities at the time. Nobody did. So there we were, the twisted Marv Albert and young, vulnerable(?) John Gallagher in NYC on "weekend leave." Marv Albert's booming voice is unmistakable, and it was so that night as he introduced himself and chatted over the boisterous press box and 18,000 hockey fans milling below. (On a side note, a fight broke out in the stands that night, and I could hear the bleacher creatures in the cheap seats yell, "Kill the fucking yuppie scumbag!" from up above. Yuppie, huh? I guess it *was* the early eighties.) I shook Marv's hand and was truly taken aback. I swear it felt like a fillet of salmon your fishmonger would hand you over the counter at Bruno's — cold, clammy, and pretty much "just fingers." *Come on, shake like a man!* I thought to myself. *You're Marv Effin' Albert.* I thought about our encounter a lot more after the cross-dressing story hit the press. I'm not saying he was hitting on me, but his handshake and demeanour were a little off-putting. Hey, whatever floats your boat, I always say.

* * *

As for Chris "Boomer" Berman, we spent a Saturday night in the Molson box during an L.A. Kings–Leafs Stanley Cup semi-final game during Toronto's memorable run in 1993. At the time he was one of the biggest names in the business at ESPN. He was a big, fun-loving bear of a man, a guy who was famous for his catchphrases and nicknames for players — Bert "Be Home" Blyleven was my favourite. There was also John "Tonight Let It Be" Lowenstein, Chuck "New Kids on the" Knoblauch, Tony "Jala" Peña, and Frank Tanana "Daiquiri."

Boomer enjoyed massive popularity in North America at the time, yet Global sportscaster Mark Hebscher would out and out steal these nicknames for his nightly 11:30 *Sportsline* show. I would make note of these so-called samplings and take the piss out of Hebscher the next morning on the Q Morning Zoo, asking, "Mark, don't you know that some other sports fans out there have cable and watch Berman religiously?" It's an unwritten law that no one can use Danny Gallivan's "Savardian Spinarama" or "cannon-ading drives" or "scintillating saves" on the air. Berman's catchphrases were in the same vein: a no-fly zone. Period. Come up with your own stuff, man! Mind you, if you're going to steal, steal from the best.

The night Berman and I hung out, the Leafs won 3–2 when Hall of Famer Glenn Anderson whacked a puck out of the air and scored with forty seconds left in overtime, sending the series back to L.A., 3–2, advantage Toronto. I should mention that the serving of alcohol had long been cut off at Maple Leaf Gardens as the clock went past midnight. Not so in the Molson VIP box, no sir. Let's just say Boomer and I marched merrily on into the night and the next day.

* * *

Bob Cole is certainly one of the most famous Canadian sportscasters of all time. The play-by-play man for *Hockey Night in Canada* since 1973, Bob has been the soundtrack of Saturday night for generations of Canadian hockey fans. Bob called over 90 percent of Leafs games on CBC from 1980 to 2008.

Best known for his "Oh baby ... there" calls, and my favourite — during Canada's 5–2 win over the United States at the 2002 Winter Olympics, when Jarome Iginla scored Canada's fourth goal of the game, excitable boy Cole yelled out "*Gore!*" (a hybrid of "goal" and "score"). How famous is Cole? He even has his own drinking game that viewers can play during a telecast. Here it is: the Bob Cole Drinking Game. Fun for the whole family!

> The Rules
> Bob: Says the right first name but the wrong family name of the player.
> You: Take a drink.
> Bob: Says the wrong first name but the right family name of the player.
> You: Take a drink.
> Bob: Says, "Oh baby!"
> You: Take one baby-sized drink.
> Bob: Gets at least one team wrong of the two that are playing.
> You: Take one drink. Take two if it's your team he gets wrong.
> Bob: Says, "Everything is happening!"
> You: Drink until everything is no longer happening.
> Bob: Asks, "Is there anything better in all of sports?"
> You: Take one drink if you disagree. Take three if you agree.
> Bob: Uses words like "dandy" or "no, sir."
> You: Take one drink for each use of those words in any one sentence.
> Bob: Says, "And here we go."
> You: Drink non-stop until we are not going any longer.

And so on. That's a lot of hooch. There are a couple of fun facts you may not know about Mr. Cole. I've been told that a maid can never enter his hotel room. Bob will not allow his room to be cleaned under any circumstances while he is in that town. Also, you *cannot* do a Bob Cole impression in front of him. I remember my friend Scott Russell of CBC telling me that he tried his Cole impression during a pre-game meeting with the *HNIC* crew a few years ago and received a stink-eye glare from the now-eighty-four-year-old. Also — and this is key — don't leave your girlfriend alone with him for a second. I learned this at a post-game party at former Leaf owner Steve Stavro's private underground lair at the ACC. I took my girlfriend Chick, who was looking quite ravishing that evening, I might add. Stavro put on a lavish affair, and he was known to be highly selective in who he invited to his parties. It was a who's who of hockey bigwigs, including NHL commish Gary Bettman. After making the rounds, including exchanging some pleasantries with Mr. Cole, I spent most of my time with Leafs coach Pat Quinn. Pat and I were sipping some fine whisky and toasting a rare Leafs playoff victory. I covered the Leafs for years while Pat was head coach, and while he was matter-of-fact with most media members, he and I would always exchange pleasantries. And a wink. I think it was an Irish thing. The fact that he always called me "Little Irish" and I would refer to him as "Big Irish" was a telltale sign. And Pat *was* big. Ask Bobby Orr how big after Quinn KO'd Number 4 at the Boston Garden in 1969. Pat also had the biggest hands I've ever seen on a hockey player. Like Yogi Berra's catcher's mitt.

Despite being distracted by Pat Quinn, I had noticed Bob Cole seriously flirting with Chick from across the room. Small talk. No big whoop. I wasn't going to get jealous of a guy who was old enough to be my father (or in Chick's case, grandfather). That is, until Chick started getting the phone calls. From Bob Cole. She played the first voicemail for me: "Hello, Martha. [Everybody called her by her nickname Chick.] It's Bob Cole ... here. I don't know what you're doing tonight, but I'd like to take you out for dinner ... oh baby ... there ... to Biff's. Call me back at the hotel when you get the chance ..." And it wasn't Bob in his normal voice — it was like he was on air doing a play-by-play! Chick hadn't even given Bob her business card, but he'd somehow tracked her down to her office, got her number, and kept calling her to ask her out. I wanted to call him at his hotel or at least confront him at the ACC suggesting that he stop this silliness, considering she was my long-time live-in girlfriend, but the messages were hilarious. Pure gold. We would later play them at parties, and our friends would be convinced they were prank calls. That's because everyone in the business, including myself, does a Bob Cole impersonation, and they all thought they had to be fake. They weren't. We even called the hotel to see if Bob was indeed staying there. He was. Now, Bob does his thing in the booth and seldom travels to the dressing room on game days, so I never saw him again. I don't even know what I would say to him. Thank him, I would think, for the pure entertainment.

Radio legend Mike Richards would make light of Cole's alleged womanizing over the years using a spot-on Cole impersonation in a segment on his show. The name of the bit was "Chicks I Like with Bob Cole." It wasn't until a little while later when I saw my friend Kathryn Humphreys say on air on CityTV something along the lines of, "You've got to be quick around Bob Cole. After all, he's quite the ladies' man." It was then that I knew he had hit on her as well. I'm sure you've seen pictures of Bob. Short, bald, fat with glasses. An incredibly talented broadcaster, but not exactly your "dream" date from that Milton Bradley *Mystery Date* board game. More of a "dud." But extra points if he announces the play-by-play of your lovemaking, ladies. Oh baby!

My final thought on all of my local and national on-air colleagues that I've befriended and respected for all these decades: I'm not knocking them, but while most morning show hosts and radio and TV sportscasters and anchors went home to their wives and kids an hour or more outside of Toronto to play it safe, I went out. I lived it. I always answered the bell and was never sick at sea. Well, almost never.

"She's got to be somebody's ooohhhhhh BABY!" Yes, Bob Cole (left), she's my baby. With the *HNIC* announcer and girlfriend Chick on the night that led to hours of Christmas party fun.

NINE

RADIO DAZED

(or, when my neighbour came over in his robe to complain about the racket at three a.m. and noticed the Harlem Globetrotters dunking baskets in my driveway, he just smiled and went back to bed) olumnist Gary Dunford was the reason a lot of us in this "business of show" read the *Toronto Sun*. Oh sure, their sports section was outstanding, but ol' Dunf on page six was a highlight not only for us in the radio/TV industry, but also because it was a great little gossip column for the masses. One of the big reasons we loved him was because Dunford loved Q107. He knew the industry well. Anyone in TV and radio looked to his column daily for a friendly shout-out, especially Q. He just adored us. There've always been a lot of "poison pen" columnists, like the *Star*'s Chris Zelkovich and the *Globe*'s William Houston. They were dour and sour, and just anti-*everything* when it came to reviewing on-air sportscasters and sports shows, in particular *Gallagher* on TSN. But Dunford was lighthearted and just hands-down funny. Zelkovich and Houston were hateful, hurtful scribes. I mean, no media personality likes to be criticized, and if they say it doesn't bother them, they're lying. But these two were trolls. I used to envision Zelkovich and Houston as vampires peeking out through the blinds each day, only to make a pained hiss as they saw the bright sun blazing down. Then, after days of sunshine, the clouds would roll in for a day, and, having gone stir crazy trapped in their crypts, they'd be out sucking as much blood from others as they could before retreating back to their dismal lairs. It's always been said that you never want to end up in Steve Simmons' column in the Sunday edition of the *Sun*, but at least Steve was entertaining. And fair. Except for one time, when he wrote that my pal former Toronto Raptor centre Žan Tabak was bawling me out after a Raptors game at SkyDome. Tabak was in fact pulling me aside to ask about trade rumours that he'd heard. But Steve more than made up for that by putting me on the cover of the *Toronto Sun* sports section when it featured a story on radio sportscasters. He made number one on his list, I might add, writing, "Gallagher has turned radio sportscasting into an art form. He is part-cynic, part-comic, part sportscaster, part fan, and he is ever the entertainer. He has grown into his stature as a cult figure among the Q107 listeners."

And he videotaped me as part of his VIP collage for his son's bar mitzvah. Sweet.

Now, as for Dunford, being an avid listener, he would routinely quote portions of the Q Morning Zoo in his page-six columns. One morning I was having some fun with a fellow morning show host, the lovely Erin Davis of ratings juggernaut CHFI. Erin and her co-host Don Daynard were part of an ongoing series of TV ads, some involving *WKRP*'s Herb Tarlek. Davis and Daynard's radio station is owned by Rogers Communications, so the commercials were just non-stop, almost on a loop, on all of the Rogers-owned TV channels. Now, Erin, along with a bubbly personality, is blessed with a large chin. Extremely large. A very masculine, Brian Mulroney–type feature. As my sportscasts were a treasure trove of silliness, for a joke, I compared Erin's protruding lower jaw to that of ex–Maple Leaf defenceman Bob Neely. Dunford later told me that he fell off his chair laughing because the likenesses of the two was astonishing and he hated that series of CHFI ads as much as I did. Sure enough, in the next morning's *Sun*, there was a picture of Erin alongside a hockey player on page six. From Q107's perch high atop the CIBC twin tower at Yonge and Bloor, which faced south to her station on Church Street, I could see the steam come out of Erin's ears.

There was a little problem, though. Dunford quoted me as saying that Erin resembled Bob Gainey of the Canadiens, *not* Bob Neely of the Leafs. Gainey didn't have a prominent chin at all. No one got the joke other than the listeners who had heard it initially. So, what does a good journalist do when his vast comedic abilities have been compromised? Well, you call up Mr. Dunford and tell him that, while you enjoyed the name drop, you were misquoted. Sooo (I know, this keeps getting better), what does Gary do in the next printing? He shows Erin Davis's mug *again*, only this time with Bob Neely's photo, not Bob Gainey's, with a correction for all to see, including the now extremely pissed-off Ms. Davis. I would see Erin from time to time over the years, but we never spoke. I wonder why? And when it came time to shoot a *Toronto Sun* Life section feature with all of the Toronto morning teams in pajamas and nighties (myself and Jake Edwards from Q, Roger Ashby and Marilyn Denis from CHUM FM, Tom Rivers from 1050 CHUM, Humble Howard from CFNY, and Don from CHFI), she never showed. Guess she can hold a grudge, eh? Obviously my comment and Gary's page-six double whammy bothered her enough for her to actually get a chin reduction. But I never knew how much it had hurt until I read an article in the *Toronto Star* about Erin and Don's last day on the air after years together at CHFI. Erin was quoted as saying, "We've loved our time together and have always had a wonderful relationship with our other competing morning shows and their announcers." She paused. "All except one: Captain Hairplugs!" Apparently, that would be me. I've heard and read worse insults over the years, and from better people than Erin Davis, but the fact that she was still harbouring resentment over my little on-air dig from over a decade before made me smile. Yes, as I always say, sticks and stones may break my bones, but words cause *permanent* damage.

✦ ✦ ✦

Q107 afternoon drive host Steve Anthony and I have been thick as thieves forever. We met in high school in Montreal and subsequently worked and roomed together at different locales across Toronto. Steve, one of MuchMusic's original VJs, is a sweetheart of a man. Blond, good-looking, and insanely talented, he's been with me for more than our share of late nights over the years. And women. When you come down for coffee and find Quebec rock goddess Mitsou in the kitchen with your Habs robe on, well, you know something was afoot the night before. Yes, Mitsou in my Canadiens robe. Smoking a cigarette. Put a plate of poutine in front of her and you have Visit Quebec's new ad campaign.

With Steve Anthony and his wife, Tanya Humphrey-Anthony, after I filled in as Steve's morning show host at CHOM FM Montreal in 1999.

The thing about Q107 is that we were winners, and we took winning seriously. At my first radio lip-synching "Battle of the Bands" contest upon joining the station, Jesse Dylan, Gene Valaitis, myself, and the rest of the Q Morning Zoo, all of us in togas, performed Sly and the Family Stone's "Dance to the Music" to a packed Copa nightclub audience. Every radio and TV station was represented. The competition was fierce. We won. Even when we didn't win, we turned a loss into sweet victory. In 1992, just a year after winning the Foster Hewitt Award for Canadian Sportscaster of the Year, I was named *worst* sports reporter by *Toronto Life* magazine. I would be "honoured" again the next year. I was, like, "Whaaa?" Devastated. Demoralized. Jesse and Gene declared, "No, no, live it. Love it. Embrace it. What do these pretentious chi-chi posers know? We'll play it up on the air. Take ownership. Don't bury the lead — bury them. Fight fire." So it began: "Now with sports, here's *Toronto Life*'s choice as worst sportscaster …"

Also, Q had an incredibly well-rounded softball team. Always one to toot my horn and my nose, I don't mind telling you that at that point in my career I was an extremely good softball player. A two-time MVP of my ballclub, the CJCH/C100 No Stars in Halifax, I actually hit a home run my first time at bat with Q107 at U of T. First pitch, over the left field fence. I always hit leadoff and, as the team's manager, pencilled myself in to play left field. There was a lot of room to cover out there. When it came to radio and TV celebrity softball teams, some stations would just trot out some technicians, all-night board operators, and maybe the weekend newswomen to play second base. I always thought, what's the sense of promoting your station softball team when nary an announcer would show up to play? Not us. The Q-Jays were stacked with on-air talent. Brother Jake Edwards, Rockin' John Derringer, Andy Frost, Joey Vendetta, and I filled a good-looking lineup. Every year we competed in the annual AM/FM softball world series over a weekend at Molson Park in Barrie. This event was the highlight of the softball schedule. For one thing, it was for radio bragging rights. Oh yeah, and it had an open bar. Wide open. It was just non-stop drinking. Now, as the guy who had to fill out the lineup before each game, I had to keep an eye on the players who were "enjoying " themselves more than others. The Q-Jays would be entered into a number of highly competitive tournaments each season but, again, the stakes were the highest for this one. This was the world series, after all. We always got to either the finals or the semi-finals, and on one memorable occasion, thanks to a three-run opposite field triple from Derringer, some stellar play at shortstop from Frost, and a series of circus catches in left field from your author, we beat CFRB 4–2 for the title. Every member of the winning team received a Wimbledon-esque silver tray engraved with the championship, team, and score. This thing would have made Martina Navratilova envious.

One year the entire morning show at the Q Morning Zoo suited up and took on the "Grey Jays," a group of men in their fifties and sixties, for a game in Dunedin, Florida, and got whopped. While we were down there, we decided to score a little sumpin' sumpin' to rev up a Friday night. I won't tell you who was with me trying to buy cocaine through a pre-arranged meeting in a mall parking lot in Clearwater, but I'm glad one of us had the sense to ask the dealer, "Before we give you the money, are you a cop? I have to ask you that, and if you are, you have to tell us." He *was* a cop and promptly told us to "fuck off and get the hell out of my sight and out of Pinellas County!" as he showed us his badge and his gun. Oops.

On another trip, one of the women from Q's accounting department who came down with us told everybody that a cab driver she'd met the night before could get lots of the "white stuff." And not just blow. Apparently he had everything from "a diddle-eyed Joe to a damned if I know." We pooled all of our money — hundreds and hundreds of dollars of it — and gave it to her to give to her new friend the cab driver. He took the money and moseyed off in his taxi into the sunset. What could she say? "Hey, he's stealing all of my drug money"? The best lessons learned are the ones you learn the hard way, I guess. Sniff.

* * *

Being a sporty on-air type has brought a lot of unexpected perks. One Saturday afternoon I was asked to play against the Harlem Globetrotters. Of course I leapt at the chance. Well, leapt as much as any aging white guy could! Cool, eh? I saw them at the Montreal Forum when they dressed the likes of Meadowlark, Curly, and Geese (they were so famous they only needed first names). I even watched the *Harlem Globetrotters* Saturday morning cartoon. I loved those guys! Before you get excited, remember, I was asked to play *against* the Globetrotters. I would be suiting up for the hilariously woeful Washington Generals, the long-time comedic foils to the Globetrotters' antics. Through the years, the Generals lost more than 16,000 against the showboating basketball tricksters from Harlem. Somehow I knew that I alone wouldn't be enough to end their record-setting losing streak. The 'Trotters did have one rule: the celebrity ringer on the opposing team (Bob Hope was one, as was Soupy Sales and even Henry Kissinger) *had* to make a basket. I was nailing some shots from past the three-point line (my specialty) in warm-up, but when I got the call from the coach, it was much different. Anyone who has met me knows that I top out at five foot eight, maybe five foot ten with my Tom Cruise–autographed model lifts in my shoes, so to be on the court with these behemoths (Paul "Tiny" Sturgess of the Globetrotters was seven foot eight) buzzing around was nerve-wracking. They kind of set me up so I had a clear path to the basket. But I missed. Then I missed again, much to the delight of the fifteen thousand or so fans in attendance. Those boards were bouncier than the ones I shot at in high school! Finally one went in and the crowd applauded politely.

Even in defeat, the Generals were a happy gang of professional b-ball players, and I invited them and the Globetrotters to join me that Saturday night at the Barracuda nightclub for my Q107 "Weekend Warrior" gig. As I recall, living legend and baseball Hall of Famer Cal Ripken Jr. and some of his Orioles teammates showed up that night. My new teammates and I had a blast, so much so that they came home with me with some women they picked up after the bar closed. The bar is never, and I mean never, closed at the "Château de Chardonnay." And here's the kicker. When they found out that I had a basketball net, we all went out to shoot some hoops on the back porch. Game of H.O.R.S.E., anyone? The fact that it was past three a.m. was of no concern to me. But it was to my neighbour, whose phone calls I was ignoring or didn't hear. When he came over in his robe and saw several rather large black men with their red, white, and blue star-studded official Globetrotter jackets on, dunking in my driveway, he just smiled, mumbled, and went back to bed. Ah, long live the 'Trotters, and especially my Washington Generals, getting pantsed and smiling about it until eternity.

* * *

Sometimes the perks come in the form of Canadian dollar bills. Lots of them. In 1994, the good people of Labatt Breweries wanted to have a meeting with the members of the Q-Zoo. They brought briefcases. Scruff Connors, Jeff Chalmers, Donna Saker, and I were asked if we'd consider an offer. Beer? No, even better. They would give each of us $15,000 if we would refrain from mentioning any other beer company for a full year. Just Labatt's and all of its other products. No mention of their fierce rivals Molson or any other brewery. For instance, the Molson Indy car race would be the Toronto Indy. The Molson Amphitheatre? What would we call that? Just the Amphitheatre, and so on. Gee, what do you think our answer was? Nice gig if you can get it. To paraphrase Harry Chapin from the song "Taxi," I stuffed the cheque in my shirt. Labatt's was also good enough to have Scruff and I throw out the first pitch of the 1994 Blue Jays season. The last pitch of the 1993 campaign was from Mitch Williams of the Phillies to Joe Carter. The next pitch off that same mound was from me. I think I jinxed the joint. MLB would end up cancelling the '94 season in August.

In the late eighties, Labatt's and Budweiser were good enough to offer me the hosting gig for Monday Night Football at assorted O'Tooles road-houses across southern Ontario. The real kicker was that listeners would put in their name for a draw that might win them an NFL football, which I would give away at the two-minute warning. The ballots would also make entrants eligible for the grand prize, which was a trip, with me, to the Super Bowl in January. I went three years in a row. They went from good, to better, to best. The first NFL championship I attended was at Jack Murphy Stadium in San Diego in 1988. I brought along the head of our writing department, Dave Barker, and producer Gary Whidden, just for fun, and we waited to meet the winner on a Thursday morning at the airport in Toronto. We looked around for this guy at the designated gate for a while, and when no one approached us (we were decked out in Q107 attire), we got a little concerned that he may have been MIA. We took a quick tour of the area and came across a guy reeking of alcohol, with his clothes all unkempt, passed out in one of the seats. He did have a carry-on bag with a name tag on it. We checked the name with our winner's itinerary. *This* was our guy. *Good God, man; get yourself together*, we thought. We just left him to sleep it off. He did finally wake up, stumbled over, and offered us some of the vodka-laced family-sized Tropicana orange juice that he had stashed

Here I am throwing out the first pitch at SkyDome in 1994. Bad karma. They would cancel the entire season a few months later.

in his bag. We passed. I'm surprised they let him on the flight. This guy was a total nightmare. Later, when we got to sun-splashed San Diego (my goodness, what a beautiful city), we went to a high-end taco restaurant, natch. So, what does Mr. Stoli vodka do, still in a drunken stupor? He finishes his meal and runs out on the bill. Well, so much for entertaining the contest winner. I don't know what drugs Gary had in his toiletry bag — I think he said it was for his migraines — but the next day we gave our contest winner some top-notch pharmaceuticals to help with whatever condition his condition was in. They knocked him out. He said he slept all of Saturday and ordered in food, and the next time we saw him was on the bus to the game on Sunday morning. But *not* before Dave, Gary, and I did what any red-blooded Canadian boys on vacation would do on a blistering hot Saturday afternoon. South to the border went the three amigos — a term that was in vogue that weekend, not because of the daft and unfunny ¡*Three Amigos!* film from 1986, but because that's what the Denver Broncos called their three young wide receivers who led them to Super Bowl XXII. The three amigos would lose 42–10 to the Redskins. We took the twenty-minute cab ride from our hotel to Tijuana, Mexico. What a shite show that was. We were not in search of the legendary Tijuana donkey shows (don't ask), which do or do not exist, or the bullfights, which do. No, just a day of bar-hopping in shorts and tank tops and watching the tourists, thousands of whom had flooded into San Diego for Super Bowl weekend and were doing the exact same thing we were: getting *pasado de copas*. Getting into Tijuana was the easy part. You see, the cabs don't come back to get you, and the Tijuana taxis (thank you, Herb Alpert) won't leave Mexico. So you've got to walk for miles once you get back on U.S. soil, with hundreds of revellers who have joined you for the day, just to flag a cab back to S.D. It was night time in Tijuana, and it was a little spooky being at the border. But hey, Super Bowl weekends are made for this kind of thing.

My third time heading to the Super Bowl was with a lucky fan was in 1990. The game was in New Orleans, making it one to remember whether you even attended the game or not. It's true; thousands of people flock to the city for the parties alone. Game? There's a game? For me, the fun started even before we left the tarmac in Toronto. As you know, Budweiser would send me down to the game, plus a contest winner, but with New Orleans being a city so small (under 500,000 in 1990) and hotels at a premium, I'd have to share my room *with* the lucky Monday Night Football draw winner. And since the airport in New Orleans was small and there were not a lot of flights accommodating the hundreds of thousands of revellers flying in and out, the trip was for six nights. *Man,* I thought, *this person better be entertaining.* Remember that sloppy drunkard who would have missed the whole San Diego trip had we not found him passed out in the airport? So, I'm at Pearson looking around and waiting for some guy to come up to me and introduce himself when this gorgeous brunette taps me on the shoulder and says, "Hi, I'm Kelly, the contest winner." Now, it may have been just an oversight on behalf of the Q107 promotions department, who figured that, since over 90 percent of the crowd at O'Tooles every Monday night was male, this Kelly person would be one, too. But this was not a man. Far from it. I knew I had a slight problem here. The morning sportscaster sharing a room with a female contest winner? How many CRTC violations would we be breaking? There could be lawsuits involved. I got on the horn to Q and explained my predicament. They agreed — not good. Kelly later remembered that while we were going through customs, I had to empty my carry-on bag, and several condoms fell out. The elderly female customs official looked up, smiled, and said, "I hope you're planning on using those." Well, at least *someone* was hoping I'd get lucky on this trip.

And so, with the wheels in motion in T.O., Kelly and I headed to freak-show central in N.O., not even knowing where we'd be staying. I'd be lying to you if I said I was hoping she'd get another hotel room. I mean, she was just recently single and I wasn't dating anybody. And did I mention she was quite fetching? I called my Q107 promotions liaison in Toronto and, ta da, they had found Kelly a room. Bonus round: this one was a suite at one of the city's best hotels, Waldorf Astoria's Roosevelt. My hotel was in another part of town and across the Mississippi River, where nothing was going on. All the action was on Bourbon Street, baby, and after a long afternoon of travel I checked Kelly into the Waldorf and put my bags there for safekeeping, and we hit the town. And what a town. There was a Mardi Gras atmosphere from the moment our rubber hit the road in the bustling French Quarter. For special occasions like this, Bourbon Street becomes a pedestrian walkway during the evening hours, so no automobile traffic — just idiots like us walking (most stumbling) up and down the street. New Orleans' open-container law permits pedestrians to walk the streets with a "go-cup" in hand (I call them travellers) filled with one of New Orleans' signature cocktails, like a Hurricane from Pat O'Briens or a Hand Grenade, both of which are 90 percent sugar. There were dozens of brass bands and drunken dancing on the street, all beneath beautiful cast-iron balconies overlooking a seemingly endless row of bars, clubs, and restaurants. It was just insane, and this was night number one. My new "special friend" Kelly and I breathed it all in. That along with the greatest food I've encountered in any of the twenty-plus states I've visited in that fine union to the south. We basically lived at Paul Prudhomme's K-Paul's Louisiana Kitchen, home to some of the best, if not *the* best, Creole and Cajun food in the world. As that day turned into the next, I could see by the people on the floor and the clock on the wall (or was it the clock on the floor and the people on the wall?) that it was time to walk Kelly back to her $750-a-night suite at the Waldorf. As I looked around her beautiful, spacious room, I thought about what lay in store for me in my little room and the $30 cab ride to get there and thought, *Wouldn't it be nice if I could just sleep on the couch and check into my hotel tomorrow?* After all, it had been a long travel day, with all of the connecting flights from Toronto. Oh yeah, and I would promise to be the perfect gentleman.

Before I could even made the suggestion, Kelly told me that she had been to several Monday Night Football events that I'd hosted, and even had friends stuff the ballot box when she couldn't make it to up her odds of winning what she saw as a hopeful "dream date" with me. Knowing that made my next "move" seem like the natural thing to do. So, one thing lead to another, and, well … Funny thing is, I never even made it to my motel across the Mighty Mississippi. Kelly and I spent the whole sun-, booze-, and football-filled week soaking in all of the colourful sights and sounds of N'awlins. Oh yes, and the extracurricular activity was indeed a bonus. Funny, we even dated for a month or so after we came back. Again, the game ended 55–10 for the Niners. The fifth-highest-scoring Super Bowl of all time. On and off the field, as it turned out. Stop it!

TEN

CITYTV EVERYWHERE

(or, as I was called in by station management and the RCMP, I soon realized how serious my day was about to become, what with a box filled with anthrax delivered to one "John Gallagher, CityTV"! Who would want to kill me?)

I guess it was fitting that, along with my duties as sports director and co-host of the Q Morning Zoo at "Toronto's Best Rock," Q107, I would join the eclectic newsroom at CityTV in the fall of 1990. But on the other hand, it was rather bizarre. You see, the fact that I was even hired to join the station was astonishing in the first place. CityTV was under the "CHUMbrella," which owned radio stations 1050 CHUM and CHUM FM. And, for the most part, Q107 and CHUM FM hated each other. During the late 1980s and early 1990s, Q's on-air personalities maintained a feud with CHUM FM, referring to it as "Scum FM," an obvious wordplay on its rival station's pronounced call letters. We, Q107, were referred to as "Screw 107" in retaliation by CHUM FM. How was I possibly able to do Q107 in the morning and CityTV at night? The simplest answer is that I got a tip from my then-roommate Steve Anthony, who was working down the hall at MuchMusic. I was one of the first people to apply, and I nailed the audition. It's as simple as that. Suneel Joshi had been hired by CFTO Sports to become that station's first non-white on-air reporter/anchor, and the ten o'clock (which would become the eleven o'clock) *CityPulse Tonight* sports gig became open. Heck, my shift ended at nine in the a.m. on Q, so I was wide open for the rest of the day. So, after a few weeks of auditions with CityTV cameramen and some skillful jockeying behind the scenes — CityTV's visionary man upstairs Moses Znaimer and CHUM radio execs tried to get 1050 CHUM to take me on as part of their morning team (they declined, thank goodness, because I did *not* want to leave Q107) — I got the call from "MZ" himself.

Moses is always armed with an arsenal of aphorisms. He's so extremely intelligent, so cerebral, that at times he says things to you that you just marvel at. And many times they'd just go over a young sportscaster's head. His phone message left on my machine late at night was one of those. I had to play it for friends to help me figure out what he was saying. Bottom line, Moses said I got everything I wanted. I now had the City sports gig and got to stay at Q107. So, there I was on *CityPulse Tonight*, the award-winning eleven o'clock newscast, in North America's now fourth biggest city. (I've never thought Mexico City should count, do you? But let's not quibble, Sybil.) CityTV was *everywhere*. We were known as Disco News. We were fun, abrasive, colourful, and years ahead of our time. Our six o'clock and eleven o'clock newscasts were, for all intents and purposes, the highest-rated news programs in the city, if not the country, in the "all-important" eighteen-to-thirty-four-year-old demographic. Technically CTV's CFTO had more people watching, but that was because over a million two-panty grannies in the neighbouring communities of Mississauga and Oakville hadn't gotten up off the couch to change the dial since 1972. That, and because there were no remote controls, so you *had* to get up! I personally think a lot of these sweet old octogenarians are afraid of "clickers." Our family once bought a new TV with a remote control for my grandmother, but she never used it. She thought if she pointed it at the TV and missed, the drapes would catch on fire. Ba-dum!

Anyone who lived in the Greater Toronto Area, or anywhere in Ontario (heck, I was told we were number two in the ratings in Ottawa!), knew that CityTV was full of characters, and I was one of them. In 1994, Peter Goddard of the *Toronto Star* called me the city's number one on-air sports personality, the "Titan of Tough" among sportscasters, writing that I was "a cross between Bruce Willis and a pit bull … a guy who calls 'em like he sees 'em, *if* he sees 'em." Rob Longley of the *Toronto Sun* added that I was "the city's best and *loudest* sportscaster." Being on television changed everything. I had done the morning show at Q for four years but, other than a dozen or so public appearances and a few TV commercials, I had done so under a cloak of anonymity. All that changed after a few weeks on *CityPulse Tonight*. It was the strangest thing. It was like I'd pulled off a mask, revealing some completely different (and pseudo-famous) person who had been under the latex all along. I was instantly being recognized all over town. For instance, the old Asian couple behind the counter of the corner store where I would pick up milk and other sundries were huge CityTV fans, and suddenly they were aghast by my presence in their store. They say that fame should be more than just getting a good seat at an expensive restaurant; well, let me say that not only are you all of a sudden getting the best seats at the best eateries, but you're no longer paying cover charges at clubs. Nice. I've regularly been bumped up to first class on trips (all you have to do is be polite and ask either when checking in or at the gate), but when it happens the first time because they recognize you and you get moved from steerage to seats 1A and 1B, it's really quite cool. In this instance, it was on a seven-hour flight to London with the new girlfriend. "Champagne for you before takeoff, Mr. Gallagher?" Yes, please.

This newfound fame also gets you certain looks from the opposite sex. Fundamentally, most women are suckers for a guy who's funny. I've met so many women who married the first guy who made them laugh in high school. And a lot of ladies are suckers for actors and TV types. This is a good thing. Watch them swoon behind the velvet ropes at red carpet events and at after-parties at film festivals like TIFF, making propositions and all that, even with D-listers like me. All you need is for a woman to either keep staring or just come right over and ask, "Where do I know you from?" Ninety-nine percent of the time it's quite advantageous, but sometimes, well … For example, I once had this one woman convinced that we'd jumped out of a plane together as members of the "Winnipeg Flying Club." The fact that I'd never been to Winnipeg did not deter her. Another time, I was sitting at the annual Toronto Maple Leafs pre-season luncheon at the Sheraton in the early nineties waiting for the team to be paraded in when an older woman, whose command of English was, shall we say, spotty, demanded that I sign all of her Wendel Clark memorabilia. She was convinced that I was the Leafs' captain. The resemblance was there, I guess. Short, stocky, balding, with a moustache. I tried and tried to convince her that I wasn't the pride of Kelvington, Saskatchewan, but to no avail. I couldn't shake her. She was a stage-five clinger. *Fuck it*, I thought, and signed everything she put on the table, even an expensive Number 17 Leafs sweater. I would have loved to have seen her face when the real Wendel Clark walked up to the head table. And again, as was the case with John Kordic, I still do get, "Hey Derringer!" and not because I look like him. It all just adds up, to some people. The connection to Q, the morning shows, and our names: John Gal-la-gher and John Der-rin-ger. Derringer and I worked on Q107 for years and still thrive in the Toronto market today, but we're still being confused with "the other guy."

While the other channels had their white, silver-haired Tom Gibney look-a-likes, we had rock-star anchors like Gord Martineau and the wonderful and talented Anne Mroczkowski. All of the sports anchors would swing baseball bats or twirl basketballs in our sports "tee-up." And everybody was always in motion. It was "We're walking, we're walking, we're walking, we're stopping and we're talking." Heck, we even had former lieutenant governor of Ontario David Onley do the weather using leg braces, crutches, or his trusty electric scooter. You see, Moses Znaimer liked to populate his on-air staff with real people, not reporters. Talents such as JoJo Chintoh, Monika Deol, Harold Hosein, Dwight Drummond, and the dearly departed John Saunders (to name but a few) were the true faces of multicultural Toronto. I know. It all seems so utterly Martian now. According to writer Ed Conroy in an article for BlogTO called "That Time When CityTV Had a Pulse," Toronto's former mayor David Crombie — who was also a huge CityTV fan — said "the city is your newsroom" in reference to the CityPulse news team's crowded Queen Street studio. For a sample of what I did there, look up "John Gallagher CityTV 1" (and 2) on YouTube.

❖ ❖ ❖

CityTV loved the cops and the cops loved us. I cannot tell you the number of times I have been let off over the years, after being pulled over by the police, because of who I was and where I worked. I got stopped several times on my way to work in the morning. I'd get out of the car (a complete no-no!) and walk to the cruiser, hoping that they'd recognize me and just wave at me to drive away. The gall, I know. And it worked. Mind you, one time on the PCH in Los Angeles, the CHiPs officers actually pulled out their guns ordering me back in my rent-a-car through their loudspeakers. They tried to nab me for "failure to stay in a carpool lane," but I weasled my way out. I pulled "The Unfrozen Caveman Lawyer" bit from *SNL* on the cops, telling them that these new lanes — which I actually had *never* seen — "frighten and confuse" me! "I don't know, because I'm a simple sportscaster from Canada — that's the way I think." And they bought it.

But most of the time that I saw the lights a flashin' behind me, it was very late in the evening. On one night, I was with my girlfriend Celeste and was pulled over after speeding up Avenue Road on the way home. As always, I got out of the car for a little of the "old soft shoe" tap dance.

After several minutes, the very nervous Celeste looked in the rear-view mirror and, to her horror, saw the cop and I armwrestling over the hood of his police cruiser. She then saw the six-foot-five officer win the "feat of strength" easily. He shook my hand and told me to play more soccer highlights on the eleven o'clock sports. Oh yeah, and to stop speeding. "On your way, youngsters!"

Another time, also heading north on Avenue, a cab driver cut into my lane and sideswiped me. (Totally his fault. Even his customer said he'd testify on my behalf.) When I got out of my sportscar to argue, I was pulled away by a cop who was immediately (and miraculously, I might add) on the scene. He said, "Johnny, I smell liquor on your breath. Here, come over to the side of the road. Now stand there and I'll take care of this. Don't let the cab driver smell the booze on your breath!" But my favourite, by far, took place in the early morning after a TIFF party (the bars are legally open until four a.m. because of the foreign press deadlines) and a cop pulled me over for speeding just about two lights south of where I lived. After a nice chat along the lines of, "Have you been drinking, Mr. Gallagher?" and me replying, "Yes," he did the most bizarre thing for me. Now, I'm not proud of this. Eternally thankful, yes; proud, no. But after sensing that it was possible I would blow over the limit, he took off his jacket and hat and threw them in the back seat of my car. He then took my sports jacket and put it on, placed my girlfriend in the back of his police car, had his partner get in the driver seat, and then jumped into my BMW convertible and drove me home safely and soundly. He just didn't want anyone to see that a cop was driving me home. Now, thanks to the fact that I don't work downtown anymore, and with the advent of Uber and my new love for the TTC subway system, I refuse to get behind the wheel after any amount of drinks. It was incredibly stupid then, and nobody should take these stories as an endorsement of drunk driving, which I may or may not have been doing. I'm just glad I wasn't given the opportunity to blow into a breathalyzer. After all, I didn't want it to tell me, "One at a time, please."

One day I got called into the big boardroom at City. I had no idea what it was all about. But I entered a room full of cops, including members of the RCMP. The station's head of security was there, too. If I was getting fired, this seemed like security overkill! Turned out that I, John

Gallagher, had been sent a mysterious parcel that may or may not have contained anthrax. A white substance was all over it. The same thing had happened to NBC anchor Tom Brokaw one week after the September 11 terrorist attacks. The anthrax in Brokaw's package infected his staff. Although my box tested negative for anthrax, no one was taking any chances. No other on-air personality at CityTV, or even in Canada, for that matter, received an anthrax threat. Just me. Hmm, maybe I *should* start running more soccer highlights.

✻ ✻ ✻

My time in this business always seems to come down to my relationship with Moses Znaimer. Whenever Moses would launch a TV network like Space, Bravo, or CP24, he would have me emcee the gala opening night. Not Gord, Anne, or Mark Dailey. Always me. I asked him about that, and, trying not to boost my ego, he said, "It's because you're loud and have a big mouth and you can quiet everybody up in a hurry." Moses knows the broadcast business inside and out. He is a visionary. Case in point: When he found out that I was leaving CityTV after eight years to host my own show on TSN called *Gallagher*, he was reportedly quite hurt. I mean, after all he'd done for me, right? When I told him how my mom could watch me from her living room out east on TSN, he responded with, "We'll send tapes of your nightly sportscasts to your mom through FedEx." He then took me through the newsroom and put his arm around me and said in front of everybody, "This is your home, John. Don't go." Then he said, "I know for a fact that TSN will be bought up by CTV in the spring and you'll be out of a job and back here begging for me to re-hire you." And you know what? That is exactly what happened. Mind you, because I still had a year and a half on my TSN contract (worth upwards of $150,000 per annum), I just went to Moses and asked for my old job back. He happily agreed, and we settled on a salary figure, but not without him giving me a little scare. You see, provocation is a particular tactic of Moses's. He's adept at posing the precise question that might rattle your chain so he can find out what you're made of, if you're worthy of his time. He set up a lunch meeting at a Japanese restaurant near CityTV on Queen (he sent his ramen noodles back *twice*, as I remember) and then promptly told me that he was having second thoughts about bringing me back. I had worked for him for close to a decade, but he still wanted me to "sell" him on John Gallagher. Huh? What was that middle part? I told him, "I've already resigned from TSN!" He was just having one of his moments. He signed me for five years. Cash on the barrelhead!

Years later, Moses had another, shall we say, "moment" when he hired me to host the morning show on his freshly acquired station, Zoomer Radio AM740, and to do weekends on the New Classical 96.3 FM (because nothing says Tchaikovsky, Bach, Beethoven, and Mozart like John Gallagher). Plus, I was doing voiceovers for his Vision TV and was the official voice for Joy TV. Yes, just like Muhammad Ali winning the heavyweight title thrice, I had been hired back by Moses a third time, and all was right with the universe. Again. At times, he is the same Moses Znaimer — mischievous, yes, but a man who has built empires and reshaped the media landscape. For a generation of Canadians, Znaimer designed the delivery mechanism for media's tastiest empty calories. And I adored him. Except for the times when we AM740 co-hosts (Bill Gable, Eva D, Jane Brown, and myself) would get simultaneous emails *during* the morning show asking, "Which of the four of you am I going to *fire first*?"

Oh yeah, and this happened. Moses and I attended Mark Dailey's funeral in 2010. I met several of my ex-coworkers and station higher-ups there. (I also got a tap on the shoulder from a distinguished-looking gentleman sitting behind me. He introduced himself. It was future Toronto mayor John Tory, who politely told me how much he enjoyed my work. Some people have zero taste, eh? Still, a mensch.) Something must've clicked between us. I think I saw a couple of lightbulbs flash over their heads, because the following week they called me into CityTV for a meeting. They asked me if I would like to be the new voice of CityTV. I thought, "Wow, what an amazing opportunity. I'll bounce it off Moses," since they'd unceremoniously fired him years before, breaking his heart. You never knew with Moses, because it was like good-cop, bad-cop with him. Well, bad timing for me that particular day, because Moses was in one of his moods when I set up a meeting to talk with him on the phone. I actually wrote the entire pitch down on paper, selling him with the idea of "Mark Dailey passing the torch to John Gallagher and continuing the legacy that you, Moses, began those many years ago." He said flatly, "No," then added, "If you'd like to leave me yet again and go back to CityTV, then go ahead, but you're not working for them and me, John. Again, no." Moses would change his mind a month or so later and give me the green light, but the job was filled. If I'd called him when he wasn't having a Frank Cross moment, it would have been different. I once asked Moses if Cross, the Bill Murray character in *Scrooged*, was based on him. It could easily have been, but it wasn't. But he told me that Ed Harris's character Christof, the manipulative, omnipotent producer in *The Truman Show*, starring Jim Carrey, was. What a shock.

I like to tell this story about my final day at Zoomer Radio (there's that *Z* again), AM740, and Classical 96.3 FM. It goes like this: Moses had myself, FM and AM music directors Michael Lyons and Brian Peroff (who had over forty years combined at programming the music at the two stations), Denise Donlon, and the one and only newspaper publisher and author Conrad Black, who hosted *The Zoomer* on Vision TV, all fired because of station cutbacks at ZoomerMedia. I heard months later that Moses didn't have the heart to tell me himself, so he had his henchman do it instead. It goes with the territory in this day and age in radio, TV, and print. I was the highest-paid announcer in the building. I even had a clause in my contract that stated that if any jock signed for a higher salary than mine, I'd get a dollar more. The problem was, Moses had taken over *CARP* magazine and renamed it *Zoomer*, as part of a multiplatform strategy to reach aging baby boomers. My question is, who buys a magazine? Not a single copy, but an *entire* magazine? Especially in this day and age. You'd walk out into the parking lot, and your feet would stick from the blood hemorrhaging from the *Zoomer* magazine offices. Mind you, there was quite a bit of the red bodily fluid pouring out on the radio side, as well. But as Cam Cole of Conrad Black's *Post* wrote of print journalists, and it augurs well for TV and radio sports types who have been losing their jobs "by the number" the last few years, "The sports columnists of my generation are the dinosaurs of the newspaper trade. And you know what became of the dinosaurs. We are the last of the over-privileged scribes who've been sent to travel the world, cover all the big events, and spend our bosses' money with impunity. And, we've known for a while now that the ride couldn't last forever." So, as the story goes, as Denise, Conrad, and I headed to our cars (on the anniversary of 9/11, of all dates), freshly fired and toting our boxes and computers, I said this to Conrad: "Hey Connie, what say we all head up to your place on the Bridle Path [often referred to as Millionaires' Row and the most affluent neighbourhood in Canada] for some drinks? We can get Barbara Amiel [his stunningly beautiful wife] into a little two-piece and sit around the pool! Are you in?" After all, Black, Amiel, my ex-girlfriend, and I had sat beside each other at the fabulous Opus restaurant on Prince Arthur in Yorkville years earlier — the night I gave my ex a pair of $4,000 diamond earrings on our fifth anniversary — and we'd exchanged pleasantries and he'd sent over a bottle of wine. So we had a history. Sort of. This time, Lord Black did not smile back. Perhaps he just didn't hear me. So I was fired from a station that played classic hits from Elvis, Sinatra, Ella, Dean, and Roy Orbison that I thought I'd spend the rest of my career at. And at the age of fifty, I vowed I would never make the mistake of being fifty again.

ELEVEN

SO FLEETWOOD MAC IS MAKING ANOTHER COMEBACK. ALSO MAKING A COMEBACK: COCAINE, WIFE SWAPPING, AND ROYALTY CHEQUES

(or, as the doors to the penthouse suite of the Four Seasons swing open, Stevie Nicks bends over and passes me her straw)

Being a host on Canada's premier rock and roll radio station meant I got to go to a lot of premium concerts. On October 19, 1987, a bunch of us from the station saw Fleetwood Mac (mmm … Stevie Nicks) at Maple Leaf Gardens. One of the station's sales execs was a close friend of the band's manager, and so we all got to meet the band backstage. Talk about a highlight! I was *this* close to two of my rock goddesses: Christine McVie and, of course, the absolutely jaw-dropping Miss Nicks. I'm pretty sure Christine was hitting on me. At the very least, she was making no attempt to be discreet while she checked me out. She may have just been trying to make her soon-to-be-ex-husband, bassist John McVie, jealous. Who knows? But I definitely recognized that look. I've been hit on before, and this was a hit. Poor Christine. I only had eyes for Stevie that night. Not that she'd ever give me the time of day. Still …

After the show, we all headed back to the Four Seasons hotel. Apparently Stevie wanted to have a little party for everyone back at her suite. Again, not saying I had even a remote chance of hooking up with one of the greatest rock vocalists of all time, but when you get a chance for a close encounter with a beautiful, famous rock star, you take it! "Reach in, dig in, but don't *fall* in," I always say.

We piled into the elevators, but by the time I got to Stevie's suite, the rest of the gang had drifted off. Probably to stop at their own rooms to freshen up. It was pretty late by then. So when I entered the suite, I was *el lobo solo*. The lone wolf. The doors swung open and Stevie Nicks was wearing a black bustier with a long, flowing gown. She was stunning, of course, but she kind of gave me a look that said, "Okay, boy. Eyes up here!"

I remember lots of candles, and good music playing from her CD collection. We had a glass of wine and sat on the leather couch chatting. Letterman was on TV in the background when all of a sudden he started butchering Stevie on air, showing her "I Can't Wait" video and a mock list of her upcoming appearances. You can see highlights of Dave's relentless assaults on Stevie online. It was part of a year-long feud he was having with her, Madonna, and Cher. He was unforgiving. Dave was one of the greatest late-night hosts of all time and one of my heroes, but he could be a complete prick. This — a repeat from when Stevie was on *Late Night* months earlier — was playing in the background while she and I sat there, me trying *not* to make googly eyes at my number-one rock goddess. She muttered something about "hating that asshole" and turned it off. We had some more wine, but I was looking for something a little stronger, without suggesting anything. Stevie Nicks was no stranger to alkaline chit chat flakes. She was once asked by ABC how much she had spent on blow, to which she responded, "Millions. Millions. And yes, don't I wish that we had that money and I could give it to cancer research today." Then there was also the rumour that, because of her deviated septum, she had one of her assistants, well ... Let's just say the rumour was about an alternative method of ingesting drugs that involves a part of the body that — well, let's leave it, shall we? For the record, Nicks denies the rumour. The London *Observer* released a "10 Greatest Rock 'n' Roll Myths" list. Coming in at number five? The allegation that Stevie Nicks had an assistant help her ingest cocaine using a straw and a part of the body not normally used for breathing in drugs. Didn't I tell you I'd leave it? The *Observer* said it, not me!

Eventually the rest of my party arrived. No one else from the band came, just some of the crew from earlier. Any chance for a one-on-one "exchange" with Stevie was gone. But this woman was so out of my league, I may as well have been a Little Leaguer pitching to the '93 Blue Jays. I took consolation from the thought that more people at the party increased my chances of ingesting a few lines. Snorting was my objective at that point. If there was any truth to those "Rumours" (sorry, couldn't help it) about Stevie, I really didn't want to see it. Or did I? That would be a great moment in rock and roll, eh? At least from where I was leaning down from.

Stevie had a better idea. And it *did* involve a straw. And drugs! A member of the crew had brought a gigantic chunk of black hash and had broken off a piece the size of a Knorr beef bouillon cube. No rolling papers? No problem. Stevie grabbed a Guinness glass and a large Fleetwood Mac '87 tour pin, bent the needle to a ninety-degree angle, lit it, and watched the plumes of hash smoke billow inside. And here it comes, kids: she took a huge suck from the straw, inhaling the hash, and while bent over passed it to me, and I did the same. This was shaping up to be an extraordinarily fabulous party with some fine (and fine-looking) people in the penthouse suite of the Four Seasons. But I could tell by the people on the floor and the clock on the wall that it was time to call it. I did get to kiss Stevie good-night. On the cheek, but hey, it still counts! After all, it was four a.m. on a school night, and I had half a dozen sportscasts to write. Not to mention that the morning show was now just a few hours away. It was totally worth it. I had a classic rock story to tell! And there's more: on the way out I did spot Aerosmith's Steve Tyler and Joe Perry getting out of their limousine and told them, "Hey guys, there's a party at Stevie Nicks's in the penthouse suite! You should go, man!" They looked at me like I was a two-headed cyborg. This stuff just writes itself.

TWELVE

G.O.A.T.: THE GREATEST OF ALL TIME

(or, "Ali, Boma Ye!")

Muhammad Ali rips the page out of my *Penthouse* magazine and tucks the rest of it in his coat pocket for later reading in his hotel room. His wife Lonnie rolls her eyes at him. Lonnie then feeds the three-time heavyweight champ of the world a mountain of pills, a quantity of medicine I wouldn't see until I was into my fifties. The champ was fighting the early stages of Parkinson's disease — an ailment that may or may not be linked to his days getting the insides of his head scrambled by the likes of George Foreman and Smokin' Joe Frazier in the 1970s.

Yes, I'm sitting next to Ali at, of all places, the Pickle Barrel in Toronto's Eaton Centre. This place ain't Ruth's Chris or Morton's Steakhouses (although I *so* wish it was), just a local Toronto family restaurant that has been around for years. My friend and fellow boxing fanatic, the late Eddie Zawadzki, had invited me along with a handful of other fans of the sweet science — Spider Jones, Paris Black, and others — just to have dinner and mingle with Ali, who was in town on a press junket. Lucky me, I got seated right beside him. We didn't speak much; heck, Ali hardly spoke at all then. For once in my life I was at a loss for words. What do you say to the Greatest? I do remember asking him how he liked his chicken, and he responded with an Andy Griffith–like "Mmm, *gooood* chicken." I had brought some sports magazine covers for him to sign and also an old 1980s *Penthouse* magazine (don't ask) that featured an article with a fantastic painting by LeRoy Neiman inside. Ali had never seen the *Penthouse* article (gee, I wonder why) and was enthralled by it. He sat there reading it (and covering it in chicken grease) until Lonnie asked him to put it away. He did, but not before taking the rest of the article from Bob Guccione's finest work and tucking it in his suit pocket. After all, the champ had some babies to kiss, hands to shake, and fan photos to pose for — he *loved* the attention. He gave me the classic James Cagney "you killed my brother" overbite pose when I put up a fist. I didn't want to push it, though. Even then, in his late forties, he could have dropped me like second-period French. Wow. I loved that man. Still do. I'm still sad that he's gone now. I can run down his entire career: dates, opponents, results, et cetera. I used to recite his poems for all to hear. For example,

Joe's going to come out smokin'
But I ain't gonna be jokin'
I'll be pickin' and pokin'
Pouring water on his smokin'
This might shock and amaze ya
But I'm gonna destroy Joe Frazier!

My recitals of Ali's poetry drove my family crazy. The fact that I sat beside him for over an hour and was actually thinking of attempting the Ali shuffle in front of him … well, that was a night to remember.

❊   ❊   ❊

Muhammad Ali tells me, "Punch me all you want. I'll still look pretty!" At the Pickle Barrel (yeah, I know) in 1988.

I've always been fascinated by boxing. My father never learned how to skate, and in turn, didn't play or watch hockey. Football was a secondary sport with my friends and family. So it was just baseball, with my beloved Expos, NHRA drag racing, and boxing for me. And to see Ali and Frazier on the cover of *Time* and *Sports Illustrated*, well, these men were like gods to me. Who has a *Ring* magazine subscription at eleven years old? Hockey cards, yes. Nat Fleischer's Ring Rankings, no. Who can name every heavyweight champion from John L. Sullivan to Ali at that age? Well, that's just not normal. The late sixties and early seventies were a golden age for the sport. There were Ali and Frazier, of course. But there were also George Foreman, Carlos Monzón, José Nápoles, and a young Roberto Durán. It was a glorious time to be a boxing fan. It's easy to forget now that in the first half of the twentieth century, the three big sports in North America were baseball, boxing, and horse racing. Now boxing is a shell of what it used to be.

Inspired by the greats, I started to "dabble," shall we say, at the local boxing club. Trust me, if the Montreal West Youth Boxing Club hadn't been five minutes from my house, I wouldn't have a great story about becoming the undefeated Golden Gloves Boxing Champion of Quebec. My brother Steve was already a provincial champ, having fought the likes of Ian Clyde and Cleveland Denny. Steve was a star in a school filled with the best young high school hockey and football players in Quebec. When Steve wanted more Elton John played at the Friday night coffee houses, the DJ didn't say no.

Our neighbourhood was an unlikely place for spawning up-and-coming fighters. As ever, most of the good fighters came from the rough areas of Montreal, Toronto, and Halifax et cetera. The problem with me is that I never trained. So I got just good enough to be entered into the Quebec Golden Gloves boxing championship in November of 1974 at the Shamrock Boxing Club, in Point St. Charles, as Irish an area of Montreal as you're going to find. *Maybe I could score some points with the judges with a name like Gallagher,* I thought as I headed to the quarterfinals on a Friday night. I would get a lot more than a few "nods" from the locals, as it would turn out. Since I hadn't fought as an amateur before, and not very well with the rest of the tweens at the club three nights a week, for that matter, I was placed in the novice category for fighters with nineteen bouts or fewer. The thing that separates boxing from even the most physical of team sports is that if you make a mistake, you can get hurt. Badly. Look at the other participation sports. A puck goes in on you as a goalie, and a little red light goes on. A ball goes between your legs, and the winning run comes in and — unless you're Bill Buckner, whose colossal boner cost the 1986 Red Sox the World Series — no big whoop. But when you get hit with a stinging right hand or left hook, it hurts. I've had to hold back tears more than a couple of times sparring in the ring. Anyone who's ever got a shot to the nose knows there are tears, and sometimes blood, so I'm here to tell you I was nervous, even a little scared. I was shaking on the drive to the Shamrock Club.

Here's how the weekend played out: Of the seven fighters in my category, one had to get a bye into the semis. That boxer was me. Score one for the Gallagher camp. A "gimmee" from the mostly Irish organizers at the Shamrock Club, perhaps? So another butterfly-filled drive to the tourney the next day and "bing bing bing!" — yet another break. The kid I was supposed to fight got cut in training just that morning. The result? I got *another* bye, this time into the championship round. So, it was Sunday and I had yet to even enter the ring. Some of these lads were 2–0 in the tournament, and I was still sitting on an 0-fer. My opponent that day was not just 2–0 on the weekend — he was 19–0 as an amateur. Say hello to Jean Francois Leblanc from Gaspé, P.Q., home of some of the hardest body punchers in La Belle Province. "Kill the body and the head will die," Smokin' Joe Frazier once said. Well, that was the way this kid had trained. And in his corner was local Gaspé legend Fernand Marcotte, the future middleweight champion of Canada and Sugar Ray Leonard's opponent years later.

I will say this about my first fight: at least I looked good. Blue satin trunks with white stripes, a glossy blue tank top, and my brother's Ali-like white boxing boots with tassels. Whatever was going to happen, it was going to happen in style. The three rounds were a blur. The Irish home crowd was of course behind a fellow "son of the sod," so cheers went up every time I landed a blow, as hard-punched as any fourteen-year-old with *zero* ring experience could muster. All I could hear besides the roars from the crowd was my brother Steve yelling, "Jab, John, *jab*!" And I was fast. Ducking and weaving. I mean, this guy couldn't catch me with a taxi.

It was late in the third round and it was close, or at least that was what my cornerman Sean Duffin was telling me. Then Leblanc hit me with a left hook, right in the bread basket, which is just below the solar plexus, near the cockles of my heart (and, for any Denis Leary fans reading, in the "sub-cockle area"). A harder punch to the stomach I have never received before or since. As the bell rang to end the fight, I started to heave. Leblanc hit me so hard I headed to the bucket in my corner, planning to spew my guts out. Duffin screamed, "Don't throw up! It will look bad to the judges." So I swallowed hard and waited for the announcer. "Le gagnant, the winner by a split decision, from the Montreal West Youth Boxing club, John Gallagher … Gallagher!" Wow, just to get through that weekend, what with butterflies, the byes to get to the final round, and the blood, but to win was indescribable. Even future Olympian Ian Clyde, with a huge smile, put the medal around my neck. Steve told me to congratulate my opponent with a "Bonne Boxe" handshake afterwards. I wanted to parade around the ring yelling "Ali, boma ye!" (meaning "Ali, kill him!" which joyous fans screamed at Muhammad Ali after he beat George Foreman in the Rumble in the Jungle a few weeks earlier). Of course, I was not Muhammad Ali. Not even close. Hell, who was? But do you know what? For a moment there, I was a champion prizefighter, and I sure felt like my hero, with a smile as big and wide as his.

The drive home was raucous, as I was the lone fighter from Montreal West to win that day and my trainers were thrilled to have another addition to their trophy case. As they dropped me off, they said something along the lines of, "Great job, kid. We'll see you at the gym Tuesday." But that was it for me. How could I possibly outdo what had just gone down? Besides, the girl I was dating from Montreal West High, told me, "I like that nose right where it is: on your face. Just saying." And with that, I passed the trophy back into the car and said, "I think this should be around *real* boxers. Thanks for everything — I'm retiring." At fourteen. What a career. And I've been milking it ever since. Hey, it looks good on the resumé. I mean, how many Golden Gloves Boxing/Provincial Freestyle Frisbee/High School Disco King champions do you know? Safe to say, none.

THIRTEEN

CAPTAIN HAIRPLUGS TO THE RESCUE!

(or, Barbara Walters announces, "We can't have John on *20/20* tonight because we're going live to the World Trade Center, where a bomb has gone off ...")

So my live interview on *20/20* is getting the sheperd's hook because of a terrorist attack? Damn you, Al Qaeda! Oh well, at least I can take this make-up off and hit New York City on a Friday night on ABC's tab. Thanks, Babs, as well as legend Hugh Downs (and Barbara's little Havanese dog, for keeping me company in the green room). Actually I wouldn't know how to respond to Ms. Walters: "A hair-waising weport" (no lie). It was 1993, and 47 million Americans had just seen most of my head spill open onto an operating table as doctors stuffed my pumpkin-like cranium with my own hair during a $90,000 hair transplant operation that ABC and CityTV's film crew had been shooting for over a year. In fact, the feature was so popular they ran it again a year later with an update on how my new mane was growing in.

Being bald sucks. Bald is *not* beautiful. Never was. Never will be. I know this from both sides of the eight ball. Let's take you back. Heck, we can go back to the late seventies when, in my teens, I could see my hair clogging up the shower drain and my comb dragging out more strands than was to my liking. My father was bald. Joe Garagiola bald. Brother Steve, three years older, was designing his own solar power landing strip "up top" with rapid movement. It was heartbreaking. Freaking bald and/or balding in my late teens and early twenties? Really? I was still "vaguely rocking."

I spent hours in bar bathrooms trying to move around the missing acreage. You had to work with what was left, but none of my girlfriend's spikey gel or hair spray could cover up the inevitable. I was turning into George Costanza. Pretty well all during the eighties I trimmed the 'do down to the minimum. Think Johnny Unitas or Leaf captain George Armstrong. Bare bones. None of this combover shite. *And* I grew a moustache. You see, that's what men do: secretly "distract" women from their balding pates by growing a moustache or a beard. That's *sure* to throw them off. I used Rogaine for years and years, but while it didn't grow any hair back, it did keep it from falling out. I was past the point of no return. What other options were there? We've all seen Hair Club for Men customers whose pieces are so bad you want to snatch them off their heads and throw them at them. Some actually look like a small muskrat has crawled up on their heads and died.

I knew about hair transplants. Nic Cage, Michael Keaton, Tom Arnold, Mel Gibson, and recently John Cleese have all had them done, but it was a chance run-in with friend and then-promotions director at Q107 Perry Goldberg that would lead me to becoming *the* poster boy for hair transplants worldwide. Perry's Toronto doctors were the famous Walter and Martin Unger, the gold standard in hair transplants. Remember in June of 1984, when Michael Jackson's hair caught on fire when a flashpot went off too soon during the filming of a Pepsi ad? Martin and Walter Unger were flown down to Los Angeles to patch him up. (It's been rumoured that the painkillers Michael was prescribed led to his life-long addiction and subsequent death years later, but at least MJ's hair looked good again.) These doctors were the very best, and Perry was one of their proud patients. Good, but gosh-darn expensive. I set up a consultation — I had enough of a "donor area," or healthy hair that never falls out in the back above your collar, and enough "elasticity" on my scalp to have the procedure performed.

And a complex and delicate procedure it was. The doctors took long strips of hair and flesh and carefully sliced them into individual hairs. These hairs and follicles were transplanted or inserted one by one into incisions in the scalp. Years ago, when the operation was in its infancy, doctors would transplant groups of hairs — or plugs — and patients would come out looking like your sister's baby doll's scalp. These new-generation grafts matched the growth patterns of your original hair. They'd even soften up the hairline so you would see a subtle hint of a receding hairline. That was why the operations were $8,000 a shot. I had seen several "before and after" photos and knew what famous scalps the brothers had worked on, so I was booked in for three operations at around $24,000. This was to connect the "Phil Collins Island" (as I called it) to the mainland. You've seen men with that little patch of hair above the forehead, like Collins and Gordie Howe. Walter and Martin were going to fill that in. Everything was all set for the first one when I received a call from the doctor's office. Change of plans. ABC's *20/20* star reporter John Stossel was doing a feature on the pros and cons of the billion-dollar hair restoration industry, and they'd chosen to cover the Ungers at their New York City offices. ABC was looking for a "poster boy" and needed a lab rat to have the operation and then be followed for several months to see the transformation. I got bumped. No biggie, but a light bulb went off. I figured, why not me? So, while still on the phone, I made my pitch, and I got invited to a little pool party the brothers and their families were throwing that weekend.

I worked the room like a pro. They, too, thought the idea was brilliant. Off to NYC I went to audition with nineteen others (all New York residents) for interviews with the *20/20* producers. I was thinking if I nailed the audition and "won" Stossel and the ABC crew over, I was in for eleven operations — $88,000 worth — *fo' free*. I mean, who wants to go to pocket? Oh yeah, and I'd also get a brand new head of hair. Time to turn on the charm. You're a morning show host and a TV star — bring it! I felt like Ali, just feeling them out for a few rounds, then *boom, boom, boom*. I had them. I love that feeling. Later that day I was chosen, along with two others (down to the short strokes, people), to undergo the operation but to have just a local anesthetic on my scalp and be awake the entire time. Sure, it was easy to be funny and bouncy in front of a room with amateurs, but could I be a hit on Percocets, ether, and that drip, drip, drip of liquid morphine? I was afraid I'd sound like the village drunk in some early Irish novel. But apparently that toxic mixture made me even *more* endearing to the *20/20* braintrust, because on the plane back to Toronto later that afternoon, Walter and Marty were informed that I was "the guy." Yes, I'd nailed the audition, so it was "Captain Hairplugs" to the rescue. The doctors had prohibited me from drinking during the entire three days in NYC. Curses! Alcohol thins the blood and raises your blood pressure, and nobody — especially them — wanted to see blood spurting all over the operating room because of me being overserved at Gallagher's steakhouse on 52nd Street the night before. So with the news of my newfound riches and apparent home-team discount — the Ungers are proud Toronto lads and I'm *sure* they had some input on who was chosen and would have to spend countless hours with them over the next year — I had a drink. Several. Good times.

With the expensive "seeds" in place and with the nightly eleven o'clock sportscast being used as a snapshot of my hair growth (ABC paid freelance CityTV cameras to follow me around for a good part of the six months), the road to restoration began. ABC actually used a time-elapsed series of shots from *CityPulse Tonight* on the *20/20* piece so you could actually see my hair grow in like a chia pet. "Chia-pet head" was an obvious and quick nickname for me. I've been called worse. National and local stories abounded regarding my soon-to-be-new locks. The *Toronto Sun* photoshopped possible end result looks and 'do's, from Michael Jackson's Jheri curls to Pete Rose to the pencil-eraser look worn by one-half of the rap act Kid 'n Play. Fred Patterson aired a hilarious commentary on the ordeal on the "Humble and Fred Show" on CFNY (now The Edge) suggesting that HE could be a donor for my hair transplants. With hair from his ass. Charmed, I'm sure. A lot was made about the fact that most hair transplant recipients would take a long leave of absence from work or wear a freaking hat for six months while "under repair." No, not me. If you're going to have it, have it. And if you're going to do it, do it big. ABC Friday-night *20/20* big. So, several months later, and with an "almost" full head of hair (hey, they're not miracle workers), it was time for me to be wheeled in on a Friday in NYC on February 26, 1993, for my American network debut. I was to be interviewed by the *20/20* panel after the twenty-minute piece on hair transplants ran. Slight problem. That day, terrorists parked a rental van in a garage underneath the World Trade Center's twin towers a few blocks away and lit the fuses on a massive homemade bomb stuffed inside. Six people died and more than a thousand were injured. As I waited backstage, and after my piece ran, Barbara Walters threw to the "live eye" at the WTC as I took my make-up off. No interview, but I was still "almost famous," I guess.

Years later, a friend told me my operation was actually running twenty-four hours a day on a TV in the window of a hair transplant clinic in Dublin, Ireland, promoting the hair transplant doctors inside. Footage they'd just dubbed from ABC and made their own. Do you smell a lawsuit? I should note that Barbara Walters *did* get in one more thoughtful, in-depth quip at the end of the show. After wondering why we balding men would go through such an expensive and painful (actually, it wasn't at all) experience, she uttered, "Babies are bald and they're the cutest." Whoa, boy. Hey Babs, don't forget to enjoy the view.

FOURTEEN

NO LONGER DESTINY'S DOORMATS

(or, when Cito Gaston asked, "Where did you get that lovely blouse?" I responded, "Your wife!")

There's a reason the Montreal Expos are labelled "Nos Amours," or "Expos — We Love You," because, for me, when it came to watching them or even covering the team professionally, I was always a fan. With the Toronto Blue Jays, it was more, let's say, businesslike. That is, until I stopped being a press card–carrying member of the media. Oh yeah, and the Expos moved to Washington. Then, all bets were off. I would party with the Jays, take women back to Robbie Alomar's hotel room/apartment at SkyDome, hang out by the pool with them for weeks at spring training, and even steal their girlfriends. (Sorry, Jack Morris, but it happened.) I considered all-world pitcher Dave Stewart a good friend. And hall-of-fame general manager Pat Gillick would routinely pop in when I had big-name wrestlers on *The Gallagher Show* on TSN. I know, Pat Gillick a WWE fan?

As a member of the media, I could have scored all kinds of memorabilia from the club. Bats, gloves, and MLB baseballs by the boxload, like other reporters would get from players. It wasn't really my jam, but I'd scoop up the odd ball here and there. Mind you, I had never caught a foul ball at a MLB game. Until 1987, that is. The Jays were in a huge battle with the Detroit Tigers that year. It was late September, and the Jays opened up a big three-and-a-half-game lead on the Tigers by the second-last weekend of the season, winning three of four against Detroit at Exhibition Stadium. I was there for the series opener, a 4–3 win with Mike Flanagan's curve ball, one of the best in the bigs, ever fooling the Tigers' stacked lineup. The game will be most remembered for Tony Fernandez, the Jays' all-star shortstop and one of Toronto's most valuable performers, busting his right elbow when he was taken out at second by Bill Madlock. Madlock rolled Tony hard to break up a double play. Fernandez flipped over and landed on his elbow, which struck a wooden divider that separates the artificial surface and the dirt surrounding the base. He came down hard. Everyone knew it was bad. Fernandez was hitting .322 with sixty-seven RBIs at the time. Even though I was there for the win, losing Fernandez probably cost the Jays the season. After the weekend, the Jays lost their last seven in a row to finish two games back of the Tigers. The Blue Jays finished with a 96–66 record, second-best in the major leagues, but to no avail.

Looking back, I know this is totally silly, but at that fateful Tony Fernandez/busted elbow/playoff-hope-ending game, I caught my first live ball. I was grabbing a cocktail at the concession stand when I heard the crack of Bill Madlock's bat and the cheer of the crowd as a foul ball came straight toward me. It hit a wall, bounced around a bit, landed at my feet, and rolled under the condiment table. I made a dive for it at the same time as a woman in her sixties. We both grabbed at the ball and struggled a bit as the mustard and ketchup containers on the table above us started to shake. Again, I could get as many balls as I wanted on the field, but this was different. This was an actual game, and it was off the big black bat of Madlock (you can still see the scuff on the ball from his Louisville Slugger) and I was going to battle for it. I rolled around the concrete trying to wrestle the prized Rawlings ball from this elderly women, tumbling over the table and sending mustard, ketchup, and relish all over both of us. My buddy Brendan Connor, formerly of CBC Sports and TSN, was with me. Brendan "reported" my antics the next day on the *Jesse and Gene Show* and of course embellished for effect. The way Connor told it, you'd think I'd put the lady in a sleeper hold or something. Whatever … Never let the truth get in the way of a good story, eh Brendan? For the record, I kept the ball. Damn straight. Not my finest moment, but I earned it and still have it.

＊ ＊ ＊

You don't want to get on the wrong side of legendary Blue Jays manager Cito Gaston. Most people don't win in that scenario. Though if you ask Cito, former Jay Roger Clemens may just have gotten away with it. Mention the name "Roger Clemens" to Gaston and be prepared to cover any virgin ears in the area. When it comes to his former ace, Gaston doesn't mince words. Words which, for decency's sake, we could never print here!

It all goes back to when Clemens was dominating the American League for the entirely mediocre 1997/98 Blue Jays. According to Gaston, it was Clemens who campaigned to have him fired and replaced by Tim Johnson. Says Cito, "I wouldn't doubt that; he's an ass himself, a complete ass. I'd say that loud, right in his face. It's all about him, nobody else but him." In his book *The Rocket That Fell to Earth: Roger Clemens and the Rage for Baseball Immortality*, author Jeff Pearlman looked at the career of the fading, multiple Cy Young Award–winner and added that Clemens was the one who pushed Jays' brass to fire Cito and hire his ill-fated successor Tim Johnson. That decision turned out to be a disaster for the team. Johnson was fired just a year after being appointed for lying about his military service. He'd claimed to have been a veteran of the Vietnam War, but he'd fabricated the story for some bizarre, unknown reason. It's a terrible thing to lie about military service. But it did provide me with a classic line on *The Gallagher Show*. Assistant general manager Dave Stewart was my guest that night and I cracked him up, while discussing Johnson, by quipping, "Let's let Saigons be bygones." He laughed so hard, he peed in *my* pants.

Gaston often had a rocky relationship with the Toronto sports media. He once accused a large handful of being racists. I was not one of them. Still to this day he proclaims, "There's a couple [of sportswriters] who continue to take shots at me for no reason at all. I just wonder if they would take the same shot at me if I was white."

Also, don't call him Clarence. He hates that. Even when I told him about the days I would watch him, Dave Winfield, Nate Colbert, Enzo Hernandez, and the mustard-and-brown-uniformed San Diego Padres at Jarry Park in the 1970s, on sunny afternoons that you'd squint at a sky so blue it would hurt your eyes just to look at it. He would tell me, "That was Clarence Gaston. I'm Cito now." Also, don't mess with his wife. Oh yeah, you would think that would seem important, or even that it wouldn't need to be said. But that was my mistake on a sunny May afternoon at SkyDome in late May of 1994. But he started it. LOL.

Before every home game, Gaston would meet with Toronto media members. Usually the exchanges were low-key and relaxed. Besides providing injury updates and the like, Gaston would often be asked to explain the reasoning behind his personnel decisions, and he was always cool. I will say this before continuing: he was in a lousy mood on the day in question because he was starting a three-game suspension for disorderly behaviour and bumping umpire Rick Reed a few weeks earlier in a game against the Angels in Anaheim. Gaston was in uniform but had to be out of the ballpark an hour before game time because of the suspension. And he was pissed off about it. I was reporting on the suspension for CityTV and I just happened to be wearing a very colourful and very expensive shirt that I had bought in a swanky boutique in Yorkville. He and I had always exchanged pleasantries over the years. Heck, I had drinks at his house, for goodness' sake.

In hindsight, I assume Cito was just in a foul mood about the suspension. He might have lashed out at anyone. But I was there and my shirt was, shall we say, attention-grabbing. Cito yelled, "Hey Gallagher, where did you get that faggotty-looking shirt?" among some snickers from other reporters. Thinking — or *not* thinking, as it turned out — of a witty retort, I blurted out, "Do you like it? Your *wife* bought it for me!" Silence. Then I heard some "wooo"-like groans go up from a few bystanders and felt a chill fill the stadium, which was strange because the roof was open and the sun was beating down on us. Cito looked straight at me and said, "What did you say?" Instead of "Nothing, Cito," I responded with, "I said your *wife* bought it for me." Yeah, I doubled down. Then Cito asked me if I'd ever heard of the "dozens." "Not hip to that one, dude," I said. He went on to explain that in pro sports, you *dozen* talk about how much money you make or what kind of car you drive, and you especially *dozen* talk about another man's girlfriend or wife. I had to look it up. Apparently "playing the dozens" is an African-American custom that can be traced back to slavery. Two male competitors just trash talk each other, taking turns insulting one another (perhaps a "Yo mama is so ugly" joke) until one of them has no comeback. Defeat can be humiliating.

Well, I was not going to start anything like that with a six-foot-three 225-pounder from Texas under any circumstances. Especially when he was being forced to leave his team to Gene Tenace, of all people, on a game day. I tried to break the ice and headed straight toward him with my cameraman, but he was having none of it. "I'm not talking to you today," he said as he got up and left his spot in the dugout, much to the chagrin of the other sportswriters and sportscasters, which left them without much of a storyline. Too bad. With my cameraman shooting the whole time, the "Where did you get that faggotty-looking shirt" and "Your wife bought it for me" lines led the sportscast that night. We just bleeped out the "faggotty" bit. Come on, we had our standards. That was the way we did things at CityTV. Make sure *you* are a big part of the story. I did apologize later, realizing my friendly banter was perhaps out of line, and he was cool with that. But not before making it the sports story of the day, on CityTV *everywhere*.

* * *

A lot of ex-athletes go into broadcasting after their playing careers. Some do well. Others should never come anywhere near a microphone. Former Blue Jay Joe Carter falls into the latter category. And he fell hard. After a short but forgettable stint with CTV providing colour commentary for the Jays, Joe Carter joined the Cubs broadcast in 2000. My goodness. Look up "malapropism" in the dictionary and it says, "See Joe Carter." And he was paired with the son of long-time Cub favourite Harry Caray, Chip Caray. Between Chip's sanctimonious attitude and non-stop chatter and Joe's butchering of the English language, not to mention boring, no-colour "commentary," you wanted to throw a brick through the screen. His broadcast career was over in a hurry. Mercifully.

Now, while he's been dining out on that series-ending home run for the Jays against the Phillies in 1993, Joe was known as a guy who was rude to fans on several occasions and not all that popular with the media. I can still remember him dodging reporters and cameras on his way to the clubhouse to avoid being interviewed when it wasn't at his convenience. But when he wanted to get something off his chest, well ... Case in point: A week before the end of the 1997 season, Cito Gaston was fired. I was at the ballpark that night when Carter wore Gaston's Number 43 on his jersey, and he would do so for the remainder of the season in part to honour him and to express his displeasure at his firing. Carter hopped around from reporter to reporter parading his new jersey and professing his solidarity with his newly fired manager and friend. He didn't get a lot of takers. Not me, anyway. It would be Carter's final week with the Blue Jays as well. After hitting .234, he was gone. He now makes a yearly appearance at his Joe Carter Golf Classic, in which he has infuriated golfers and sponsors alike by hiking up prices to astronomical amounts, doubling and tripling foursome fees over the years. You really have touched them all, Joe, at least when it comes to golfers' pocket books.

FIFTEEN

I KISSED A MAN (ROBBIE ALOMAR) AND I LIKED IT

(or, how a little nudge from my BMW could have won the Jays their first world title) became quite friendly with a number of the Jays during my time covering the team. During spring training, you could often see Roberto Alomar and I gallivanting around downtown Toronto together. A hot spot in those days was a fabulous "meat market" called Alice Fazooli's. It was a baseball-themed establishment. For instance, they displayed a bronzed baseball that allegedly was the one Babe Ruth hit into Lake Ontario — his first home run as a pro — at nearby Hanlan's Point in 1914 (it wasn't) and a life-sized statue of New York Yankee outfielder Dave Winfield with seagull shit on his shoulder. If you recall, in August of 1983, Toronto police officers arrested Winfield for killing one of the thousands of gulls, or "shit hawks," at Exhibition Stadium while tossing a ball between innings. As ridiculous as the charge was, Winfield co-operated with the authorities and went downtown; he was booked, and bail was set at $500 dollars. It was completely accidental and nowhere near as violent as the time fire-balling lefty, and former Expo, Randy Johnson caused a seagull to literally burst into pieces upon being hit by one of the Big Unit's 99 mph fastballs. One of my first assignments in Toronto was to interview Winfield at his hotel room when the Yankees were in town. He was promoting a book he wrote called *Turn It Around*. I showed up to the interview with no batteries in my tape recorder. Curses! He was so cool about it. I ran down to buy some, did the interview, and when no one else from the media (no *New York Times*, *Post*, or *Daily News*, or *Toronto Sun* or *Star*?) showed up, he ordered up eggs benedict for the two of us. Classy and classic.

The Jays players loved it in Toronto. Perhaps not the tax structure, but there was a bevy of single girls in the city who adored them. And their money. Not to sound overly skanky, but the boys and I loved to set sail toward poontown. Robbie and I were at Fazooli's on one occasion as I "geared up" (with a glass or two of wine) for my upcoming sportscast on CityTV. I convinced Robbie to join me on the sportscast for a hoot just after eleven, and he agreed. The place was a snowball's throw away from City, but he insisted on being chauffeured over in his stretch limousine instead of walking. Hey, if you've got it … Now at this point in his career in Toronto, Robbie was beyond the new "it" athlete in the city. On the field, he was a twelve-time All-Star and had won more Gold

Gloves (ten) than any other second baseman in baseball history. Toss in four Silver Slugger Awards and a couple of World Series rings and you've got yourself a Hall of Famer and an all-time great. He was one of the most popular athletes in the city and the country, if not *the* most popular. Any baseball fan who watched him over and over, game in and game out during his prime years in Toronto, could make the case that his skill set — remarkable defensive range, hitting for average and for power, superior base-running, and insightful, instinctive understanding of the game — was nothing we'd ever seen before. Off the field, with his male-model looks and his deep Puerto Rican accent, he was a heartthrob, a hero, and he was idolized by millions. Seriously, women swooned at the sight of him. Even after his ill-advised *Toronto Sun* Sunshine Boy photo in a Speedo. He was a rock star.

His arrival caused quite the commotion at the TV station. And after getting his make-up done and getting him mic'd up, I had him co-host the sportscast with me. We killed. I could just see the news directors and station managers from rivals CFTO, Global, and CBC screaming into their collective monitors, "Damn it! Gallagher's got Robbie Alomar live on the air … and he just *kissed* him!" Hey, I'm a touchy-feely, kissy-face kind of guy. Some men aren't. I am. And yes, I kissed him on air. After the sportscast, I just leaned over and squeezed his face like your grandmother would when you're five, and I planted one on the cheek. The newsroom erupted in laughter and applause. Today something like that would have been a YouTube sensation. Back then, you actually had to sit down and write a letter, then fax it or put it in an envelope and send it. People did. And it wasn't all good. How dare I kiss a man who was not only the best Blue Jay of all time but also quite possibly the greatest second baseman in MLB history? We did get a lot of angry letters about the on-air kiss. But hey, it was a legit bromance and a really great spontaneous bit of sportscasting.

It didn't happen a lot, but sneaking women up to his SkyDome hotel room, where he lived for the five years he spent as a Jay, was hilarious. (He even had a special route that bypassed the lobby after games and on occasions like ours.) Robbie actually had two huge hotel rooms with knocked-down walls. One room looked like Elvis Presley's "jungle room," with leopard-print wall paper.

Our friendship cooled in the spring of 1995, Alomar's final year as a Blue Jay. And to be honest, it was all his doing. I was just doing my job. We were having a leisurely chat at the Jays' complex in Dunedin, and instead of planning a night out on the town, Robbie told me that he'd gotten engaged over the off-season. Wow, how terrific for him, I thought, and mmm, what a scoop that would be for me if I could announce the upcoming nuptials on air. Reporters were always looking for breaking news and exclusives in those days. Robbie Alomar and I had a bond, so with a little nudging, he decided to announce on the air that he had popped the question to a lovely Puerto Rican women over the Christmas holidays. Perhaps he should have thought it through. Since it was during the opening days of training camp, when pitchers and catchers arrive, no one else had heard the news. I don't even think he had told any of his teammates. Here's why I know this. The day after my story ran on the six and eleven o'clock news on CityTV back in Toronto, Robbie's phone blew up. You see, the Love God of the Big Smoke had inadvertently forgotten to tell the bevy of beauties he had been "seeing" back in the 416 that he was off the market. Sweating, almost ashen, he spotted me the next day, pulled me aside from the batting cage, and asked, "What the fuck did you say about me getting married?" "Me?" I retorted, totally confused. "*You* said it!" "Well," he says, "you've ruined my life." Our relationship was a tad frosty after that. That's okay; the Jays won seven of their last fifty games that year and finished dead last. He was a Baltimore Oriole a few months later. His reputation took a major hit during his first season in Baltimore when he spat in the face of umpire John Hirschbeck at SkyDome. Not only did he blatantly spit in Hirschbeck's face, but after the game he said Hirschbeck was just bitter because one of his sons had recently died and another had just been diagnosed with a terminal illness. Yikes. Talk about a career-limiting move! Eventually all was forgiven when, in 2011, he was the first Blue Jay player inducted into Cooperstown. It's nice to see Robbie back in the Toronto fold, too. Now twenty-five years removed from the spitting incident, it's like it never happened. In retirement, he's once again a golden boy. Also, try getting THAT close to players during today's ever-changing media landscape.

✦ ✦ ✦

As the baseball world knows, the Jays won two World Series during their history. (Besides the Joe Carter home run in the 1993 World Series, the single greatest hit in Jays history was the homer Robbie hit against Dennis Eckersley in Oakland in the 1992 ALCS, leading them to their first.) But with a little — okay, big — nudge from this author, it could very well have been three. It's true. I wrote about the Jays and A's and the controversy involving Bob Costas ("Elvis has a better chance of coming back in this series than the Jays") in 1989 earlier in this book, but it could have turned out better. A lot better. That's if I'd killed Dennis Eckersley with my car. Maimed, killed, it doesn't matter. No small feat, mind you, but the task was there for the taking. Let's relive this, shall we? It was the first week of October, and the Jays limped home after losing the first two games of the ALCS in Oakland. It was on a Thursday, an off day for both clubs, when the strangest thing happened. I was driving to SkyDome to do a story on Game 3, about to park in the underground garage, when I noticed this guy jogging right next to me under the Gardiner Expressway. It was a gorgeous sunny day and I had the roof down in my BMW. After a double take, I realized the man running next to me was exactly who I had thought he was. The green and yellow stirrup socks were a dead giveaway, but so was the long brown hair and the big, unmistakable moustache. It was future Hall of Famer Dennis Eckersley, the A's (and all of baseball's) top reliever. A pitcher the Jays just couldn't figure out. Heck, who could? This was a guy who gave up five earned runs in the entire 1990 season, resulting in a microscopic 0.61 ERA. He was the American League's Cy Young Award winner and Most Valuable Player in 1992, a season in which he posted fifty-one saves. Mind you, he also gave up Kirk Gibson's game-winning home run when his A's were upset by the underdog Dodgers one year earlier. Either way, I had him right in my sights.

Yes, I was lining him up for a sudden introduction to a giant pillar under the Expressway. And this isn't utility infielder Lance Blankenship, this is all-world closer Dennis F. Eckersley. It's funny because I was wondering why he wasn't just running around on the turf inside of the ballpark or at least around the mezzanine area, where there's lots of room. I guess he needed the fresh air. It should be noted that most non-A's fans *hated* Dennis Eckersley. Heck, *I* hated him. Years later, seeing him give up that game-tying home run to Roberto Alomar in Game 5 of the 1992 ALCS was one of my all-time favourite sports moments. We all remember how he'd huffed and puffed at the Jays' dugout just an inning earlier. To most baseball fans, he was an asshole. And there he was, running a few feet away from my car. Mmm … I have to be honest here. Never in a million years would I ever strike down a man with my car. I looked it up so you don't have to: the maximum charge in Ontario for dangerous driving when an injury occurs is ten years in prison. I have to tell you, though, for a split second (I know it sounds absurd) I thought of giving him a little tap. You know, just to let him know I was there. The worst that could happen was that he would have hit a guard rail or the giant pillar and died. That would be bad. But how about a little trip? A dislocated shoulder? Sprained wrist? Lower body injury? Can you imagine the headlines the next day? "Local Sportscaster Closes Down Closer!" "Eck Just a Speck After Smashing Through BMW Windshield!" "Gallagher Wins ALCS for Jays — Promoted to Assistant GM!" At the red light approaching SkyDome, I let him get a good head start and watched as he ran past. Eckersley was near-flawless in saving the final two games of the series — 6–5 and 4–3 Oakland wins — giving up a single to Kelly Gruber but otherwise retiring the side, getting pinch-hitter Lee Mazzilli to pop out to end Game 4, and striking out Junior Felix to finish the last American League baseball game of the 1980s in Game 5. And the Jays were through. One slip of the wheel and it could have ended so much differently. Question: What would you have done? No, seriously. A raging Blue Jays fanatic might have done differently. Never fear. I took the high road. Well, actually, it was Lake Shore Boulevard. Ba-dum!

SIXTEEN

SMUGGLERS' BLUES

(or, as I bend over with my pants around my ankles, I hear
the "snap" of an RCMP officer's rubber glove. Oh-oh.)

My career as a broadcaster almost ended before it really got started. Now that you know me, you can probably guess that it involved drugs and partying. I landed a sportscaster gig at CJCH, the top station in Halifax. It was a major upgrade in status from the Saint John station I'd been at. The job came my way in part due to a favour from a past romantic interest (Deanna Nason) and in part due to the drunken antics of CJ sportscaster Garnet Martin. One of the biggest rules in the business is "Don't miss broadcasts." Well, Martin loved the booze, and it started to affect his work. He was getting wasted and missing his spots on air. He got canned, and lovely Deanna put in a word and I was on my way.

Upon landing the gig at CJCH, I became fast friends with CJ's superstar morning host Brian "Philly" Phillips. Philly and I decided to go on vacation together in Jamaica. Specifically, to the infamous clothing-optional Hedonism II. The thing is, two weeks in Jamaica at a hugely popular resort was rather pricey for a young up-and-coming sportscaster who hadn't cracked the $20,000-a-year mark in his career. I've loved Jamaica from the first moment I saw it. I would return to Hedonism II a decade later when the Q107 Morning Zoo hosted a week there with some contest winners. Since we've already established that I'm somewhat of a scoundrel, let me proudly say that I had sex with three different women, all Q107 contest winners, on that trip, including a pair of sisters. I know, I know, "We get it Gallagher — you bedded a lot of women — puh-lease. Move on!" But, talk about a bucket-list achievement! Casual sex was rampant at Hedonism II then.

I slide that juicy tidbit in because ten years earlier, in 1984, at the same resort with Brian, it was definitely not. It seemed that the two weeks we were there, the entire state of New Jersey had moved south. Eighty percent of the resort was made up of men from New Jersey or Philadelphia. Think of those douche-waffles from MTV's *Jersey Shore*. Got it? Now add two hundred. It was brutal.

There were some single women there, one of which I was unlucky enough to meet on the very first morning. Being a tanning fanatic, I was up early and by myself running in the SPF 4. (Hey, it was the eighties!) Just as I was settling in, this woman — let's call her Snooki — pulled a chair through the sand and put it right next to mine. She couldn't have plunked herself down where all of her other friends would be for most of the day; no, she decided she needed some early morning company. Snooki, I'm sure, was a fine woman, sister, and perhaps even mother back in the Garden State, but let's just say she was in the "no-go neighbourhood." Oh, it got better. Snooki put her towel down on her lounge chair and promptly took off her bikini top. Just the top. "Snooki, don't untie those bikini bottom strings," I prayed. She didn't. I thought, there IS a God, and he's Rastafarian. Now, I don't want to get too graphic, but yamma hamma! I wish I could bleach the image out of my brain.

Don't get me wrong; Hedonism II is a fabulous place, and I would return several times. Plus, Negril is a funky little town and home to the greatest sunsets on the planet. One of my favourite spots in Negril is Rick's Café, which is located on a steep cliff in town. Perfect for cliff jumping and getting blow jobs from some of the "local talent." I took part in neither, thank you, but I had to laugh when Brian came back to his barstool one night at Rick's with his hair all out of place, a huge grin on his face, and big red lipstick kisses all over the front of his white shorts. Fuck, I laughed. There were a few nights of dancing and smooching with women at the resort, but nothing amounted to a hill of beans. "This is not what it said in the brochure!" I wanted to scream. Yeah, no penetration for me on that trip, but there would be some on my return!

Now, I've done some stupid things in my life, but the stunt I pulled on my way back to Toronto takes the prize. Marijuana has never been my thing, but I did briefly partake in some of the local ganja when I was there. Just enough to get a nice little buzz. But I have to tell you, it was the finest herb I have smoked or will ever. I had to take a tiny dime bag back to my friends in Halifax. I know. You're thinking, "Da fuck was Gallagher thinking?!" My plan was simple enough. Just wrap the $20 worth of "stuff" deep enough under the insoles of my running shoes (I even glued them shut) and breeze through customs at Pearson Airport. The strangest thing is that I had caught a nasty cold the last day in Negril, and by the time the plane home hit 30,000 feet, I was a mess. My ears were so plugged up from my sinuses that I could not hear a single word anybody said. Plus, I was sweating like a stuck Irish pig by the time we got to customs. "Anything to declare?" asked the customs agent. I couldn't hear a thing, so it was, "What? What? I'm sorry, what?" That, plus the flop sweat, made me a marked man. Add to the fact that customs officials were actually finding bags of Jamaica's finest in the suitcases of morons who'd hardly tried to conceal it and, well, this was going to be a free-for-all. There were dozens of busts. It was happening all around me. At least *this* moron had it hidden deep inside a running shoe, so I was safe. Or so I thought. There was a random check of luggage by customs officials. Brian was waved through. Not me. "Next in line, please!" I gulped hard as a woman started going through my luggage and came across a pair of cowboy boots and checked to see if there was anything inside. There was. Two pieces of John MacArthur's ID fell out. *Big* red flag. John was, and still is, a good friend who lent me his driver's licence so I could, and did, get a student standby rate for a round-trip ticket to Toronto from Halifax. Back then, driver's licences were just pieces of paper with no photo ID. But out drops the driver's licence. Apparently that was an indication that drugs would be mailed to this John MacArthur person by me at a later date. Drugs?!

Then, it happened. The next item the lady pulled out of my bag — deep, deep, deep out of my bag — was my left running shoe. She then proceeded to peel back the Dr. Scholls undersole to find, under the glue … let's call it Exhibit A. What are the chances? Go through some shorts and socks and we'll call it a night, but no, no, no. *Busted!* I went completely numb. I knew this was bad. Really bad. I was quickly escorted into a room to meet the Canadian Border Services Agency, all the while wanting to go out kicking and screaming like Billy Hayes in the film *Midnight Express* — "For what? For whaaat?!" — but I thought better of it. The officer handling me was a total hardass. He promptly demanded that I take all of my clothes off and bend over for a cavity search. There was no asking or saying please. As if getting probed wasn't bad enough, Officer Poky-Finger got out his baton and threatened to hit me in the stomach so hard that all of the marijuana-, coke-, and heroin-filled condoms that I'd swallowed before takeoff in Jamaica were going to spill out all over my file on his desk. Really? I'm a sportscaster of a morning show in Halifax. Heroin? In my sweaty, deafened haze, I tried to convince him that I was just bringing back a little sample of Jamaican ganga to my friends back home. Somehow he bought it, or he had to go interrogate the *real* traffickers who were also on my flight. Either way, I was still in the hands of the police who told me, in no uncertain terms, that the maximum charge for bringing marijuana — *any* amount — into Canada was five years in prison less a day. I was told I was going to spend the night in jail, perhaps more. I was starting to think this would be all she wrote for my broadcasting career.

Then, like the angels in blue they were, two cops started going through my wallet. One of the officers found my lifetime membership to the Billy Club. This was a cops-only hangout in Dartmouth, N.S. And how did I get a membership to this cops-only club? You see, once a week, Brian and I and the morning team would go out to several of the area's businesses serving up coffee and doughnuts as part of the "CJCH Brew Crew." It just so happened that the Billy Club was one of our stops. The cops there loved our show and made us members. The two cops who were about to put handcuffs on me and take me to the crowbar hotel not only were both from Halifax, but they were also members in very good standing of, you guessed it, the Billy Club. I mean, what were the chances? They asked me how damaging getting arrested and charged with possession would be for my career back home. I assured them that if this got out, my mugshot would be on the cover of next morning's newspapers. They then left the room for ten minutes, came back, and told me — quite sternly, mind you — that if I ever, *ever* tried a cheap trick like that again, I would be thrown in the clink "faster than a rabbit gets *fucked*!" (I guess they had seen *Scarface* — Google it). After several hours, I was free. Still quite sweaty, totally deaf, and walking a little off-kilter thanks to the anal probe, I quickly called Brian at the airport hotel and told him I was on my way. We met for a drink at the hotel bar. Boy, did I need one.

SEVENTEEN

YOU CAN TAKE THE GIRL OUT OF THE TRAILER PARK, BUT YOU CAN'T TAKE THE *WHAT* OUT OF HER MOUTH?

(or, Q107 wordscramble: Here's Robert Palmer
with "You're a DICKHEAD of Love!")

I've always liked the line, "There. I've said it; I'm glad." I suppose in this chapter it should read, "There. I wrote it; I'm glad." It usually holds true for me unless what I said gets me parked in the boss's corner office the next day being asked the question, "What did you say, and are you still glad you said it?" Worse yet if what I said leads to a lengthy off-air suspension, and worse even still if it means getting eighty-sixed while I'm in the prime of my life and broadcasting career.

It was a whirlwind of a time, co-hosting the Q Morning Zoo on Q107 in the a.m. and being sports anchor for City at night. Throw in public appearances at up to $10,000 a shot, and your humble high-school-dropout "on-air" putzlehead was making over half a million dollars a year. I loved the attention, the notoriety, the fame, and the fortune. And I loved covering sports. Yes, they were paying me nicely to go to sporting events and then go live on TV and radio to describe what had transpired. Gimme some a' dat! Don't forget, fellow sports fanatics shell out thousands of dollars to see major sporting events live. I got in free. And all expenses paid for. Super Bowls, World Series, Stanley Cup finals, World Championship boxing matches? Free, free, free, and free. Plus I got to hobnob with the world's finest athletes and stars. This was before the Internet, before you had dozens of all-sport channels and PVRs. Now you can stream live sporting events and sportscasts on your smartphone twenty-four hours a day. Back then, if you wanted the night's highlights, damn it, you tuned in to John Gallagher at eleven every night.

It was a simpler time, and safer for that matter. Safe as far as what was acceptable in the life of an on-air "personality." Lordy, lordy, lordy, the things we got away with on and off the air back then would shrivel some men's testes into raisins. Today you can be fired for anything and everything. Here's a good example. Not long ago, my friend and fellow sportscaster Damian Goddard was fired from Sportsnet for tweeting his opinion on same-sex marriage. One wrong tweet or post on social media and "ya burnt!"

The "Gallagher Files" contain a similar incident. We're all familiar with Tonya Harding, the American figure skater who ruined her future in the sport when she was implicated in clubbing fellow competitor Nancy Kerrigan before the 1994 Winter Olympics. Back then everybody was taking shots at her. Including yours truly.

The "kicker" story is the last segment of a broadcast that usually features a bizarre or humorous "bit" intended to end the news or sports on a lighter note — think Ron Burgundy and the waterskiing squirrel. I wrote that night's kicker. I was going to make a Tonya Harding joke. I forget if it was during one of her celebrity boxing fiascos, but I decided to weigh in on how far Tonya's "star" had fallen, so at the end of the sportscast I read the wonderfully insightful *bon mot* that I had worked on all night. Minor thing — it didn't come out as intended. Not even close. The sports cast ended thusly: While shaking my head and smiling at the Harding clip, I uttered, "You know, you can take the girl out of the trailer park, but you can't take the gum out of her mouth." That's what I wrote and that's what showed up on the teleprompter. Only I didn't say "gum." Instead, I slipped up and, well ... I accidentally said "cum." I didn't know I'd said it, but I heard the cameraman and the floor director groan "Oooh," so I turned to the late and great legendary newscaster, Mark Dailey, and said something like, "That's it for sports." But Mark knew what I had said. If he'd been quicker, he could have said, well, "That's it for you," but instead, red-faced, he mumbled something about the weekend weather forecast coming up with Harold Hussain. Probably best. That, or breaking out laughing.

Jeez, Louise. Dozens of times I would arrive at CityTV and the news director, nicknamed "Hurlabuse," and his cronies would be huddling around a TV monitor going over my previous night's sportscasts. This was one of those times. Since I did write "gum" in my script and it was indeed in the teleprompter, and they did believe me when I said it was just a slip of the tongue, I got off with a subtle warning. After all, on Q107, we'd feature the daily "wordscramble" and substitute, for example, Robert Palmer's "Addicted to Love" with "You're a Dickhead of Love!" Everyone I've talked to recently admits that, twenty years ago, Caitlyn Jenner would have been an hourly punchline. Had that happened in today's climate, it probably would have been, "Buh bye, Johnny."

EIGHTEEN

BLUE MORNING, BLUE DAY

(or, Mediocrity, thy name is Expos)

To quote the late Rick James, who I imbibed with during a fun-filled afternoon at the Rainbow Room in L.A., "cocaine is a helluva drug." It certainly is. And apparently during the heady years of the best run of seasons in the history of the franchise, many of the Montreal Expos' star players agreed. It was an upbeat time for Montreal baseball. The team was actually "beyond" good and attendance was regularly hitting the two million or more mark. Cocaine started to stream into the Expos clubhouse. By the wheelbarrow. It's been documented that Tim Raines learned to slide headfirst into bases because he didn't want to break the vile of coke he carried in his back pocket. And there were others. Several others. So many that the great teams of the early eighties failed to bag a title because of their heavy cocaine usage. In fact, manager Dick Williams's autobiography relates his fear of players being caught smuggling cocaine over the border and even possibly stashing their supply in his luggage. Can you imagine? The teams competing against the Expos had their share of cocaine addicts, but Montreal supposedly had the biggest coke problem in the entire league. John McHale, president of the Expos, said that eight or nine of his players were using cocaine in 1982. Told of McHale's comments, Whitey Herzog, the manager of the St. Louis Cardinals, said his team had an even bigger drug problem than the 1982 Expos when he took over in 1980. In fact, Herzog said that the Expos had one player on the team who was not only a cocaine user, but a cocaine dealer. Herzog said that in one game in Montreal his pitcher hit said cocaine dealer by accident, whereupon he was admonished by an infielder in an impromptu conference for endangering the team's chances of buying cocaine from that player after the game. Get this: the Cards skipper also claimed that he would do his best to inspire his team to win the first game of a series in Montreal because by the second game the team would be so high on cocaine that they wouldn't perform well.

Which brings me to a one-on-one interview I had with Ellis Valentine, perhaps the biggest and brightest star on the Expos horizon in the late seventies and early eighties. The guy was the complete package, a "five-tool" guy. Before I knew the evils of cocaine and the telltale signs of what it did to you, I interviewed Ellis. It was after a game in the early eighties in which he didn't play — that happened a lot. I could see by his demeanour and facial expression that he was definitely "on" something. I could see his dilated pupils, the contorted jaw grinding, and the endless sniffing. And he was pretty chatty. I think it was Bill Lee, the Spaceman, who joked that once between innings he noticed Ellis Valentine had made the left field white chalkline disappear. Then there was Ron Leflore, the ex-convict turned big-league star who was played by LeVar Burton in the film *One in a Million* while a member of the Detroit Tigers. This guy was really going to turn the Expos into contenders. Instead what he did was turn the Expos into cocaine fiends. The stories are rampant about how he took several young Expos under his wing and turned them into addicts. It boggles the mind how good the Expos could have been had they not been high on cocaine all the time. Yes, it's true. Mediocrity, thy name is Expos.

Around Montreal, the Dodgers' Game 5 victory in 1981 has come to be known as "Blue Monday." And I was there for it. First hand. I remember heading down to the clubhouses, still stunned by the Expos coming so close to the World Series. I could hear the Dodgers taunting the Expos by singing the Montreal rally song "The Happy Wanderer" — "Val-deri, val-dera" — from the hallway as their cookie-cutter Hollywood wives shared champagne outside the room. I was interviewing everybody save for Youppi, the mascot. Eventually I had a chat with Dave Van Horne, the soothing voice of the team and the soundtrack of my summers through thick and thin (usually thin), through the ups and downs, since opening day 1969. It was almost like your uncle taking you aside at a family funeral and reassuring you that everything was going to be all right. It wasn't just the fans who would never forgive Rick Monday, the man who clinched the series for the Dodgers. Every time the Dodgers and Rick Monday flew into Trudeau Airport, Monday had his passport checked and re-checked by immigration officials. It was as if he was on some kind of terrorist watch list.

The 1994 baseball strike shut down the season with the Expos sitting at 70–40. They had the best team in baseball by a wide margin. The team had a monster offence led by the best outfield in baseball: Moises Alou left, speedster Marquis Grissom in centre, and Canadian Larry Walker right. Their starting pitching staff was led by solid veteran Ken Hill and a very young future Hall of Famer by the name of Pedro Martinez. Their bullpen, led by John Wetteland and Mel Rojas, contained two of the most dominant shutdown arms in the league. In other words, the table was set for the Expos to win it all. But the labour dispute killed the season with the Expos having won twelve of their last fourteen games and starting to pull away from the rest of the pack. It killed their best chance at a title since 1981.

When baseball resumed in 1995, gone were Walker, Grissom, Hill, and Wetteland. The Expos just couldn't afford those guys. Gone was their chance at greatness. I remember hearing about the 'Spos yard sale while standing around the batting cage covering the Jays in Florida and thinking, "Wait. What? They traded who?"

As Sean Gordon wrote in the *Globe and Mail* when Tim Raines was voted into the Hall of Fame, "The team may not exist any more, but that doesn't mean folks have stopped caring…. Things ended badly for 'Nos Amours,' what with the deserted stands and the losing teams, but there is a residual nostalgia in Montreal for Canada's first Major League Baseball franchise, and in a lot of ways it is underpinned by Raines. He played with Rusty (le Grand Orange) Staub, the original Expos superstar, and with Vladimir Guerrero, the franchise's last great player." Yes, we Expos fans will always remember Tim "Rock" Raines for a ready smile and an easy manner, somewhere between the always-on persona of "Lights" Carter and the reserved, soft-spoken Dawson. Now all three are in the Hall of Fame. Where they belong. By the way, Expos, we still love you.

NINETEEN

YOGI, TEDDY BASEBALL, THE YANKEE CLIPPER, SPACEMAN, AND THE DUKE

(or, is George Bell's butt STILL purple, but more importantly, does he still want me to kiss it?")

overing sports now is nothing like it was in the halcyon days of the last century. You know, the glory years of the forties, fifties, sixties, and seventies. Or even, for that matter, in the eighties and nineties, when I first started covering them. More and more, as I listen to myself, I think I'm sounding like Grandpa Simpson shaking his fist at the clouds. Sometimes I sound like one of those "Get off my lawn!" geezers, but it's true. This was before half a dozen all-sports-and-news radio and TV stations popped up. Not to mention the Twitterverse, bloggers, a host of live podcasts, streamers, and the daily barrage of newspaper reporters and cheerleaders who seem to be in the press box so they can tell the players how great they are. Not that long ago, we in the media had full access to players. We had one-on-one interviews and more than a few intimate and interactive moments with the biggest stars of the day. We dined with them. Accepted invitations to their weddings. Got calls from them after a sports-cast inviting us for cocktails. And I'm not talking about fourth-liners or utility infielders here. Big names. The biggest in the business. Blue Jay ace Dave Stieb would routinely call after my sportscasts on Q107 to agree or disagree with my daily "Q comment." The phone rang one Friday night at CityTV and it was Pat Burns, head coach of the Leafs, inviting me to Montana's for drinks.

It was endless. I was at one of the many parties celebrating the 1982 MLB All-Star game, and there, leaning up against the Olympic Stadium tarp, minding his own business, was "Mr. Baseball" Bob Uecker. Bob is one of the most humorous and entertaining men in the business. Because the doors hadn't opened for the public and it was just the players and the media, he was all by himself taking it all in. Bob had yet to score it big as Harry Doyle in the *Major League* movie franchise and (unfortunately) on the sitcom *Mr. Belvedere*, but his Miller Lite ads and multiple appearances on Johnny Carson's *Tonight Show* made him an easy and approachable subject for an aspiring radio announcer from Halifax. I just hoped he'd say yes.

"Got a second, Mr. Uecker?" "Sure, kid," he responded as he read the call letters on my microphone flag. "C100 and CJCH — where's that, kid?" "Halifax, Nova Scotia," I said. Then a long pause. "Nevvver *fucking* heard of it." Classic. Every other word was "fuck"! He was notorious for his foul language off the air. When he found out I was originally from Montreal, all he wanted to talk about were the city's famous strip clubs. "How about the big tits on the French chicks at Chez Paris, eh kid?" On and on he went, and it was hilarious. But he was a pro, so when I hit the record button on my tape recorder, he was all business. The interview started as a garden variety one-on-one, but I soon realized this was not going to be your average friendly banter. This was Bob Uecker in pre-game mode. It was like he was just getting warmed up in the bullpen, getting ready for the big mid-summer classic on national TV. And he warmed up to the cub reporter from out east, for some reason. Lucky me! The man was a gem. I didn't even have to set him up. He just launched into his routine. "Career highlights?" he asked. "I had two. I got an intentional walk from Sandy Koufax and I got out of a rundown against the Mets." *Bing!* "I signed with the Milwaukee Braves for three thousand dollars. That bothered my dad at the time because he didn't have that kind of dough. But he eventually scraped it up." *Boom!* "One time I got pulled over at four a.m. I was fined seventy-five dollars for being intoxicated and four hundred for being with the Phillies." It was like he was on *The Tonight Show*, only with a different Johnny.

Just then, it happened. Here comes the payoff pitch. In the middle of the interview, the All-Star Game umpires, Doug Harvey and Marty Springstead, as is custom, were sizing up Olympic Stadium for the managers of the National and American leagues. The basic stuff: the field dimensions, where the foul areas are, and how many feet down the lines to the outfield wall. Now, these were no ordinary All-Star Game managers, and neither were the two honorary captains of each team who tagged along. So here came — are you ready for this? — Tommy Lasorda of the L.A. Dodgers, from the defending NL champs, along with Billy Martin from the defending AL champion Yankees, plus honorary captains Yogi Berra and the "Duke of Flatbush," Duke Snider. You couldn't help but notice them as they walked by me and Bob, but Ueck being Ueck, he decided to stir the pot a little bit. As they passed right by us, Uecker said to all of them — and this is all on tape, mind you — "Look at these fucking clowns here. I bet you all fit into the same miniature fucking clown car on the way here. Where's your fucking rainbow wigs and red plastic noses?" My microphone went limp.

I stood there in shock. But it got better. A lot better. If you thought for a second that any of these men — who, save for Springstead, were all Hall of Famers — were going to take that flack from a career .200 hitter turned TV celebrity, you'd be sorely mistaken. Here they came, starting with battlin' Billy Martin. "What the fuck did you say to me?" Soon all of them were taking shots at Uecker; all in jest, mind you. Everybody loves the guy. You want to talk about banter. The air hovering above the eight of us was getting pretty blue with F-bombs, mofos, and cocksucker remarks, but it was hilarious. Okay, I thought to myself, there would be some serious editing back in the studio, but I wasn't going to stop Billy, Tommy, Yogi, The Duke, et al. from some good-spirited pre-All-Star-Game riffing. And hey, Uecker started it. I couldn't ask for a better double foursome. It was just out and out luck. Why didn't this happen to Howard Cosell, who was standing twenty feet away, or any of the hundred or so accredited media types with film crews and sound men? Pure luck.

Well, the umpires did have a job to do, and after a few minutes they whisked everybody away. But not before a couple of "fuck yous" to Uecker. Then the strangest thing happened. Yogi Berra was shuffling off, and he turned back to me and asked, "Where are you from, kid? I don't recognize your station." "Halifax, Nova Scotia," I said proudly, again. To which Yogi leaned in and said, "Nevvver heard of it." I thanked Bob for his time. Heck, I should have knelt down and kissed his 1964 World Series ring. He had inadvertently set all of that up with just a few wisecracks. But hey, as they say, timing is everything. He gave me a wink and wished me good luck in my career.

I did have another chance one-on-one with one of the game's greats. I seated myself next to Pete Rose, then of the Philadelphia Phillies, on the National League's bench at Olympic Stadium. I remember I asked him, "Tell me, what makes Pete Rose tick?" He blurted out, "What makes me tick?" and looked at me like I was a two-headed serpent with sinister intentions. As he was struggling for an answer, I gently passed my twenty-dollar camera to a newspaper reporter, who snapped a photo of me interviewing baseball's all-time hits leader. Just then, Chuck Tanner of the Pittsburgh Pirates, serving as one of the NL's coaches, tapped me on the shoulder and said, "Interview's over, kid, 'cuz Pete's gotta come in for a team meeting." As Pete got up, I thanked him and thought of saying,

"See you in the Hall of Fame!" but didn't. Good thing. You know, some day I'll rummage through all of my old packed-up boxes in the garage and find that photo of Pete and me, and that classic interview with Ueck and the gang.

* * *

Montreal Gazette veteran Tim Burke was the consummate pro. The dean of Montreal sportswriters had been to my house in the mid-1970s in Montreal West doing a front-page story on my brother Steve, who was battling it out for the Golden Gloves boxing championship in the province. (Steve would go to France and go undefeated for Team Quebec against their best. He would tell his kids years later that "I fought for my country overseas." Great line.) Burke introduced me to Canada's foremost political cartoonist Terry Mosher, a.k.a. Aislin. Terry's work has garnered him worldwide fame through publications like *Time* and the *New York Times*, but the *Gazette* and Montreal is where he still calls home. Aislin is a terrific character, a Canadiens and Expos fanatic and self admittedly, quite fond of the grape.

During my years adoring the Expos, there was one player who stood out from the rest for me and for millions of others: Bill "Spaceman" Lee. Lee was one of the most colourful and zany players in Major League Baseball history. How cool was he? Rock god Warren Zevon included the song "Bill Lee" on his 1980 album, which had perhaps the greatest title for an album in that decade: *Bad Luck Streak in Dancing School*. Lee was a lefthander. Gee, what a shock. He once said, "You have two hemispheres in your brain — a left and a right side. The left side controls the right side of your body and the right controls the left half. It's a fact. Therefore, lefthanders are the only people in their right minds."

The Lee story you probably know. He pitched for the Red Sox from 1969 through 1978 and had three straight seventeen-win seasons from 1973 to 1975. The Expos got him in 1979 for something named a "Stan Papi" and he won another sixteen games, but in 1982 he was unceremoniously kicked out of the game and blacklisted, according to Bill in his book *The Wrong Stuff*, co-written with Richard Lally. This happened a few months before the All-Star Game. After protesting the release of his good friend and Expos second baseman Rodney "Cool Breeze" Scott in May, Lee left Olympic Stadium — in full uniform, mind you — and went across the street to bang back a few beers and play some pool with a friend. This wasn't the first time Lee had pulled this stunt. He had done it years before with the Bosox. Paul Flannery of the website Deadspin described it this way: "Lee didn't just talk tough. He stormed out of the clubhouse and left the Red Sox when the team sold his friend Bernie Carbo to the Indians for $15,000. They responded by burying him in the bullpen and then trading him to Montreal for a utilityman named Stan Papi, who had a grand total of 117 at-bats for the Sox after the 1978 season." For the record, for years the rallying cry in Boston over losing season after losing season was, "Who the fuck is Stan Papi?"

Back to the Scott incident: When Lee "returned to the clubhouse, the Expos said he was in no condition to pitch. Lee said he'd had only … three and was ready if necessary. This was strike two, but he was out. The Expos released Lee after general manager John McHale found the pitcher waiting for him the next morning in his darkened office sitting in the lotus position. Lee spent two years wandering the wilderness playing for teams like the Moncton Mets and an outfit in Venezuela. There were a couple of sideshow MLB tryouts that never came to much, and then reality set in. It was all over. It wasn't until much later that he grudgingly admitted that he had overplayed his hand."

The man he was playing pool with at Le Brasserie 77 was none other than Terry Mosher, my new "occasional" drinking buddy. Terry told me the story about that day with Bill and after more than a few rounds suggested I get in touch with him. "You should call him; I'll give you his number." He did. I called. He answered. I set up a meeting at his house the next day. His absolutely stunning girlfriend Pam (whom he left his wife for) welcomed me in, and I would spend hours upon hours with the man, the legend, Bill "Spaceman" Lee over several icy Heinekens from his fridge. Aaah, the Spaceman. (He preferred "Earthman," BTW, and that's how he signed a 5-by-7 colour glossy for me: "Bill Lee, Earth, 1982.") I'll tell you, the man is insanely funny. Now, at that time in his "career," two months after his release, he was playing as many as three games a day as a first baseman or right fielder for several local softball teams and with a team in the tiny Quebec Senior League, les Senateurs de Longueil. He told me, "I

With "Spaceman" (Earthman?) Bill Lee at a celebrity softball game at Christie Pits in Toronto.

pitched in the 'show' for fourteen years, but I enjoy this more. I go out every day and then go have a beer with the guys. And it's a beer that means something. It's a good life."

The conversation never stopped. We talked about him admitting to sprinkling marijuana on his buckwheat pancakes every morning. He was fined $250 by MLB commissioner Bowie Kuhn but sent them $251 just to throw off their books. His years in Boston and fabled Fenway feuds with manager Don "The Gerbil" Zimmer, and the 1975 World Series with the Reds, perhaps the greatest seven-game set in baseball history, were also hot topics. Before Game 7, Reds manager Sparky Anderson announced that his starter, Don Gullett, was going to the Hall of Fame. Lee responded, "Oh yeah, well I'm going to the Elliot Lounge." In that final game, Lee threw an ill-advised Eephus — "spaceball," or "moon ball" pitch, as he called it — to Tony Perez of the Reds with the Red Sox up 3–0. Oops. It resulted in a towering two-run home run over the Green Monster that Lee told me "is still rising." (There was another great line Bill told me about seeing the Green Monster for the first time as a rookie. He asked, "Do they keep that thing up for games?") The Red Sox would go on to lose the game 4–3, costing them the chance for their first World Series championship since 1918. He also talked about the 1978 Bosox, who had a fourteen-game lead over the Yankees before a huge collapse. That was the famous Bucky "F%&$ing" Dent game. He told me he was glad the Sox had traded him to Montreal after that season, saying, "Who wants to be with a team that will go down in history alongside the '64 Phillies and the '67 Arabs?" He also told me a bizarre story about helping Bob Dylan's wife lock Dylan out of his house. I know; what the eff? When we were finished, I had a stack of cassettes and hours of tape to whittle down to two minutes for a radio feature, and one of the most memorable moments of my career. And it had just started.

* * *

Another baseball highlight, in a career filled with dozens of them, came in 1991 at another Canadian-hosted All-Star Game. This one, the sixty-second, was played at SkyDome in Toronto, and it was a week-long boozefest. There was a gala party on Toronto Island, where I posed with my mom's all-time favourite player, Hall of Famer Johnny Bench of the Cincinnati

Redlegs, then working radio for CBS. I hobnobbed with former Montreal Expos Al "Scoop" Oliver and Ron LeFlore and their wives during a lavish affair on Toronto Island. I should mention that if I'd known then what I know now about LeFlore, I would have chastised him for introducing a young championship-calibre 1980 Expos squad to cocaine (and the several other drugs he reportedly supplied) that all but squashed their chances at a World Series title. Again.

One true supersized highlight was covering a memorabilia signing by my all-time baseball hero John Wesley "Boog" Powell of the Baltimore Orioles. At six foot four and three hundred pounds plus, Boog was, to say the least, a formidable figure. My first baseball memory was watching the New York Mets beat Boog and the O's on TV from Shea Stadium and seeing thousands of crazed Amazin' Mets fans pour onto the field. I watched it with my mom, a huge baseball fan, and thought, wow, there must be something to this sport to get people *that* excited. Boog, the 1970 AL MVP, would crush the Reds the next year. I figured the O's had the momentum to win four or five titles in a row during those years. Mind you, momentum in baseball, Earl Weaver used to say, is tomorrow's starting pitcher. Jim Palmer said about Weaver, "The only thing Earl knew about big league pitching is he couldn't hit it." Still, that began my long-time love for the game, baseball cards, and big Boog. Powell and I got along cordially. I was afraid to ask him out for drinks and steaks because I'm sure the tab would have been in the thousands. He'd, as comedian Denis Leary suggested, upon ordering his cut of beef, say, "I love to eat red meat. I'll carve off what I want and ride the rest home!"

The '91 All-Star Game itself was nothing to call Mom long-distance about. One of my childhood heroes, Andre Dawson, homered in a 4–2 AL win. Cal Ripken Jr., my future drinking buddy, was named the MVP, and — this was great — Hall of Fame catcher Carlton Fisk hit a bloop single in his twelfth and final All-Star Game. At forty-three, it made him the oldest All-Star ever to get a hit. Good ol' Pudge. Although I did love the fact that George Bell, then of the Chicago Cubs and pinch-hitting in the ninth, facing Dennis Eckersley, struck out as boos rained down onto his purple ass, while the hated Eckersley of the A's received big cheers. Years earlier, Bell had famously told Blue Jay fans and the media to "kiss his purple butt" after he was booed for committing an error. The next day a fan brought a sign that read, "George, we're behind you all the way." Classic. I hated Bell's defiant "one tough Dominican" stance and would rip him on air whenever possible.

Now, the highlight for young Master Gallagher the night of July 9, 1991, took place before the first pitch. I must have been in the clubhouse just taking it all in, trying successfully to rub shoulders with All-Stars old and new, so I was a little late getting to my seat in the press box. I was all by myself waiting for one of the elevators when I heard "bing" and the doors opened. Three figures were inside. One was a big, burly security guard who could have easily waved me away and asked me to wait for the next elevator, considering who was also inside, but he didn't. I was smiling from ear to ear and literally felt a warm glow as I entered the lift. The two gentlemen (not the bodyguard, who was *all* business) meagerly smiled back. Are you ready for this? There I was standing beside Hall-of-Fame Boston Red Sox slugger Ted Williams and New York Yankee hero Joe DiMaggio. Just the four of us. How cozy. I knew they were throwing out the first pitch and I knew I'd see them from high atop the field. I just didn't think I'd be breathing the same air as two of the greatest names in sports history. The two were making the rounds in '91, attending White House dinners and all-star games marking fifty years since the legendary summer of 1941, when Williams batted .406, becoming the last player to hit .400 for a full season, and DiMaggio stroked base hits in fifty-six straight games, a record that still stands. The two said nothing, which was normal considered they hated each other. I reached into my sports jacket for one of the twenty-dollar disposable cameras that I would have with me the entire All-Star week. Twenty-four exposures and memories that would last a lifetime. The security guard leaned in for a peek, *not* like I was pulling a Saturday-night-special shotgun out at the Oval Office, but just to take a closer look. After all, he was guarding Ted "the Splendid Splinter" and Joe "The Yankee Clipper" who, outside of Babe Ruth, were the two most famous baseball players on the planet in the twentieth century. When I showed him my camera, he relaxed, said nothing, but shook his head to signify, "ah, *no*." If he had been a local guy, maybe, but this larger-than-life Bubba Smith lookalike was New York City–based MLB security to the highest degree. I stuffed it back in my coat pocket. The three got off at field level as I headed to the press box, dejected. The biggest brush with greatness of my life (bigger than Ali, Pete Rose, David Bowie, Brad Pitt, or Led Zeppelin? There's an order to it, if you squint) lasted one floor and without exposure. From my camera, anyway.

TWENTY

YES, MR. GALLAGHER, YOUR NET IS READY

(or, Ken Dryden whispers in my ear,
"You're starting the third period," and I'm thinking,
"That's something you don't hear every day.")

Ken Dryden is my all-time sports hero. Always has been, always will be. Growing up in Montreal, hockey is a religion, and Ken Dryden was god. So to have the five-time NHL All-Star, five-time Vezina Trophy winner, and six-time Stanley Cup champion (in just eight years in the league, mind you) tap you on the shoulder and tell you to get ready to start the third period of the game celebrating the twenty-fifth anniversary of the '72 Summit Series between Canada and the Soviet Union, it's kind of a big deal. This was all pre-arranged. With Dryden and his fellow Canadian netminders Tony Esposito and Eddie Johnston (not to mention Soviet netminders Vladislav Tretiak and whoever his backup was, who didn't get a sniff in the series) having long hung up their oversized goaltending jockstraps, it was left to a few former NHLers, Leaf announcer Joe Bowen, and yours truly to "tend the twines." Joe and I were each going to play five minutes to start the third period. And with Dryden behind the bench and a packed house looking on, this was perhaps my defining moment in a life filled with great sports memories. As another drinking buddy James Earl Jones said in the film *Field of Dreams*, "Memories so thick that you have to wipe them away from your face." Screw the memories. At the time I just hoped I didn't get killed by a 100 mph Dennis Hull slapshot. So, how had I got there? How is it that Yvan Cournoyer, Frank Mahovlich, and '72 series hero Paul Henderson were lining up five feet in front of me to take an important faceoff that had me and everybody else wondering when the first goal was going to go in?

I'd always wanted to be a goalie. When I knew I wasn't going to make it as the starting centrefielder for the Montreal Expos, I turned to something a kid who would grow up to be all of five foot eight could be good at — goaltending. There were and still are several vertically challenged netminders in "the show." But in the sixties and seventies? Rogie Vachon, Gump Worsley, and Johnny Bower were all pipsqueaks compared to today's standards. Well, I was small, and just not very good. Serves me right for not strapping on my first set of goaltending gear until I was seventeen! Oh sure, we played street hockey in NDG and Montreal West for years, but when it came to expensive goalie equipment, my father opted to give me a broomball set for my twelfth birthday instead. Yes, broomball — the sport of the future. If your future is playing in the Special Olympics. I had to use my sister's white figure skates at the local rink, in the dark well after the rest of my friends had gone home, just to get some turns in.

As my skating got better, everything changed. There's a popular fallacy that goaltenders don't have to be very good skaters. Growing up, coaches would line their twenty-odd players up at one end of the rink and have them sprint two hundred feet. The two worst skaters would always be the goaltenders. That was just a big bowl of wrong. You have to be quick and agile, with cat-like reflexes, and be an incredible skater to be a good goalie. I was none of those things. But I worked at it, and after a series of injuries to goaltenders on my high school team, I eventually found myself sitting on the bench as backup as we ran roughshod over some of the best and worst schools in the league. One afternoon, with the local rink packed because it was *the* place to be, my team, the Crusaders, was leading 12–0 late in the third period of a late-season game. I had yet to even make it into a game because, well, I still skated, again as Danny Gallivan would describe it, "gingerly." Basically, like a giraffe on roller blades. Sensing automatic victory, a murmur came up from the crowd. My nickname

Who needs a goalie stick to lean on when you have me? With my all-time favourite boyhood hero, HHOF member Ken Dryden, on one of our numerous nights out together.

in high school was "Johnny Wow." Remember the *WKRP* episode when Washington got a gig at a local radio station and his mentor was George Carlin as "Wally the Wow"? Well, come Monday morning, Johnny Wow was born. I hated that freaking nickname, but since everybody knew I wanted to be a radio announcer, it stuck. I still get it when I go back home, but now I just go with it.

So, right out of the movie *Rudy*, based on the life of Daniel "Rudy" Ruettiger, who dreamed of playing football at the University of Notre Dame, the chant began. Not "Rudy, Rudy, Rudy!" but instead, "We want Wow!" "We want Wow!" "We want Wow!" So, with time ticking away, my coach, Gary Murphy, pulled the same move Dan Devine does in the film and put me in. We scored three quick goals to make it 15–0 and I saw little action. No beautiful kick saves, no flashy glovework, just a few goalmouth scrambles that I was able to cover up. But there was a problem. I was so nervous making my high school debut that I had the worst case of "cotton mouth" you can imagine. I had no spit. I could hardly swallow. And this was the late seventies, before goalies had Gatorade bottles on their nets for a quick squirt. But I needed water — now. So during an enlongated period when my teammates were peppering the opposing net with pucks — remember, it was 15–0 and the shots were 62–12 — I made a mad dash for the bench to get a drink. My coach lost it. You see, I wasn't aware that leaving the net is a two-minute delay-of-game penalty. The team was fighting for top spot and needed to run up the score and get a shutout because of the goal differential in case we finished tied for first. The coach was screaming, "Get the fuck back in the net, Gallagher, or that's the last time you'll ever see it! Hurry or you'll get a penalty — *fuuuck*!" I had to sprint back to the net with my throat closing off due to dryness. The local newspaper was there to cover it, and Monday morning I hustled to get the sports section. There was the result: at the bottom, it read, "KVHS goaltender shutout — Dave Hearn, Johnny Wow." Fuckers.

Later I would try out for and get cut from a Junior "B" team in Halifax, but I kept up appearances in local beer leagues. One great thing about netminders is that we never pay for ice time. Ever. Oh, we might bring a few cases of beer for the last game of the season, but goalies never go to pocket. Mind you, my so-so goaltending career, along with my sports celebrity status, combined on one glorious day that would see me make an appearance on ice at Maple Leaf Gardens. So, there I was starting the third period at the Gardens after Dryden gave me the "tap." He became a regular guest on my CP24 show, but on this afternoon, he was my coach, and I just didn't want to disappoint him.

The Paul Henderson line was starting for the red team. I was in that classic white jersey with the big red Canadian flag. And here came Henderson. Great. As most Canadians know, Paul scored the Summit Series winner in Moscow, culminating those now-famous twenty-eight days in September in 1972. If you recall, he scored the winners in the final three games, including his late Game 6 tally on a one-on-three break, splitting the defence, the one he would later admit to being the finest of his career. But he was just warming up. Paul Henderson will be forever immortalized in hockey history as the guy who scored the biggest goal in what became arguably the greatest Canadian moment of the twentieth century. Not bad for a guy who was actually one of the last players to make the team. If he could score like that on Vladislav Tretiak of the USSR, he was going to toy with me like a cat playing with a mostly dead mouse.

Paul and I would become pretty pally over the years. He always called me "Tiger," but I'll be damned if I know why. Perhaps my on- and off-ice antics reminded him of ex-Leaf Dave "Tiger" Williams, another future teammate of mine. Paul has been milking that '72 series-winning goal for over forty years now. Free drinks and dinners? You know it. This is is a true story. When I invited him to be on my CityTV talk show one Sunday night, he suggested in return I pay for dinner one night for him and his wife. I happily agreed. When he showed up for the interview, he handed me a bill for $150 from a dinner he and Eleanor had *just* finished on Queen Street. I'd figured dinner *some* night, not *that* night. Still, a terrific man and fine hockey ambassador for this country. I was glad to have the station pick up his tab. So here came Henderson, gliding down the ice, and he had Leafs greats Ron Ellis and Darryl Sittler with him! Dryden, knowing I'm a huge Canadiens fan, countered with Habs legends Frank and Pete Mahovlich, and Yvan Cournoyer. Talk about a dream come true!

The five minutes are a blur. Ron Ellis *did* score after barrelling me over in the crease, but the goal was waved off by hall-of-fame veteran and legendary hard-ass referee Bill Friday. The pucks kept coming and nothing was going in. Every bounce was going my way. Pucks I didn't even see were hitting my pads. Deflections careened off my stick, blocker, and skates. I've always jokingly said, "I may be small, but I'm slow," but I was having one of my finest nights as a goaltender. Here came Stan Mikita, J.P. Parise, and the aforementioned Dennis Hull and his 100 mph slapshot. (His brother Bobby would record a 119.5 mph slapshot, and Dennis had one that was not far off.)

Oh yeah, here came Hull — he was scoreless and didn't look happy about it. Dennis Hull broke free and was all alone in over the blue line, but instead of winding up and shooting from out there, he skated in another ten feet and gave the fans what they'd all paid to see: the shot. I wish *I'd* seen it. All I heard was it buzzing past my left ear. Top shelf, where mom hides the bad sports clichés. Red light on. Shutout over. Dennis even wrote about that goal in his book, *The Third Best Hull*. When he was a guest on TSN's *Gallagher* show, we'd replay it from several angles. Later on I'd sit at the back of Wayne Gretzky's and drink into the night with him, out and

Team Canada '72, twenty-five years later, with (from left) Ron Ellis, Paul Henderson, Frank Mahovlich, me, Yvan Cournoyer, and Pat Stapleton. Funny how I got all the Montreal players on my team.

out crying at the on- and off-the-record stories of his days in the show and as one of the most sought-after dinner speakers in North America. I would spend some quality time with several members of Team Canada over the years. And I'm not talking about the time that I booed Vic Hatfield (who bolted on the team in Russia) every time he touched the puck one night when he played against the Habs at the Forum. Phil Esposito and I co-host the *Next Sport Star* show twice a week with Bill Watters, Perry Lefko, and Frank D'Angelo and get together over some Stolis when he's in town. Ron Ellis, Gilbert Perreault, and I have skated in several "celebrity" old-timers games together. Marcel Dionne was a guest on *Gallagher* and brought several sweaters from his hockey-themed clothing line. I love when they do that. Just don't call it schwag. And I mean NEVER. J.P. Parise and I re-enacted his near stick-swing incident with German ref Joseph Kompalla for a CityTV sportscast. Pat Stapleton and Bill White were guests on my CP24 show, and Pat told me exactly where the game-winning Summit Series puck is — hidden in a safety deposit box somewhere.

* * *

Membership does have its privileges. In the summer of 2017, when a bunch of us celebrated the greatest sporting event during the 150th anniversary of Canada, I was back with my old teammates. Cowboy steaks and a half crate of wine in the Distillery District with Phil Esposito, Yvan Cournoyer, Frank and Pete Mahovlich, Wayne Cashman, Jean Ratelle, Brad Park, et al. I'm telling you, it was like having an audience with the Pope. Or the Godfather. Well, let the wine pour and the yarns begin, I say. Speaking of the Corleones, this one from Esposito: "I was up for the role of Talia Shire's husband in *The Godfather*! The guy that James Caan beats the crap out of. But Francis Ford Coppola was going to shoot the movie in April 1971 and the Bruins were gonna have a long run to the Cup, so I had to say no." To which I reminded him, "You should've taken the part cuz the Habs knocked you out the first round." While Esposito pinched me on the cheek like a grandmother scolding a five-year-old — only a lot harder — Yvan (who won one of his ten cups — ten! — that year) smiled. Cournoyer, my teammate in the '72 series twenty-fifth anniversary game, came up with this gem: On the tenth anniversary of the Summit Series, he was sitting at a bar with

100-year-old Foster Hewitt, who'd butchered the Road Runner's name throughout his career and for the entire month of September 1972. Foster just happened to order a Courvoisier cognac within earshot of Yvan. He pronounced the word perfectly. Yvan asked, "Let me get this straight: you pronounced the names of every Russian on that '72 team dead on but called me, a Canadian, Corn-NOY-er my entire career *and* you just *nailed* Courvoisier like nobody's business? Tabernac!" Laughter exploded. But my favourite moment was with Wayne Cashman. He and I were speakers at a sports celebrity dinner in the early 80s in Halifax. We had a limo and were barhopping all through the city. Now, I saw the best and worst of Wayne Cashman over the years. The good, in Montreal for a coffee when he was head coach of the Philadelphia Flyers for the 1997/98 season, and the bad. That would be the night in Halifax. At the end of the night, Wayne, a notorious booze hound at the time, was dropped off at his hotel. And like Jack Nicholson in the movie *Terms of Endearment*, he fell out and cracked his head on the pavement. Cashman staggered to the lobby with blood dripping everywhere. In the summer of 2017 I asked him about that night and he

At Mike "The Ultimate Leaf Fan" Wilson's Night for a Change — Stop the Bullying gathering in 2016. With HHOF member Phil Esposito, Cup-winning coach Mike Keenan, and poon hound extraordinaire Ron Duguay.

looked me straight in the eye and said, "John, I have never been to the city of Halifax in my life!" Now, I've had mornings when I've had to think about what I did the night before, but I've never been blacked out for an entire weekend like Wayne did in Halifax. True lies? No, CJCH afternoon host Dave Cochrane remembers Cashman in Halifax. "He came in and read the sports. We helped him with proper pronunciations of some of the names. Oh, he was there." In body, at least. I asked Phil Esposito about Cashman's "late nights" and he told me that in 1987, he said to Wayne, "if you don't stop your drinking you can stop being assistant coach of my New York Rangers." Phil told me "he hasn't had a drink since. Thirty plus years."

My good friend Frank Mahovlich was also at the gala. The "Big M" always reminds me that he was the final guest on *The Gallagher Show* on TSN in 1999. I like to say that *no one* remembers *The Gallagher Show*, but Frank does. Mahovlich is as sensitive, proud, and intelligent a hockey player as I've ever had the privilege of meeting. It's been said that Frank could do stupid good things in a hockey rink. It just didn't always seem to occur to him to do them. He told me a funny story about his days in the WHA. Mahovlich was placed on an unproductive line with enforcers Frank "Seldom Been Beaten" Beaton and Dave Hanson, one of the Hanson brothers who had been in the movie *Slap Shot*. According to John Brophy, when a reporter asked Mahovlich what was wrong, he replied, "I don't know, but I seem to play a lot better with Gordie Howe and Alex Delvecchio." Years later, on my talk show on CityTV, I had Frank and his son Ted, who was promoting a book about his famous dad, on. I asked Ted what he would do if Frank's old coach Punch Imlach — who made his father's life a living hell, deliberately mispronouncing his name, calling him Ma-hal-o-vich — was a guest on the show, sitting right next to him. What would he do? Ted said, "I'd knock him right off his chair with a right to the jaw." And he would have, too.

※ ※ ※

My time in the limelight was coming to an end. The clock was ticking close to the allotted five minutes I was given, and I could see another former Leaf, Mike Palmateer, getting ready to return to his rightful crease at the Gardens. Time for one more improbable and perhaps impossible save? Perhaps off

541-goal scorer and HHOF member Stan Mikita? Cue the cheesy inspirational music, because here comes one more goalmouth flop and a pad stacker to stop Stan in a mad scramble. Big saves all around. Disaster in front of the Maple Leaf Gardens faithful averted.

I received a huge ovation from the Gardens crowd. After all, the failed Junior "B" early training-camp cut/token celebrity sportscaster "fill-in" netminder was supposed to have his jock not only handed to him but also thrown into the grey seats. So they knew and appreciated a "spirited effort," we'll call it, when they saw one. And my hero, Ken Dryden, had put me in. Don Cherry has said, "Show me a good goalie and I'll show you a good coach," and, "Ninety percent of the game is goaltending. Unless you don't have any, in which case it's 100 percent."

I skated to the bench, and again I bring you back to the film *Rudy* and one of the final scenes. In it a young Vince Vaughn makes a play just to get Rudy, played by Sean Astin, into his one and only Notre Dame game. I pointed to Dryden behind the bench and uttered the line from the movie: "*That* ... was for you." If all truth be told, *that* was for me.

TWENTY-ONE

KILLER INSTINCT

(or, "Gallagher! Burns, Gilmour, and a pair of
naked women armed with bottles of hooch are riding
a luggage cart through the hallways on the penthouse
floor. You've got to come down here and cover this!")

My first few months covering the Toronto Maple Leafs were, in a word, engaging. Getting a bear hug from an old friend who just happened to be the Leafs coach, John Brophy, on my first trip ever to the Gardens was a highlight, to be sure. After that, well … There was the time when Ken Wregget pulled me aside and told me that I had made his wife *and* kids cry over breakfast earlier that morning while they were listening to a comment I made about his goaltending flaws (and there were several) on Q107. Getting hit by a cane swung by Harold Ballard while he was exiting his bunker after another Leafs loss? It happened. I wish I had the scar to prove it, but the feeble old despot ruler didn't have the umph. Ballard's years running the team was a time of such total stupidity and nonsense. And it seemed to last forever. Truth be told, the guy was a bigoted, crude, misogynist nincompoop. My CityTV colleague Jim McKenny used to say that those seventies teams he was on were just two good players away from contending but that Ballard was too cheap. And an idiot. How could you let goalie Bernie Parent go for $10,000? That happened, too. Parent left the Leafs for the WHA, but when his teams in Miami and Philly folded, the Leafs got his rights back. When he asked for an extra ten grand, Ballard fumed and sent him to the Flyers for Doug Favell and Bob Neely. Parent would win his first of two consecutive Conn Smythe and Stanley Cup trophies months later in Philadelphia.

It always seemed like there was something cheesy about the whole organization. Even the sandwiches in the press room. On the odd occasion when the Leafs hosted, for instance, a Canada Cup news conference with a lavish spread, Ballard would ruin it by announcing, "Help yourself to lunch, gentlemen, but you better get there before this fucking fat ass does," pointing at unassuming reporter Bruce Barker. On the night of my encounter with his cane, he was being helped into his wheelchair at the Gardens as I approached him with my tape recorder. Still steamed after another Leafs defeat and obviously not taking any questions that night, he hit me with his cane while screaming, "Get the fuck out of here!" Unlike broadcaster Bob McKenzie who pressed charges when Phil Esposito hit him in 1993 at the same MLG, I exploited the encounter and aired a bleeped-out edition of the interview on Q107 the next morning. Harold would die just months later.

Irish Mafia alert! With HHOF Habs/Leafs coach Pat Burns at Montana's in the mid-nineties.

After years of complete futility, the Toronto Maple Leafs were finally good again during the 1992/93 and 1993/94 seasons. When the Leafs went on that roll in the early nineties, it was a glorious time to be up close and personal with the local heroes. Yes, I had a front row seat. And unlike covering sports these days, reporters had a real "hands-on" relationship with players. Some of us got rather friendly with them. The guys and their wives and girlfriends would watch my nightly sportscasts and wake up to me on Q107 in the morning. We'd go out for drinks and dinners with them, go to their weddings (thank you, Doug and Amy Gilmour), and bring dates to Wendel Clark's hot tub parties at his place on Madison Avenue, and I even double-dated with all-star Dave Ellett. I know it still happens today with reporters, but not nearly as much as back then. By the way, that phone call I received at City late one night about Burns, Gilmour, and two naked "fans" actually happened. I'm not so sure the guy was making things up, but what was I to do? Was I tempted to call either of them on their cell phones and ask if they could order up a bottle of Aussie chardonnay and let me join in on the fun? Yes, maybe I

There are a lot of Stanley Cup rings on these goaltenders' fingers. Just not on mine. With (from left) Bernie Parent, Johnny "The China Wall" Bower, me, Mike Palmateer, Gerry "Cheesy" Cheevers, and Glenn "Chico" Resch.

should have called them. The fact that I had *both* of their cell numbers dumbfounds sports reporters today.

The Leafs in those days were an odd bunch. Talented as all get out, but a strange mix. Burns and Gilmour were right in the centre of things and were giving long-suffering Leafs fans something to cheer about following the disastrous Harold Ballard era. It started with the hiring of the fiery Burns as head coach. Then there was the absolute steal of a trade to bring Doug "Killer" Gilmour to town in exchange for a bunch of spare parts.

Gary Leeman was the biggest name heading to Calgary in the trade. He'd had some really nice seasons in Toronto. He was just the second Maple Leaf to hit the fifty-goal mark at that time. Sadly, he never regained anything like that form in Calgary or any of his other stops, although he did win a Cup ring with the '93 Canadiens, one that he has even let me try on. His career was derailed by a series of devastating head injuries, and the poor guy is still suffering to this day. But there were other important contributors to the revival. General manager Cliff Fletcher made trades to bring in goaltender Grant Fuhr and forward

It's *The Late-Late Show with Doug Gilmour!* Just before this shot, "Killer," then of the Canadiens, smuggled out his game-worn Number 93 autographed Habs jersey and stuffed it in my trunk, whispering "Don't tell Amy"!

Glenn Anderson from the Edmonton Oilers. Fuhr was then flipped for Dave Andreychuck of the Sabres. The Fuhr trade made sense because the Leafs had a young up-and-coming goaltender in Felix "The Cat" Potvin. Mind you, anytime I talked with Felix, all he wanted to discuss was my chocolate Labrador retriever, who he had seen on one of my nightly sportscasts on City. Potvin had several Labs at home. Strange for a guy nicknamed "The Cat."

For the first time in a generation, the Leafs were relevant. And the city, including several of its attractive female residents, was catching Maple Leaf fever. It was during this time that I spotted Anderson at a downtown bar surrounded by a bevy of beautiful women. Ever the ladies' man and a gentleman, he made introductions all around. Two of the women were Suzanne Kean and Sharri MacDonald, who remain my good friends to this day. Suzanne and I went out for a year or so. Fun fact: On our first date, she was the page-three *Toronto Sun* Sunshine Girl (who looked stunning in a red bikini), and we were naked before the night was over. That has to be some kind of unique dating trifecta, doesn't it? Sunshine Girl, first date, sex. Speaking of, Dave Ellett, "The Natural," and I were having a late night at Gretzky's restaurant. He and I always hit if off because, despite being from Cleveland, he was, like me, a huge Montreal Expos fan. On this evening, it was well after closing time and a bunch of us were milling around with some of the local "talent" when all of a sudden Dave went missing. Shortly after there was such a banging coming from the restaurant that some of the dozens of liquor bottles that lined the wall in the bar area started to tumble down. Ellett and his new lady friend were in a booth behind it, getting overly frisky. Ellett was also part of one of my brother Steve's favourite stories. He had always been wary of the tall tales of my rumoured celebrity friendships in the big smoke, but it was during a trip with his friend Ian from Moncton, N.B., during the Leafs '93 playoff run, when this happened: in 1993 Dave and Wendel Clark were departing the Leafs dressing room after a win over the Blues when they spotted me and said, "Gallagher would know! Hey John, where's a good Chinese restaurant around here?" Minutes later Dave, Wendel, Steve, Ian, Leaf forward Rob Pearson, and I were in a couple of cabs heading to my favourite spot on Spadina and soon digging into huge plates of steaming Asian cuisine. Steve didn't doubt me again after that.

As for Wendel, he would save his best game in his entire playoff career for Game 6 of the Kings series in L.A. Clark would pop three goals at the Los Angeles Forum, his third tying the game up 4–4 and sending it into OT. But of course Toronto, one goal away from its first Stanley Cup final berth since 1967, loses on a play that is still a thorn in the side of Leaf fans to this day. Wayne Gretzky high-sticked Doug Gilmour, but referee Kerry Fraser didn't award the Leafs a power play, even with Gilmour bloodied. Gretzky of all people scored the clincher for the Kings, as Kurt Russell, Goldie Hawn, Mary Hart, James Wood, John Candy, and even Ron and Nancy Reagan (WTF?) leapt from their seats (okay, Ronny didn't leap anymore at that point), sending the series to Game 7 in Toronto. What a series it had been up to that point. There was Burns, fired up and having to be held back from going after Kings coach Barry Melrose between benches. And this actually happened: during a packed post-game press conference after Game 5 of the L.A.-Leafs series at Maple Leaf Gardens, someone brings up the Montreal Canadiens, who had made short work of the New York Islanders in the other Conference final earlier that evening. Burns' old team! With Toronto leading the best of seven 3–2, one more Leafs victory would have set up the first Habs-Buds Cup final since 1967. Burns looks around the room, spotted me, pointed, and said, "So the Canadiens are in the final. Well, that ought to make you happy, eh Gallagher?" I was just standing there minding my own business! Heck, I hadn't even asked the question. When Burns pointed me out as a blatant Canadiens fan (and, in Toronto, an obvious evil-doer), everyone just turned their eyes and cameras on me. We're talking CBS, NBC, ABC, ESPN, and all of the local channels. It was like that scene in the wonderful film *Notting Hill*, when all the cameras focus on Hugh Grant. I can't see Julia Roberts in the part of Pat Burns, but still. Of course I loved it, and I used it in my story that night.

Giving the Leafs the "business" was something I enjoyed over the years. We all did. Just recently, ESPN named the Toronto Maple Leafs the worst franchise in North American professional sports. They won that distinction for three out of four years. The Leafs finished 122nd out of 122 teams and ranked near the bottom in every single fan experience category. They were a joke. Loveable losers, yes, but they were such an easy target. From Leafs GM Floyd Smith saying on the day he fired Doug Carpenter,

"I have nothing to say and I'm only going to say it once," to yours truly on Q107, when bumbling ex-Leaf GM Gerry McNamara (who'd had a steel plate embedded in his head after a hockey accident) was fired, "At least he can come up to my cottage in the summer. With that huge steel plate, we can lean him up next to the satellite dish and get HBO for free," I tried to nail them at every turn. And I didn't get the job as official Leafs public address announcer? Blimey.

TWENTY-TWO

"LISTEN, BUDDY. IF YOU SAY ANOTHER WORD, I'M GONNA KICK YOU OUT AND DRIVE THE FUCKING THING MYSELF."

(or, my John Brophy "slapshot" story)

You've seen that look before. Like the one your father gave you when you brought home a bad report card. There were few faces in professional hockey as glowering or even as recognizable as John Brophy's. I thank the hockey gods that John Brophy loved me. And I'm here to tell you, that was a good thing. You do not want to be on the dark side of John "The Godfather of Goonery" Brophy. He was the head coach of the Nova Scotia Voyageurs in Halifax for three years, starting the same year I hit town in 1981. Our station soon signed him to come in on a weekly basis during the season for a segment called "Coaches Corner." Yeah, so sue us. Brophy was a gem. As rough and tough an exterior as he had on the ice, the man was a pussy cat when away from the rink. I guess it was because he was a good Maritime boy. He always brought a big box of doughnuts for the morning crew. But get John to the rink, and it was an entirely different environment. Don't ever cross him. I did one night and felt the wrath of probably the toughest customers in pro-hockey history. Tough doesn't cover it. He racked up nearly 4,000 penalty minutes before he retired.

In Kent Russell's article, "Enforcers: Soul on Ice," the author interviewed an old-time hockey fan in Brophy's home province of Nova Scotia. "This one fox-faced old-timer lifted his head from his breakfast and said, 'I'll tell ya right fuckin' now … I saw a fan spit one on Brophy, right? He spits one on Brophy, and then later Brophy makes like he's digging the puck away from the boards in front of the guy — they didn't have glass separating you from the ice back then — and Brophy butt-ends the guy right in the teeth. Right in the kisser. And then how does he go? He goes, '*Now* spit, mother-fucker!'" When fans threw batteries at him when he coached, the security guards would have to stop him from going after them. According to Kent Russell, some fan even shot a gun at Brophy. They say he laughed when the bullet came to a stop near his feet.

I always thought they should make a movie about him. Well, they did. Mmm, kind of. Remember Reggie Dunlop (played by Paul Newman) in the movie *Slap Shot*? That was based on "Broph." The scars on that man's face, my goodness. You could tell he'd been through a few wars. Ex-Voyageur John Chabot was a good friend of mine in those days. He remembered when he played for Brophy: "We weren't allowed to lose to either Moncton — who were Toronto's farm team — or Fredericton — who were Quebec's. One night we went into Fredericton and played well, but we blew it at the end and lost 3–2. Brophy was livid after the game. He had a $10,000 Rolex that he placed on the floor and smashed into smithereens. He took off his jacket and tore it to shreds. He sat at the front of the team bus, and as we started to pull away, he punched a hole in the double-paned window beside where he was sitting. We had a six-hour drive to Halifax, and the bus driver told him, 'If you ever do that again, you're getting out.' Broph looked at him — he gave him one of those long, scary glares — and said, 'Listen, buddy. If you say another word, I'm gonna kick you out and drive the fucking thing myself.'

"Another time, we played Moncton in Halifax and lost. The game before, we'd had some disabled kids come down to the room. One of them was a huge Voyageurs fan. Everybody loved the kid. He ended up getting invited back for the next game, too. He was wheeled into the room after the loss and put near the door. Broph came in ranting and raving and screaming about us being a bunch of invalids. He spotted the fellow in the wheelchair and said, 'What the fuck is he doing in the room? We got enough of these fucking guys sitting right here!' He opened the door, put his foot on the back of the wheelchair, and booted him out of the room, sending him across the hallway and into a wall, shrieking, 'Now stay the fuck out!' Then he smashed our weight machine to pieces, ripped the stick holder off the wall, and broke every stick we owned."

I know that feeling. In my case, I underwent the wrath of Brophy when I was chosen to pick a Voyageurs game's three stars one night at the Halifax Metro Centre. My mistake? I picked a member of the visiting New Haven Nighthawks as the first star. He had scored late in a 2–2 tie, beating the Vees' goalie Mark Holden. The fact that Holden had close to fifty shots on goal and stole the point for his team was obviously lost on me. And Mark was a friend of mine! Mind you, I always thought that he'd hit on my then-girlfriend one too many times, so maybe that had something to do with it. Kidding. Still, dumb move on my part. Now, the fact that Brophy's players were in the running for the Molson Cup, which was based on a point system for first, second, and third-star votes, was extremely important to him. He hated to lose at *anything*. His Vees were also competing with teams from Fredericton and Moncton for the same cup. When Brophy found out that Holden, who was a top candidate for the trophy that year, was picked as second star, he ripped into me, and good, as the team boarded a bus to take them to another exotic AHL destination. I still have the scars. Emotionally, anyway. LOL.

But he knew we had to be in the same air again soon, so he softened up. We always got along well. In fact, one year, I tried to convince Broph to let me play backup for the Voyageurs. His backup goalie had got hurt in a practice the day of a game, and I called him up to offer him my services. I tried to convince him that it would be just one game. I could turn it into a big media event, just like George Plimpton did dressing for the Bruins in a pre-season NHL game or as QB of the NFL Detroit Lions in *Paper Lion*. Again, I wasn't a great goalie (I got as far as trying out for Junior "B"), but I wasn't going to see a minute of action. I'd just get my name in the newspaper and the record books, and I'd have a day as a professional athlete. It was a long shot, but the wily old coach thought about it. He kept asking me, "What if our starter goes down and *you* go in? We'll be fucked! I can't chance it." The team signed a college netminder to a one-day contract before calling somebody else up. It would have been cool.

Brophy's Voyageurs were a strange collection of players, and I'd get to know them quite well while cruising the Halifax scene. My station had a contest called "Dinner with the Vees" at a swanky downtown restaurant. A limo would pick me and the contest winners up at our houses and we'd meet the player downtown. Now, while the dinners were evenly spread out among the on-air announcers, half of the announcers preferred to stay home with their wives and kids and let me fill in. A $500 dinner, complete with limousine and professional hockey players? Yes, please. I got to know the players quite well over the many bottles of fine wine and the fine dining. And even better was the fact that they would listen to my sportscasts every morning on the number one and number two stations in the city: C100 and CJCH. Now, the Voyageurs were a team that had a history of sending Larry Robinson, Guy Carbonneau, Rod Langway, Yvon Lambert, and Steve Shutt, among dozens of others, to the Stanley Cup–champion Montreal Canadiens over a decade or so. Brophy's teams were different. He and upper management had assembled a ragtag, colourful bunch of players who would never have any superstar success in the NHL. There was Mike McPhee, a tough thirty-goal-scoring Cape

Bretoner who always came back to Halifax to hang with his friends, myself included. He had some solid years with the Canadiens. Brian Skrudland, who always called me Jim for some reason, had a cup of coffee with the Vees and went on to win two Cups with the Habs. Remember, it was McPhee who set up Skrudland for the game-winning goal nine seconds into overtime in Game 2 of the 1986 Stanley Cup finals, which changed the entire course of the series. The Habs, down 1–0 after a Game 1 loss, did not want to go to Montreal down 2–0. That goal was huge. Quick, but huge. They wouldn't lose another game in the best of seven and took it in five. "Dangerous" Dan Daoust was another one of them. He had some good years in the bigs, but nothing spectacular.

Big red-haired flake Dave Allison was a fan favourite, who writer Michael Farber wrote a story about for a book on hockey's craziest characters. Once the Vees hired a guy named Normand Baron, a good-looking kid from Verdun. He was a professional bodybuilder and was Mr. Quebec one year. His skating wasn't good at all, but that wasn't why he was called up. He fought. A lot. And I must say he struck quite a figure after a shower in the dressing room. And then there was Jeff Brubaker, a brooding, strong, silent, tough-as-nails winger from Lansing, Michigan. When he was with the Voyageurs, it seemed everybody was in awe of him. Even his name put fear into anyone who crossed his path — Brubaker. But aside from one season as a fan-favourite with Brophy's Toronto Maple Leafs in 1984/85, Brubaker was just another footnote to the final years of the Vees in Halifax.

John and I would arrive in Toronto the same year, 1986; he as coach of the Maple Leafs and me as morning sports director at Q107. I went to my first practice at the Gardens after the season started in the fall. It was a crazy day because Harold Ballard's dog Puck wandered onto the ice at Maple Leaf Gardens. Practice came to a standstill as half the Leafs team and Brophy yelled and chased it. I'm thinking, *does this happen every day?* Now, during a scrum with several reporters, Brophy spotted me, stopped the interviews, and gave me a big hug. The toughest, meanest SOB — again a man who was speared, spit on, and even shot at during his career — and he pulled that off. That was the kind of man John Brophy was. A fun fact on Brophy: Only the legendary Scotty Bowman has more career victories as a professional hockey coach than John.

There's another hockey figure who made his mark on the Leafs, and on me for that matter, in my years of covering the game. I'm talking about Lou Lamoriello. This was before his days in Toronto. At the time of our "encounter," Lou was Team USA's general manager (as well as manager of the New Jersey Devils) at the 1996 World Cup of Hockey in Montreal. With Canada up 2–1, I stood in shock as the USA scored four times in the final 3:18 of the game, including two lightning-quick goals from Brett Hull and Tony Amonte (both illegal in my view, as Hull's was batted down by a high stick and Amonte's was kicked in), and Canada was done. Even Curtis Joseph says Amonte's goal was kicked in. What I saw also was Lou race by me in the media box, pound on the door of the Molson Centre war room as they reviewed the illegal (in my mind) goals, and scream something along the lines of, "Don't you dare call that [Hull] goal back. Don't you try and fuck us!" He did it again with the game-winning "kicked-in" goal from Amonte. He was also general manager of Team USA at the 1998 Nagano Winter Olympics, the same team that crashed, then trashed, their rooms, leaving the team and their country in disgrace. Under Lou's watch, the lads broke furniture and busted up the dorms where the team was staying in Japan. No one player was ever found to be responsible, but ask me over a drink or two and I'll name names! Pissed at what I'd just seen, as Lou, still red-faced, with veins bulging, walked by, I mumbled something like, "Shut up and sit down, you big, bald fuck." I could have also added something like, "And your New Jersey Devils ruined pro hockey for everybody in the mid-nineties with that pussy-ass trap and made games as fun to watch as the *John Tesh — Live at Red Rocks* DVD." (Basically, the trap is a defensive alignment that tries to take away passing lanes in the neutral zone and cause a turnover. The Devils played the trap like a Stradivarius.) Which they did.

I'm not sure if he heard me, but in the summer of 2016 I was one of a handful of hopefuls from around the world (including play-by-play man Joe Bowen) to audition for the Leafs public address announcer's gig after Andy Frost was fired after seventeen years. (Andy's close friend and ex–Leaf assistant GM Bill Watters said that Andy was overly critical of the Leafs once too often on his post-game radio call-in show and Lamoriello was having *none* of it.) Lou, the new GM of the Leafs, had the final call on the decision on the PA job. It was down to five people. I didn't get it.

But did I want to work for Lou? During his decades in sports, Lamoriello has enforced a persnickety list of rules that are resented enough that employees have a nickname for their author: "Tal-Lou-ban." (For example, no moustaches or beards on players, no one wearing the number 13, no media allowed on players' planes, trains, or buses, and no rookies being interviewed on game days.) Plus the gig payed under $300 a week. And that's for just over six months. Ok, so, what does a Foster Hewitt award and nine straight *Toronto Sun* Readers' Poll wins as favourite sportscaster get you with Lou Lamoriello? Well, that along with $3.25 gets you a ride home on the subway.

TWENTY-THREE

THE KID STAYS IN THE PICTURE

(or, fresh from dropping out of high school, I was hosting the CBC six o'clock sports at nineteen. At nineteen, you like to leave yourself a few goals in life)

Sometimes — and I say this with tongue planted firmly in cheek (hopefully someone else's) — I'll saunter into my favourite bar and ask my old friend Johnny, quietly and succinctly, "Who do you have to blow to get fucked around here?" You've heard me say that in this business of show that I'm in, it's definitely *who* you *know*. And that is how I got to this place in my life. After decades and decades of extremely fine wine, women, song, and sports, it's all come down to who you know, and, along those lines, not pissing anyone off. Actor Bruce Willis, who I have met and who is one of the biggest wankers in Hollywood, once said, "You can go three years in this business being an asshole, but that's it." I went through those years but thankfully kept enough contacts in the biz to keep moving on and moving up.

If you don't think it's who you know, dig this. Granted, I'm a true believer in making your own breaks in life, but, to wit: 1979, I'm not only freshly dropped out of high school and my entire family hates me, but I'm hustling tables at the Hotel Nova Scotia in Halifax for tips when I get *the* phone call. You know, the one that changes your life. My former hockey coach Gary Murphy was the general sales manager at CHSJ-TV and radio in that hotbed of romance and intrigue, Saint John, N.B. He knew that after that "non-graduation thing," I was on the waiting list of a pretty good broadcasting school in Halifax, a city with its fair share of fine universities and colleges. He asked how school was going, and having not taken a single class, I responded, "Oh great, coach; I'm learning something new everyday." That was bullshit. I could make a heck of a cherries jubilee, but I didn't know how to splice and edit tape with a white grease pencil for the life of me. No worries; he needed a fresh new face to do sports at CHSJ, a CBC affiliate, right away. The radio morning show and the six o'clock sports province-wide? And for $12,500? Yowzah! I'm here to tell you, it's who you know.

That's just the start. A year later, I'm dating the all-night announcer from the same station, who gets a promotion to the biggest and best radio stations east of Quebec — the CHUM-owned CJCH/C100 — and tells me she'll keep an eye open for me. A few months into her stint, their long-time morning sportscaster, Garnet Martin, gets blottoed at the week-long Canadian National Brier curling tournament, misses several days, then threatens to kill both the news and sports directors by impaling them with a commemorative silver CN "golden spike" from Pierre Burton's railway book when they knock on his door at ten in the morning after he missed another shift. We have an opening. A month later, I'm starring in a TV spot with some up-and-coming hockey player named Wayne Gretzky. It's who you know. Years later, I strike up a friendship with a talented gent named Brother Jake Edwards from the opposing radio rival, who gets a *huge* promotion to do mornings on the Q Morning Zoo at Toronto's Q107, and when I ask his ex-softball teammates how "the brother" is doing, I'm told that while he's fabulous, the station *is* looking for a sportscaster co-host. How do they know? They'd both applied and were turned down. I call Jake and he quickly goes to work on making me his new sidekick. Yeah, I know … it's who you know.

People sometimes ask me what my best day ever was in this business of show, and, well, as Madonna once sang, it's a material world and I'm a material kinda guy, so I easily narrowed it down to this one. Let me just preface this with the fact that this moment almost never happened because I was almost fired three weeks into my gig co-hosting the Q-Zoo. Who gets the station sued for over half a million dollars in his first month and lives to tell the tale? I do. But I digress. It was July 1989, and I was into my third year as sportscaster/co-host of the *Jesse and Gene Show*, hosted by Jesse Dylan and Gene Valaitis. The boys received a huge offer from competing station 680 CFTR and jumped at it. "These are Ted Rogers dollars," Gene told me, smiling. CFTR was more of a George Michael, Rick Astley, Whitney Houston, Tiffany Top-40 station, and I'm a rock and roll man. Radio DJs come and go with such dizzying quickness, it's ridiculous. Think of the "Dr. Johnny Fever" character on *WKRP*, who's worked in just about every market in the USA. He's been Johnny Duke, Johnny Style, Johnny Cool, Johnny Midnight, and even Heavy Early. (Most of these names appear on the side of Johnny's coffee cup.) So with Jesse and Gene leaving the "out of control" room, we waited for some talented Johnny Fever–type to fill their talented Tom McCann penny loafers. But here's the thing. The owners of Q107, B.C.-based Western International Communications Ltd., or WIC, got word that Jesse and Gene were taking yours truly with them. Mmm, that was the first I'd heard of that. No matter; never mind. The word from Vancouver on the "Gallagher File" was, *"Keep him."* So as Jesse and Gene left GM Don Shafer's office to say goodbye that July morning, I was beckoned. Don is a man of integrity. Don's an ex-broadcaster who has been integral in running several well-known stations across the country, including Q107. My station. This is where it gets good. With the big boys convinced that I was leaving to go across the street to CFTR, there wasn't much of a conversation; more of a negotiation. I believe I walked into Don's office at ten a.m. making just under $40,000 and driving the Q107 ski team Jeep Cherokee. I walked out just after noon, after a few beers, making well over $90,000, with the keys to a BMW 7 series. Oh, *and* the Jeep Cherokee. Don was throwing money at me $10,000 at a time like he had it in his briefcase in a scene out of a gangster movie. Nice. Oh, and I was twenty-seven years old.

But let me say this about that. I almost didn't make it to that fateful day in 1989. My career in Toronto almost ended in a flash three years prior. Question: Have you tuned into your favourite local radio station lately? Forget the sportscast. Listen to the newscast. At the end you'll hear twenty or thirty seconds of sports scores, et cetera. Maybe the starting pitchers for the game that night. Boy, has that gone the way of the Brother newsroom typewriter. Save for the all-sports stations, the day of the local radio sportscaster is long gone. Hell, when I started, we all did split shifts: five to nine a.m., then three to six in the afternoon. And the sportscasts were four and a half to five minutes long. One of the big challenges was coming up with a one-minute sports commentary. Every day. These days I don't have an opinion on one thing in a week, let alone one every morning. Hey, dem's the rules. Come up with something fresh, funny, thought-provoking, and sporty every day or we'll find someone who can. Well, then. First of all, I want you to meet rough, tough legendary American football lifer J.I. Albrecht. Famous for telling it like it is, chewing on an ever-present cigar, and walking his bulldog everywhere, J.I.'s sporting life spanned over five decades working for half a dozen teams. In the CFL he served as general manager for the Grey Cup–winning Alouettes and Argos. He even worked for "my" Oakland Raiders. He made an attempt to bring a CFL franchise to the Maritimes in the mid-1980s, which is where I came in. J.I. was an interesting old coot. A bald, one-eyed, gruff, Howard Cosell–sounding SOB who many believed was trying to scam the city of Halifax into putting millions of dollars into the Maritime Schooners football club. Including me. I always thought he was a flim-flam man. A carnival barker. And not overly friendly. I remember having him on my radio show in Halifax. We did a call-in segment, and a woman argued that a CFL football team was the *last* thing taxpayers should be paying for. Albrecht replied, "Honey, why don't you go make me a pie? Don't worry about this football team, the grown men will take care of that; just go out to the kitchen and *make me a pie!*" That was J.I.

Once I asked him what the J.I. stood for. After a lifetime of telling people his name was just initials, he finally told his friend Earl MacRae that J.I. actually stood for "Just Incredible." Oh my Lord. Well, he was a striking figure, and I had several opinions about the man, none of which were good. Which brings us to September 30, 1986, two weeks into my new life back in Toronto at the Mighty Q. I should mention that we were all on a three-month probabtion period. Bill Carroll, a fixture in Toronto radio for years and now in Ottawa, started two weeks after me. Same deal with him. General manager Gary Slaight was a radio wizard, but he wouldn't think twice about firing an announcer/newscaster or sportscaster who wasn't up to the task. We were just hoping to get past ninety days, let alone the first two weeks — which I almost didn't make. I mean, I had just spent five years in Halifax, sold the condo, and packed my bags for Hogtown. I was in "the show" and there was no way I was going to be sent down to triple "A" ball in Buffalo. All of the local sportscasters were writing commentaries: Bill Stephenson over at CFRB, Fred Patterson at CFNY, Rick "Podge Lodge" Hodge at CHUM FM, and Bryan Henderson at 1050 CHUM. Heady competition. But if it meant bruising a few egos and stepping on a few toes to get ahead, well, so be it. Ahem, everything within CRTC guidelines, of course. Lawsuits? They weren't uncommon for Q (heck, even Toronto Blue Jay mascot BJ Birdy — one of the worst mascots in the history of professional sports — sued me when I suggested he be impaled on a skewer and barbecued on a spit on the pitcher's mound before a game). But a whopper for over half a million dollars? Two weeks into your dream job? Helllooo!

I remember the day like it was yesterday. J.I.'s photo (again, he wasn't exactly "this year's model") was in the *Toronto Sun* sports section for some odd reason. I needed a subject for my morning commentary, and he was our "it" boy, later to become "the tool of the day" on Q. The comment started maturely enough: "Whose ugly mug do I see jumping out from the pages of this morning's *Toronto Sun*? Why, it's J.I. Albrecht, the *thing* that wouldn't leave." I went on to rant about his misdealings in Halifax and his having been escorted out of town on a rail, but not before being tarred and feathered and so on and so forth. I called him name after name, all of which I still thought were deserved. It was hard-hitting, to be sure, and perhaps a little over the top. The piece ran again in the afternoon. No harm, no foul, right? Wrong. J.I.'s son was in Toronto going to school and was a big fan of Q107, but he was a bigger fan of his father. Less than a week later, I was escorted into the corner office (you know the one) and told that J.I.'s "team" was suing the Mighty Q for $500,000 and one John Gallagher personally for $50,000 for spoken defamation, or slander. Nice. The next letter home to Mom was going to be a hoot! "Sooo ... how's Toronto treating you? Are you going to mass every Sunday?" Mmm. The lawsuit ran on for months, then years. Q's law team, along with Slaight and program director Bob Mackowycz, quickly found out that while most of the things I'd said about J.I. were true, he was indeed a complete dick who they were *not* going to give a dime. And that's exactly what he got. We proposed several out-of-court offerings, and he stood, puffed up like the bullfrog that he was, and eventually got nothing. Score one for Q107 and a *big one* for Johnny G. I could see him on his deathbed à la Orson Welles in *Citizen Kane*, but instead of repeating the word "Rosebud," he was whispering, "Gallagher ... Gallagher ..."

TWENTY-FOUR

JUST. GREAT.

(or, how I became Wayne Gretzky's personal
"have mic, will travel" emcee)

So, I was sitting at the bar in that hotbed of romance and intrigue, Brantford, Ontario. It's late on a Friday night in the summer of 1990 and in stumbles *Beverly Hills, 90210* teen actress Shannen Doherty, who sits next to me and orders a cocktail. It was a double vodka. Even though the drinking age is twenty-one in California, I'm sure it was not the teenager's first (or last) adult bevvie. Heck, I was certain it wouldn't even be her last drink of the night. The waiter asked her for ID, but six-foot-seven-inch and 265-pound Super Bowl–winning defensive end Bubba Smith, who was sitting on the other side of me, said to him, "It's all right, she's with us." *You* say no to All-American Bubba Smith. Not me. No thanks. The celebrities are pouring in from the airport for the annual Labatt's Wayne Gretzky Celebrity Sports Classic softball game and I've been asked, along with Jake Edwards, to be the game's announcer. (We would have done it again in the summer of 1992, but Wayne postponed and then cancelled the event after his father, Walter, suffered a near-fatal brain aneurysm that destroyed his long-term memory.) This weekend would be the beginning of a long, fun, and fruitful relationship with the greatest athlete that any sport in any century has ever seen. It was going to be a beautiful weekend in Brantford. Nothing but sunny skies for the crowd, packed into the stands at Wayne Gretzky Sports Centre's baseball diamond.

Jake was in charge of announcing the lineups and I was the roving reporter, interviewing the big names on and off the field. And what names! Besides Shannen, Bubba, and the Great One, there was one of my first Hollywood crushes, Terri Garr, whose breakthrough came in the Mel Brooks comedy *Young Frankenstein*. (Of course, I made a "What knockers!" joke with a baseball bat in my hand. Cue the laughter.) Mike Myers was there, as was Tony Dow (Wally in *Leave It to Beaver*), *Knots Landing* star Donna Mills, actor D.B. Sweeney (Shoeless Joe Jackson in *Eight Men Out*), and Peter Weller, who drove in from Toronto, where he was filming David Cronenberg's dark, moody science fiction drama *Naked Lunch*. Weller (who was also in *Robocop*) was a complete and utter dick the entire time he was there. I do have a classic shot of Brett Hull, Sweeney, Weller, and I lounging by the pool post-game.

"Twisting by the pool" after the Wayne Gretzky Celebrity Sports Classic with HHOF member Brett Hull and actors Peter Weller (*Robocop*) and D.B. Sweeney (*Eight Men Out*).

The recently departed Alan Thicke was the emcee of the gala dinner held in a hangar out by the airport. I wasn't alone when I fell off my chair, floored by Thicke's after-dinner speech. You wouldn't know it from his lame (sorry, but they were) but popular sitcoms and talk shows from years ago, but Thicke was perhaps the funniest emcee I have ever had the pleasure to observe. And I have attended several after-dinner speeches on the rubber chicken circuit.

All of Wayne's high-priced NHL talent was there: Grant Fuhr, Mark Messier, et al. I got seated at the "cool" table with all of Janet Gretzky's Hollywood friends. Sunday was get-a-way day (which was always a little slow after popping from hotel room to hotel room the night before until "stupid o'clock" in the a.m.), and it was off to the Gretzky farm for his grandmother's perogies. It was there where I bounced a little Paulina Gretzky on my knee. It should be noted that she was wearing Huggies and was all of a year and a half old. Paulina has grown up to be an absolutely stunning and successful model, celebutante, and, now, mother. When I last saw Wayne, all he could do was beam when I asked about his first grandson, Tatum.

After that, Wayne's people would hire me for a series of hosting gigs. One was a Coca-Cola-sponsored all-star pickup game for some lucky contest winners in Richmond Hill. The pickup game had some true NHL royalty, including Denis Savard, newly acquired by my beloved Montreal Canadiens for star defenceman Chris Chelios and a second-round pick. (It was a transaction that has since been considered a steal in Chicago's favour, as Chelios would produce some of his best seasons as a Blackhawk, while Savard's career was on the decline. But with rumours that Chelios had been sleeping with the wife of a member of the Canadiens upper management and murmurs that the police were getting tired of protecting him after one too many coke adventures, Montreal had to let Chelios go. Plus he, like Savard, was coming off a serious knee injury.) Either way, to announce Denis Savard's name on the loud speakers in a hockey arena, a la Canadiens' long-time public address announcer Claude Mouton, was an absolute thrill: "Number 18, numero dix-huit, De-*neeese* Sa-*vaaard*!"

I'd see a lot of Wayne over the years. The fact that I hosted *The Gallagher Show* on TSN at Gretzky's restaurant on 99 Blue Jay Way was

I love this shot. Wayne and I and brilliant emcee Alan Thicke (1947–2016) at the Brantford airport during Gretzky's Celebrity Softball Weekend, 1991.

a big help. We did a one-on-one interview that was one of the show's highest-rated episodes. The CBC's Peter Mansbridge called and said it was the most insightful Gretzky interview he had ever seen. I thought that was a nice touch. Here's a handy tip: If you really want to impress your new girlfriend on your first date, take her to a Maple Leafs game when the Rangers are in town (well it did work for me). It was just before Christmas in 1998, December 19, when I took my statuesque girlfriend, Robin, to see a Leafs game. She wanted to get down to ice surface to get a better look when we heard, "Johnny, hey!" It was Wayne. He skated over, and after I introduced him to Robin, he took his glove off and shook her hand, then mine. Not a fist pump or a casual hello; a genuine handshake. Usually players are in full "beast mode" before a game and have no time for pleasantries with anyone. But what I didn't know, and Wayne would joke about it after his retirement, was that this was to be his final game at an arena he'd frequented and adored as a kid and against a team he'd cheered for in nearby Brantford all of his life. He was soaking it all in and enjoying his final pre-game warm-up at fabled Maple Leaf Gardens, and I just happened to amble by. Wow, talk about impressing your new "friend" on a first date.

It happened more than once. I was emceeing a championship body-building event in Brantford one weekend with another new girlfriend and gave my old buddy Walter Gretzky a call upon arrival in his fine little town to see if he wanted to catch up. He invited me to the old Gretzky homestead for drinks. It was the same little house on Varadi Avenue that became known as the birthplace of Wayne's skating skills. The rink his father built for him behind it is a swimming pool now. When we walked into the Gretzky home that Friday night, there was Wayne sitting on the couch with his socked feet up on the table and a big grin on his face. That was so unexpected. I mean, what were the chances? He and the family had just flown in from the Wimbledon tennis champion-ships and had popped in before flying back to L.A. We played a little ball hockey out front with kids Ty and Trevor, while Wayne's now-deceased mother Phyllis played with the youngest of the Gretzky kids, Emma. My girlfriend was beside herself, especially since it was all so random. Walter took me on a little tour of the rec room, and it was as if we had stepped into the "Gretzky wing" of the Hockey Hall of Fame. Many of the Hart,

Art Ross, Lady Byng, Lester B. Pearson, and Conn Smythe trophies were on display in the basement.

There was also an odd-looking item that I had never seen before: a home Toronto Maple Leafs sweater with "GRETZKY" and the number 99 on the back. In the summer of 1996, Wayne was extremely close to becoming a Leaf. He told Sportsnet 590 The FAN, "At one point we were close to Toronto. Cliff Fletcher [the Leafs GM at the time] really dug in deep and tried to make it happen.... My agent at the time, Mike Barnett, and I were leaning to go to Toronto and be part of the Toronto Maple Leafs.... Timing is everything, and unfortunately at that time they were trying to raise money to move out of Maple Leaf Gardens and move into a new arena, a new facility, and the ownership just felt at that time they needed to concentrate and put more of their resources into building an arena than to sign me ... I thought it was going to happen; unfortunately

"Midnight at the Oasis." Wayne Gretzky and I on his rooftop patio (Oasis) at Gretzky's restaurant in 1998.

it didn't." Wayne had the Leafs uniform made for Walter so it would be the first one "off the rack." He ended up signing with the Rangers. I sent Wayne and Janet an enormous bouquet of flowers for his final game in April of 1999. I'm sure they ended up in a big pile in the players' wives lounge at MSG. Wayne and I have shared each other's company over and over since his retirement. And now, well over thirty-five years since we were posing for photos together and filming TV ads, trying to make it in our respective professions, I always look forward to seeing my friend and shaking his hand.

TWENTY-FIVE

COMEDY ISN'T PRETTY

(or, Sam Kinison comes barging out of the
bathroom with long lines of cocaine on the sleeves
of his black sweater and says to me ...)

Sam Kinison was an absolute larger-than-life character, as outrageous and funny a man as I've ever had the pleasure to meet. Just outrageous. A former preacher, he forfeited his soul for a coke and booze habit and a few jokes about Christ on the cross. He was very wrong about many things. His routines were rife with a black streak of misogyny. His politics were of the jocko, right-wing variety. He prowled the deepest, darkest sewers of obscenity and taboo with the zeal of a holy man turned about as unholy as you can get. And those who saw him will swear that to do so was to laugh, laugh till you thought you were going to asphyxiate, laugh in surprise and disgust with yourself at the sheer toxic glee of it all. It was like that footage of the exploding whale — audiences would be drenched in Sam as the body parts of his raging demons showered the room. He was very possibly the funniest man who ever lived. He was also perhaps my favourite comedian. Ever. I saw him in Las Vegas in the summer of 1990 when he was going through a(nother) drug- and liquor-filled time of his career. He stumbled onstage and was mumbling incoherently. (Oh, what was it? It was just teeming with professional comedic brio, something along the lines of "What am I doing here … gurgle … gurgle …") and my girlfriend Lindy and I wondered if it was all part of the act. It wasn't. He might as well have been wearing his bathrobe. I'm thinking, "There goes a couple hundred bucks on tickets." But he did eventually "wake up" enough to launch into his act, finishing with a full rock band in tow performing The Troggs' "Wild Thing."

We took in the show with a good friend from Toronto, comedian Tim Conlon, who drove in from L.A. and stayed with us. In L.A., he had a recurring role on *The Arsenio Hall Show*, and he took us backstage on the Fox set to look around. On that day, LL Cool J was doing a soundcheck for his new single and Grammy-winner "Mama Said Knock You Out." Cool. Even cooler was the fact that a guest for that evening's show walked by. It was Captain James T. Kirk of the USS *Enterprise* — William Shatner. He stood next to us and repeated LL's lyrics in *full* Captain Kirk mode: "'Mamma said … knock … *you* … out …' I like that." Before I could even tell him that we went to neighbouring high schools in Montreal (albeit thirty years apart), he was whisked away to make-up. Tim asked me if I wanted to meet that pompous, no-talent, ass-kissing hack "Arse"-enio. I politely passed.

Okay, fast-forward to a few months later, and Sam was in Toronto performing at a rock and roll bar in Mississauga called Superstars, and Tim was opening the show. Sam had sold the venue out. Five thousand rabid Kinison fans, including me, filled the place for two shows. Club manager "The Original" Kid Rock (Keith Correa), Toronto's friendly ubiquitous postman/rock star wanna be without portfolio, got me backstage hours before the event to meet Sam, and for some reason we just hit it off. The weasel that I am, I made arrangements with Sam, his brother (and manager) Bill, and his entourage to go out to a big, popular steakhouse after the ten o'clock show. He was his usual ball of sweat when I came backstage. I remember Sam excusing himself and then coming out of his dressing-room bathroom with a long streak of what looked like the white chalk you'd see down the lines of a baseball diamond on the sleeve of his black sweater. Of course it was his cocaine, which he'd leaned on in the can. And like he was a guy who had something stuck in his teeth, I pointed out his little "wardrobe malfunction." He just said, "Oh yeah, thanks," and dusted it off like it was fluff. Bizarre. Kid Rock remembers, "I asked for a photo in his dressing room, and before we could pose, his brother pours out an entire gram of coke on the counter. Sam did it in one line. One line. Then he said, 'Okay, let's take that shot.' I remember we had a late, late night with him."

On a humorous note, the next night, a then-little-known comedian named Jerry Seinfeld played in front of four hundred fans. Kid Rock asked Jerry if he had anything coming up. "Yeah," said Jerry, "I'm working on a pilot for NBC. It's still in development." Mmm, I wonder how *that* turned out. Funny, years later when *Seinfeld* was at its peak, Jerry returned to Toronto for a huge sold-out show and announced that it was his first time *ever* in the city, completely brushing his badly attended debut from years earlier under the carpet.

Back to Kinison. After several lines of Toronto's finest alkaline chit chat flakes, Sam whispered to me, "I don't know about that steak. Maybe just a salad." It got a little cloudy after that, and we just ended up partying at the club. I do remember there was a limo involved. There's an old expression, "If you remember the sixties, then you weren't there." Well, for me, the same could be said for the eighties and nineties. My motto (okay, I probably stole or borrowed it. Or at least "re-worked" it.): Nothing succeeds like success, and nothing exceeds like excess. I couldn't believe when I heard about Sam Kinison's death. On the night in question, in April of 1992, Kinison was completely sober and drug-free at that point in his life, but the teenagers barrelling down the wrong side of the highway were smashed out of their minds. I mean, what are the chances? Sam had seen the truck coming, but he wasn't wearing his seat belt. At impact he was thrown into the windshield and suffered multiple traumatic injuries. This is where it gets spooky. In the first moments after the crash, Kinison seemed as if he were going to make it, but within minutes he appeared to know he was about to die. Kinison appeared to be holding a conversation in which he stated, "I don't want to die," and then finally, "Okay." Then he died. He was just thirty-eight years old.

* * *

Recently Andrew Dice Clay has been enjoying a wonderful renaissance period in his career. For a decade or so, the man couldn't get a gig filling in as an extra for a police lineup. Clay appeared with Cate Blanchett in Woody Allen's terrific film *Blue Jasmine*, and he was fantastic in the short-lived HBO series *Vinyl*, where few characters were as memorable — and none wound up as dead — as Clay's cocaine-crazed radio station mogul "Buck" Rogers. His acting has come a long way from when he played the lead role in the 1990 film *The Adventures of Ford Fairlane*, which I saw at a theatre. Opening night. What a mutt that was. I saw him in person at Bally's in Vegas in 1990, the same year he became the first comedian to sell out Madison Square Garden two nights in a row, hosted *SNL, and* got "banned for life" from MTV. Good year. That still looks pretty good on a resumé, though, huh? Clay was a humungous star at that time. You remember the Diceman and "the look"? The black leather jacket covered in shiny studs, with the word "Dice" spelled out across his back. All that. And he did something I've never seen before: he would come out and just stand on stage, smoking a cigarette, for what seemed like five minutes before starting into his material. Although the whole "Hickory dickory dock" nursery rhyme thing is so outdated and unacceptable now, back then Clay was the bomb. So much so, that the night I was there, Arnold Schwarzenegger and his wife (Kennedy royalty) Maria Shriver were two booths down from us, and the future Governor of "Caleee-fore-nia" was overly enthralled. You couldn't get to him for a photo or a handshake because "Ah-nold" and Maria were flanked by a pair of large bodyguards, but you could hear him! He was laughing louder than anyone around him. I glanced over and saw JFK and RFK's niece roll her eyes a few times because his laugh filled Bally's like Herman Munster's, from the sixties TV series *The Munsters*. Heck, Arnold, knock yourself out.

* * *

It's insane how much Canada has contributed to the world of comedy. Every form of comedian. From the good — besides the *SCTV* and *SNL* heavy-weights (I consider Martin Short, an alumnus of both, perhaps the funniest man on the planet), there's Ron James, Jeremy Hotz, Shaun Majumder, Harland Williams, and Norm Macdonald — to the bad: actor/douche salad Jason Jones, who once went on Colbert's show (he was a long-time *Daily Show* contributor) and had the audacity to desecrate his former citizenship and Prime Minister Justin Trudeau. And he wasn't kidding. A few years ago

Martin Short and I take advantage of a big sale at Thrifty's! A fellow Irish Canadian who stands alone in the comedy firmament, adored by Hollywood's elite as the funniest, nicest, and best of them all.

at TIFF, and then shortly afterwards in Halifax for a junket, I met the loathsome Mr. Jones (who's married to Samantha Bee) and found that he was one of the rudest and unfunniest members of my profession that I've ever had the displeasure of meeting. His "people" later told me he had just woken up from his nap. Both times. Fuckwad.

Another is the vastly overrated and unfunny Howie Mandel. Word has it that, with his career in shambles and his stand-up routine old and stale (oh, do little "Bobby" again!) in 2003, while Mandel was deciding whether or not to quit show business and come back to Toronto to become a carpet salesman again (he ran a carpet sales business of his own in the seventies), NBC offered him a summer fill-in game show, and he took it. (It was supposed to go to Arsenio Hall — *that's* how low they were scraping the barrel.) The show was *Deal Or No Deal*. God, spare us all.

Many believe that for a long time, *SCTV* was funnier than anything *Saturday Night Live* was doing in the late 1970s and early 1980s, late Friday nights on NBC. And the same could be said of *The Kids in the Hall* from 1989 to 1995 (on CBC in Canada, and CBS and HBO in the United States). In my opinion, *The Kids in the Hall* was a fantastic alternative to *SNL* in the early nineties. I've heard it called subversive. I've heard it called post-modern. Whatever you call it, that comedic sense definitely was paved back in the day in comedy clubs in Toronto. They mastered the fine line of cringe humour. They were the David Letterman to *SNL's* Jay Leno. I fell right into it. And they were always around. I worked at CityTV and Much, and they worked at the Rivoli a few blocks away. You'd run into the five troupe members everywhere in Toronto. They are as fine as any comedic ambassadors that Toronto or this country, for that matter, has ever seen. And because they're Canadian, like everyone on the list, they're the nicest human beings you'll ever meet.

A lot of the big-name comedic talent to come out of Toronto grew up watching CityTV and listening to Q107. Rick Moranis and John Candy loved us. John would randomly drop by the studios at Yonge and Bloor to do voiceovers and station IDs. In fact, the week I started there, he got into Dr. Tongue mode and recorded an audio greeting to my family declaring that I had made it to Toronto and was doing fine. How's that for some instant affirmation from a comedic god, huh? Years later, in late July of 1991, John and I would have several drinks during the CFL Argos' opening night post-game party at the Horseshoe Tavern (John, Wayne Gretzky, and Bruce McNall had bought the team). What an event that was.

The celebrity lineup included Gretzky, Jim Belushi, Mariel Hemingway, Martin Short, and Brett Hull. Hull and I had gotten pretty tight earlier that summer after he and I spent another booze-filled weekend at the Wayne Gretzky celebrity softball tournament in Wayne's hometown of Brantford. He and I drove people crazy that evening reciting the lyrics from "Rubber Biscuit" that the Elwood Blues Revue, featuring Dan Aykroyd and Candy on vocals and harmonica, had just performed. "Bow bow bow!" I was live from the bar on CityTV that night and jumped up on stage during the closing credits while they performed. Timing is everything, huh? That's me. "Look, a live camera. I'm over here!" John Candy. Man oh man, I could see how John was sweating when he came off stage. You haven't seen that much sweat since the Nixon/Kennedy debate in 1960. I freshened him up quickly with a nice cold cocktail. John was big and he did everything big. Friends would tell me stories of legendary dinners with the man featuring course upon course and bottle upon bottle. I was so sad when I heard he died. It was March 4, 1994. I was at spring training sitting outside getting some sun in the parking lot of a Blue Jay game in Dunedin when a Jays fan from Toronto told me. John was in Durango, Mexico, filming the forgettable *Wagons East* and, against the advice of his doctors, John had allowed his girth to swell to 375 pounds with a waistline of fifty-nine inches. He would bring his own chef to the Durango set, vowing that he'd eat healthy, but he soon fell back into his old unhealthy habits. He died of a heart attack in the middle of the night. John Candy was forty-three.

Jim Carrey was another comedian who liked to come home to Toronto just to hang out with his friends. It was even better when he dropped by the Q107 studio to promote something. Heck, anything! Oh, like *In Living Color*, where he was making huge strides as a young up-and-coming comedian. The show launched the careers of Carrey, the Wayans brothers (all of them), Jamie Foxx, Tommy Davidson, David Alan Grier, and a little-known "Fly Girl" dancer named Jennifer Lopez. Jamie and I would have a memorable night of our own while schmoozing with Toronto Raptor Vince Carter and Mo Pete (Morris Peterson) years later. Foxx was in town filming a little ditty called *Ray*, which would win him an Oscar.

Jamie Foxx in 2004 promoting a little movie he would do quite well in called *Ray* (he won an Academy Award for Best Actor). *Django Unchained* is better.

Carrey was making the rounds of the local TV and radio stations and pretty well co-hosted one afternoon with me and John Derringer. He was supposed to be on for five minutes. He stayed for hours. And why not? I remember one break lasting so long, the news was nine or ten minutes late! And for some reason he kept repeating the word "chowder" all afternoon. It was his favourite new radio word: "Chowderrr." Don't ask. It made no sense to me, either. Later that day, I was sitting on a sun-drenched patio on Queen Street down from CityTV after the six o'clock sports, and he ambles along. Jim had just finished an appearance on MuchMusic and was looking for a frozen yogurt place. He recognized me and stopped to say hi. My date's jaw just dropped. We then went into a series of (the crazed and supposedly immortal) Fire Marshall Bill impersonations, right there on Queen Street. "Let me show you something!" People actually stopped to watch. That had them all in stitches. Carrey would go on to kill in major productions *Ace Ventura: Pet Detective*, *Dumb and Dumber*, and *The Mask*, as well as out and out stealing *Batman Forever*. Here's the thing that always baked my beans

Actor Jim Carrey just after he almost threw himself out of a cab at Yonge and Bloor while holding onto the cab door, swinging to and fro, with Jake Edwards and I still in it, yelling, "Oh, does it matter? Alllllrightythen!"

regarding Jim Carrey. He starred in *The Truman Show* in 1998 and *Man on the Moon* in 1999 and both times won (he wasn't just nominated, but *won*) a Golden Globe Award for Best Actor. Yet, he wasn't even considered for an Academy Award nomination for either film. Sorry, that just doesn't fly at all.

* * *

Some of the world's top comedians have floated in and out of the dozens of radio and TV stations I've worked in over the years. Some quick thoughts. Penn and Teller were a smash hit the morning they rambled into the Q-Zoo studio. I will say this of my five minutes with them on the Q Morning Zoo. Teller does speak, but only off the air. Good thing. The man had the worst case of halitosis of any human being I've met outside of Howard Cosell. Canadian comedy legend Mike MacDonald once did a classic bit on family vacations in "My House, My Rules," which was comedy gold, but on his visit to the Zoo he seemed distant and reserved. Mmm, maybe it was because we brought up his CBC flop the semi-unwatchable *Mosquito Lake*, which was canned mid-season in 1989.

Now, co-hosting the morning show at Canada's premier rock station and hanging out in the halls of the country's only music video station, MuchMusic, in the City building at night, you can come across the absolute elite in show business. On the same block of the CHUM-City building at 299 Queen Street was a funky little bar called X-Rays, which was owned by Dan Aykroyd and his good friend "X" Ray. On slow nights, Dan, Ray, and whatever celebs were in town would actually park themselves out in front of the bar trying to entice passersby to come in for drinks. And it worked. One night, I spotted Chris Farley, the budding *Saturday Night Live* standout, gladhanding on the sidewalk. Well hell, let's go inside for drinks! Better than hanging out in a van down by the river. Hey-yo! Chris was exactly like his character on screen — loud, boisterous, and easily the funniest guy in the room. Now, in his final years, the cracks in Farley's

The huge and hugely charismatic Chris Farley posing outside Dan Aykroyd's bar X-Rays in the mid-nineties — just before we smoked a big doobie in his van down by the river.

buoyant façade were apparent to friends, family, and fans. His weight had ballooned and his voice had grown raspy through years of substance abuse, despite several stays in rehab. He died just before Christmas in 1997. He was thirty-three, the same age as John Belushi.

Denis Leary and I have crossed paths a bunch of times over the years. We hung around for beers after his "No Cure for Cancer" concert at the Danforth Music Hall. (We posed for a shot, and in the background you can see an almost unrecognizable Sean Cullen with long curly brown hair and a Davey Crockett jacket on. Cullen, another one of Canada's finest comedians and a finalist on NBC's *Last Comic Standing 6*, turned out to be the worst hockey defenceman helping to defend my net in any celebrity hockey game that I have seen or ever will see.) Years later at CityTV, knowing Denis was a huge Boston Bruins fan who hated my Montreal Canadiens, I presented him with a Bruins jacket (an old, beat-up but official relic that a fan had sent in as a joke). When I presented it to him, he looked quite touched. He just adores the Bruins. Just to get his goat, I told him that John Wensink (a big afro-haired seventies Bruins thug) was "a pussy." Startled, he looked into the camera and said "I've *got* to get a copy of this tape and send it to Wensink. He'd love to hear you say that to him and then hunt you down." I enjoyed reminding him about the fact that between the time the Allied forces knocked out the Nazis in the mid-1940s and 1987, the Montreal Canadiens knocked the Bruins out of the playoffs eighteen straight times, including seasons when the Habs had no reason beating them. Hello, 1971! Denis had to laugh. He lived through a lot of those series in the sixties, seventies, and eighties. Hey, he got a nice parting gift, eh?

But my comedic pièce de résistance was the night, in the late eighties, when Q's Bro Jake and I hosted a comedy gala at the Four Seasons in Toronto. This crowd ran the gamut from Henny Youngman to Jim Carrey and from Joe Piscopo to Gilbert Gottfried. Jake and I sat on the dais next to *SCTV*'s Dave Thomas, who, for some reason, was in a nasty, nasty mood. He was openly mocking the great Henny Youngman while Henny was doing his shtick! Sure, Henny was in his eighties, but have a little respect. The man was in *Goodfellas*! I wanted to say to him, "Dave, you'd be lucky to tune Henny's violin!" It may have been the open bar or perhaps the fact that he was a tad perturbed that his career had somewhat plateaued (to say the least) at that point in his life. "Hey Dave, I hear Disney wants to use your Bob McKenzie voice for a talking moose in a couple of years. What?" Thank goodness the rest of the Second City crew were absolute sweethearts. And I've met them all, with the exception of Joe Flaherty. I still don't know how he's escaped my grasp after all these years. I golfed with Eugene Levy. We had Rick Moranis on the air with us a number of times — we let him intoduce a few tunes on Q as Jerry Todd. Google it, youngsters. I schmoozed with Martin Short (and his alter ego, the ridiculously "stupid funny" Jiminy Glick) after his one-man show *Fame Becomes Me.*

Andrea Martin would always be in town promoting one of her shows and we'd invite her in. She gave me her email, and I would contact her whenever the hugely underrated cult film *Hedwig and the Angry Inch* came on TV. It was fun chatting with her online. Upon getting to know her better after her frequent guest appearances, I gave Andrea my phone number. I loved that she didn't call. It just made her that much hotter.

TWENTY-SIX

SPANNING THE GLOBE

(or, as I'm being detained at the airport in Sydney,
Australia, I explain I'm not the John Gallagher
who thinks he's Jesus Christ)

Yes, I've spanned the globe to bring you the constant variety in ... well, you know the rest. I've been everywhere, man. And usually by myself. Really. Travelling alone makes me feel exhilarated. It's my prescription for dealing with real-life back home. I come back happier, energized, and feeling healthy. I'm a completely different person when I'm travelling alone. Plus, I make friends fast. Extremely fast. Since the early eighties I've travelled to Europe by myself several times. Japan? El lobo solo. Australia, Fiji, and the South Pacific? Sans girlfriend. I've been to dozens of different countries, twenty U.S. states, and all of the Canadian provinces and territories with the exception of Manitoba. Sorry, 'Peg. (In 1991, CityTV offered to send anyone from the sports department to Winnipeg to cover the Argos' 36–31 win over the Stampeders. And we all said no. I was hosting a party on the Sunday for Q107 fans at SkyDome for big cash, so I declined.) Sure, I've been around the world with ex- and current girlfriends, but travelling alone is my ticket to ride. It's where you find real adventure. I can take you to Tokyo, Japan, where of the over thirteen million people living there, less than 2 percent are *gaijin*, or non-Japanese. A fascinating city where only college students speak English, eating and walking at the same time are frowned upon, and geisha girls who you go out on dates with giggle and pull your moustache because they've never seen one before. Oh yeah, and Tokyo's Narita Airport is over two hours from downtown and they don't tell you that.

How about jumping, fully clothed, into a moat with your new boss, TSN president Keith Pelley, after a cocktail-filled dinner at a castle-themed restaurant during the 1998 World Hockey Championships in Zurich, Switzerland? Or trying to get high drinking kava, the mind-clearing national drink of Fiji (one cup and it's as if your dentist had applied topical Novocain)? Don't forget to drink it in a single gulp, clap and say, "*Bula!*"

But first, let's take you to Europe in the mid-1990s. We're starting out in swingin' London, baby, where it feels nothing like the "London Fog" trenchcoat TV ads. Of the five times I've been there, it's always been sunny and hot. No complaints from this thirsty traveller. I have my favourite spots (the Punch & Judy pub — built in 1787 — overlooking Covent Garden's piazza is a must-see), and I've gotten to know the city well over the years and its customs. I wasn't hip to one in particular upon my first visit. Do not tip your barkeep as a rule! It is changing now, but twenty-five years ago, when I gave the bartender at the John F. Kennedy pub in London a tip, he pushed it back and said, "We don't want your money here, Yank!" "But hey, I'm from ..." I started to explain. "Oh never mind. Welcome to London," I muttered. Still with Jolly Old England, I'll admit at times I've had a laissez-faire approach to travel: I'll get there when I get there, boarding schedules be damned. And in turn, this has led to my missing more than my fair share of planes, trains, and shuttles — or rather most of the share.

Once, my then-girlfiend Chick and I were enjoying a fabulous spring day bar-hopping under Big Ben on the banks of the Thames river before jumping on a train to Heathrow for our flight back to Toronto later that afternoon. Lots of time, right? Mmm, well, we didn't count on our train breaking down, forcing all passengers to exit and wait an hour. Bottom line? Not even an O.J. Simpson–like hundred-metre hurdle through several gates could get us in under the wire. (Heathrow is massive, BTW.) We missed the last flight out of London to Toronto and had to stay the night, sleeping in the airport. Once we closed all of the airport bars, Chick and I found refuge and comfort on the pews of St. George's Chapel inside Heathrow. Some comfort. Sound asleep, the two us were awoken in the middle of the night by the English equivalent of a S.W.A.T. team poking at us both with high-powered rifles now aimed at our heads. This was just months after 9/11, and these gents were on strict orders. "Are you here to pray, mate?" he asked. "Huh? Can you kindly fuck off?" I answered back as I rubbed my eyes, not noticing the wrong end of the assault rifle saying, "Good morning, Mary Sunshine!" He snapped back, "Well, you better pray that you don't wind up in the dock talking to me like that, Yankee." Oh boy. Dishevelled, we sleepily headed to our gate.

Let's head to Paris, shall we? They surely can't be anymore shockingly rude there, huh? I'm joking. Of course they can. So, I'm buying a ticket to board the slick new Eurostar supertrain that travels over three hundred kilometres an hour to get you to the City of Lights in under two. The average fare in coach was under a hundred pounds, but for two hundred you would get a first-class berth with champagne, dinner, and an open bar. Well, I'm by myself. A single, strapping, vaguely rocking Canadian lad in his early thirties — perhaps I'll meet a single, beautiful (aren't they all) Parisian woman and we can cocktail and laugh all the way under the English Channel and through the rolling French countryside, exchange numbers, and I'll have a lovely tour guide once we get to the most romantic city on God's green earth. Oh yeah, and we'll fall in love. It's Paris, mon cheri, come on! It would be as simple as that, right? Ahhh, the best-laid plans. As it turned out, ninety-nine of the one hundred berths in first class were booked by a group of elderly Japanese tourists, who didn't speak a word of English. Not one. An hour in it was, "Some more champagne, Mrs. Yokomuto?"

If you've never been, Paris is a city like no other. I've been there four times. Elegant, sophisicated, pure decadence. I must tell you that while I love being on my own when I set sail, when it comes to Paris, travelling *with* a girlfriend is best, what with the walking and seeing the sights and such. I mean, think about it. A high percentage of the people there speak French and only French, and besides, the women there are waaay out of my (or anybody's) league. That way, you don't have to deal with how rude the French can be. My contention is that most Parisians think all of us touristy English-speaking gents are vile American pigs. Even we nice Canadians.

True story. This actually happened to me just minutes after checking into my hotel and quickly waving down a cab, all excited to see Paris for the first time. I got in the back of a cab driven by Lebeau, we'll call him (a nod to the character from *Hogan's Heroes*), and I asked him to take me to the Eiffel Tower. Hey, if you're going to start somewhere. Hello? He turns to me and looks at me like I had just given a Polaroid picture to an Australian bushman. *"Qu'est-ce que c'est?"* asks Lebeau. "The Eiffel Tower, monsieur! *S'il vous plait,"* I retort. This guy then goes into this mostly French but broken English diatribe on how I should correctly pronounce the Eiffel Tower and the fact that he won't take me to it until I say it correctly. And he's serious *"La Tour Eiffel!"* shouts Lebeau (with Eiffel pronounced eee-FELL, as opposed to EYE-fell.) This goes on for minutes. I'm literally pointing out his window *at* the Eiffel Tower, which you could see from everywhere in Paris, including over his dashboard "There it is — *take me there!"* *"Non!"* says Lebeau defiantly. Remember, at this point I had just paid close to three hundred Canadian dollars to ride for two hours with ninety-nine Japanese tourists on a train. I was in no mood for this guy. I wanted to reach over and grab the loaf of fresh bread (*"une baguette"*) that he had in the front seat and knock that silly little French chapeau off his head! (Too cliché?) Fine. "Please take me to *le Tour Eiffel, Monsieur Sucker of le Cock!*" Welcome to Paris. The trip got better after that, and in a hurry. Gee, do you think? I ran into some Canadian journalists I knew from Canadian Press in Toronto, who set me up with media passes to the French Open tennis tournament. These guys knew the city and where to drink and dine, and were a huge help.

From there it was off to Belfast, then to Edinburgh in Scotland, on the Hoverspeed Cross Channel Seacat (which, sadly, is no longer running), then back to Dublin. One day in Dublin, I experienced all four seasons in one hour. I was staying a block from the Lansdowne Road stadium (now the Aviva Stadium), where I saw an Irish World Cup soccer qualifier one glorious afternoon, when I headed out for a walk. It started out sunny, then turned to rain, hail, snow with high winds, and then sunny again. Oh, this is funny. I was in a pub having a drink, and when I headed to the washroom, I heard two gentlemen say, "Johnny Gallagher's in our pub! It's Johnny freaking Gallagher." (In Ireland, it's pronounced Galla-her, by the way.) I thought they were "taking the piss" (joking) but they were just two Irish brothers from Toronto back home visiting family and they recognized me from CityTV. The next several rounds were on them. The last time I was there — and this is the way to do it, folks — my girlfriend and I bounced all over Europe sleeping in the extra bedrooms of relatives. We hopped from Danny (my ex-brother-in-law) in Paris to Renée (my brother's ex-sister-in-law in Dublin) to an ex-girlfriend's flat in London. It's the only way to fly.

While getting to Paris wasn't half the fun I expected, I'm here to tell you that your seating arrangements on planes and trains are important and can be quite advantageous. Case in point. Los Angeles to Sydney, Australia. The flight is fourteen hours. On this flight there were half a dozen movies and meals and an endless supply of Australian wine, which has been all I've been drinking for the last twenty-five years. Part of my vacation was touring the finest vineyards in the "Land of Oz," home of Wyndham Estates, and maybe a zip on over to say hi to Wolfie Blass. (Trust me, if you've been drinking Wolfgang Blass wines as long as I have, you can call him Wolfie.) Keep the wine coming. Funny, I was in the very back row of the plane next to an empty seat, so they just plunked an ice bucket next to me and left me alone. That empty seat was important because more than a few Aussies sat down next to me during the marathon trip to have a quick cigarette (I was a casual smoker back then, but only if I had a drink in one hand, which, on a plane ride with an open bar, I invariably did) and then scurry back to their non-smoking section. Remember when you could smoke on planes? This was one of those times, but only in the final row (a lot of good that's going to do for the people around you, but hey). I'd strike up conversations with a few of the lovely Sheila who sat next to me, received some valuable Sydney touring tips, and got more than a few phone numbers.

I must tell you that Aussies are some of the most fun-loving people on the planet. The men love to drink, watch, and play sports and they love to party and "mingle" with good-looking Aussie women, who all look like Elle McPherson. And of all the accents I've heard in my life, the Australian variety instantly make my knees go weak. I quite enjoyed the parade of them walking to the end of the plane to have a quick "fag" with me. Mind you, on arrival in Sydney I was detained for hours trying to convince customs officials that I was *not* the same John Gallagher from Ireland who thought he was Jesus Christ and was trying to convert people to Catholicism one twelve-year-old boy at a time. *That* John Gallagher was deported and tried to get back several times. I had to assure the good people at Sydney International that this wasn't one of those times and I wasn't Jesus Christ our Lord and Saviour-slash-pervert.

Well, I made it to Sydney, one of the greatest cities in the world and future home to the greatest Olympic Games ever held, but I almost didn't. Let's take you back two days prior. After smoothtalking some Air Canada reps at the gate, I got bumped up to first class. Again. By the way, the trick is to ask *at* the gate, or even once you've boarded. In my situation, airlines knew that the kind gesture of putting John Gallagher's butt in seat 1A would perhaps lead to a mention on air once I got back home. And I always thanked them. So, Toronto to L.A. was spent in the big, plush, cushiony seats with champagne handed to you before you even sat down. Plus, first class was wall-to-wall with my friend Mark Breslin and his stable of new up-and-coming Yuk Yuk's comedians, who were heading to L.A. to test the warm waters of the dozens of legendary comedy clubs there. But five hours in the air boozing with these guys, albeit hilarious, turned into trouble. For me anyway.

As mentioned, I smoked back then, and that was a no-no on that particular flight, so I made a beeline to a smoking friendly bar at LAX to light up. I should have seen the telltale signs, but I was lit up like a Christmas tree. I sat down at the bar, ordered a drink, put my carry on bag on the stool beside me, and then, *boom*, some guy sits down right away and strikes up a conversation while politely asking for a cigarette. A friendly guy with a cowboy hat. He seemed harmless enough. He wasn't. They must have seen me coming up the pike a mile away. By the time I had even had a sip of that drink, my bag, which had been right next to me, was gone. These guys work in teams by distracting the poor soul (me) at the bar with a diversion (bumming a cig) while his partner snatches the bag. That's all I wanted was to spend the next several hours at the airport while Sunset Strip and Hollywood awaited me just a few miles away. My long-time comedian friend, the hugely talented but ever-underachieving Tim Conlon, was throwing a party for me on my only night in L.A. that evening. Instead, I spent the night in a hotel at the airport awaiting word on my lost bag that never came. And in the middle of the night, I woke up in a flop sweat, suffering what would be my first panic attack.

It gets worse. My passport was in that bag. No passport, no trip to Australia, or anywhere else, for that matter. I had to get the Canadian consulate to open their offices on a Sunday morning at nine a.m. and issue me a new passport, pronto. A $50 U.S. cab ride each way. I must say, my new best Canadian friends were terrific and quick! I hustled to LAX and waited for hours to get another Qantas flight out of there, all the while thinking, *Screw it, I'll just cash in my ticket (it was a $5,000 trip) and go to Vegas for a week and call it even. But damn it, I'm this close. I'll just keep calm and carry on.* Not to mention the fact that I was going to puddlejump back from Australia and hit Fiji and Hawaii on the way home. Damn the torpedoes, full speed ahead. Smart move. I wished I had made the original flight, and as a result, I missed my hero's welcome at the airport. An old friend of mine was tight with the Canadian consulate general in Sydney who turned out to be a big sports fan and loved my work at CityTV and Q. He, his wife, and some friends had arranged a surprise welcoming party with balloons and a big banner to welcome me to Australia the day before. I wasn't on that flight thanks to my "drinking buddies" at LAX, so the air went out of that party. We did hook up a few days later and I even stayed at their mansion outside the city for a few days. I brought them Blue Jays memorabilia. They were huge fans.

But Australia. My goodness, it is everything they say it is and more. I went in January, which is their summer, and it was like a tropical paradise. Not to mention hot. Did you know it's against the law in Australia to neglect to lather your kids up in suntan lotion before they even leave the house for school? The ozone layer in Aussieland is as thin as a sheet of Saran Wrap, apparently. The two weeks was a series of cricket matches, winery touring, and getting close enough to Uluru (Ayers Rock) to worry about a dingo eating my baby! This "baby" would be a pretty young thing I met at the Hard Rock Café in Sydney who kept staring at me from across the bar. I noticed the Canadian flag on her backpack and put two and two together (being from Toronto, she recognized me from TV), and we hit it off immediately. She was doing the same touristy thing I was, only she was staying at the local hostels and such. We continued on a pub crawl through the Kings Cross area of the city, getting more than a little soused. We even hit a carnival downtown with a roller coaster, which may or may not have resulted in what happened an hour or so later. My new special friend and I would take it back to my hotel room for some late-night silliness. We had hit several of Sydney's finest watering holes, plus some rides, so it'd already been quite a night. Of course, there's always room for extracurricular activities.

The reason I'm telling you about this night of passion in one of the greatest cities on Earth is because of what happened next. So my young friend (please excuse me if I can't recall the woman's name) and I were playing flippy flop in my bed (nice first day, eh?) when I think I hear some unpleasant grumbling sounds permeating from … her? Yes, her. At this point she's on top of me, bouncing away, when I'm thinking, uh-oh, I've seen this movie before. Just not while fucking. This girl is going to hurl, something fierce, and like it or not, I'm getting a ringside seat. And here it is, projectile vomit coming at me. I successfully ducked to get out of the way as she tumbled off me and attempted to hit the washroom. Albeit unsuccessfully. All I remember after that is the concierge on his hands and knees, with a bucket and a scrub brush, while Junior Miss Wonder-Heave took refuge with a marathon sit-down shower. I do remember her joining me and sleeping it off, but she was gone (I'm sure from sheer embarrassment) when I woke up. Plus, she stole my passport and all of my money. Really? No, not really.

TWENTY-SEVEN

SPRING IS SPRUNG, THE GRASS IS RIZ, I WONDER WHERE THE BLUE JAYS IS?

(or "It's not spring until Gallagher arrives with the roof down in his convertible with a beautiful blonde or two in the back!" — Richard Griffin, *Toronto Star*)

During my days at CityTV and Q107 in the nineties, one of the highlights was going to spring training in Florida to cover the Blue Jays. The Jays camp is located in the blue-rinse capital of the USA, sleepy little boring Dunedin, Florida. The good part is that Dunedin is less than a ten-minute drive from Clearwater Beach, home to thousands of spring breakers who would swarm the area every year. I once worked for a radio station that professed to be the perfect station to listen to at the beach. It was C100 (in Halifax) "Reaches the Beaches" — well, when I hit the sands in Clearwater, it was John Gallagher "Reaches the *Peaches*." If I didn't bring down a girlfriend for spring training, which was often, there was an abundance of local and "shipped in" talent. I don't know what it was, but I did have a lot of luck with attractive waitresses in the area, which drove some of the other TV, radio, and newspaper reporters nuts. My friend Richard Griffin of the *Toronto Star* would always say, "It's not spring until Gallagher arrives with the roof down in his convertible with a beautiful blonde or two in the back!" I loved that. CityTV would send three reporters down. If you wrangled it the right way, you got sent down first to A) get all of the good stories (i.e., hot-shot rookies, sexy free agent signings, etc.), and B) choose the rental car, which was almost always a Mustang convertible. Who wants to spend an hour at the airport having to exchange the four-door minivan the first assigned reporter rented, when you could be at the beach, you know, reaching the peaches?

One of the minor drawbacks back in those days was the weakness of the Canadian dollar. At it's lowest in 2002, it hit 61.9 cents to the U.S. dollar. Now, while we were all on a per diem, it didn't cover late-night bar bills and shopping at places like T.J. Maxx. I had a solution: American Express travellers cheques. I'm not even sure if they make them anymore. I know most stores won't even accept them. Back then, that's all I used, and I will tell you why. There was a time when U.S. and Canadian travellers cheques were almost identical, with just "U.S. currency" or "Canadian currency" in the top corners of the blue-coloured bills. You really had to look closely. This was a time before they printed cheques with "CANADIAN DOLLAR" in shocking pink to counter the antics of flim-flam men like me. Here's why. I'm not saying I condone this, but at 61 cents on the dollar ... hey, a man's got to shimmy when he's got to survive. At first I would stock up on shorts, tees, and assorted summerwear. Let's say the bill came to $200, which it usually did. You made sure the young lady behind the counter accepted Amex travellers cheques. Sometimes she had to check with her manager if they accepted said cheques. They would never say no. You always gave them a U.S. cheque — just one to, you know, check. Then you gathered the rest of the payment — *all* in Canadian cheques — from your wallet and handed them over. Remember, all she saw was a U.S. cheque, and her manager has given the okay. Heck, sometimes I'd speak in a 'Murican accent just to throw them off the scent of the swarthy, deceitful, little man standing in front of them. The young lady would count them up and slip them under the till. It was a bonus if the bill came to, let's say, $202.50, so you could slip them a $50 Canadian bill and get $47.50 back in U.S. dollars! Hell, I was *making* money down there.

Another scam I used to pull was driving by the fast food joints in the area. You drive up, get a burger and a soda for $4.99, and lather, rinse, and repeat. It's the same thing: hand them the $50 U.S. cheque and have the person consult with the manager — remember, this is a drive-thru and hungry customers are behind you, so it's go go go, and he gives the thumbs up. You ask for a pen to sign it. Have a Canadian cheque on your lap ready for the old switcharoo, add your "John Henry" and Yahtzee! I would pull that off a dozen times a week. Do the math. Let's say it's ten times. That's $500 in Canadian money magically transformed into U.S. funds. At a rate of 41 percent back on the dollar, that $500 turns into over $700, plus munchies. You're a bad man, Johnson, a very bad man. Hey, McDonald's made over ten billion dollars in 2004. Sue me.

Another memorable trip was when my co-host Brother Jake Edwards and I headed to Ocho Rios in Jamaica for a week to stay in a villa that our station, Q107, was considering for a "Win a trip to Jamaica with the Q-Zoo" promotion. There were friends of ours from 99.9 The Mix on the same trip — two women from their promotions department — so we hung out with them, one of whom I was quite smitten with and casually dated, as friends, when we returned to Toronto. On one hot, sunny day, the four of us decided to rent a Jeep and head to Bob Marley's birthplace in a tiny little town an hour or two away. It was well worth the trip to see the landscape and the real Jamaica. This was a closeup of how most regular Jamaicans live.

The drive was bumpy and the roads were narrow, but we were all huge Marley fans, so it was hammer down, southbound to Bob Marley–town! And we were well prepared, with a huge ice-filled cooler filled with liquor and some of the local ganja to keep us all entertained. This was a time well before GPS, so it was a huge flip-and-fold map of the island for us. Now, I don't know if it was the extracurricular goings on with the drinking and toking or these godawful back roads, but we got lost … several times. And let me tell you, the cast of characters that we stopped to ask for help was something out of a bad B-movie.

Miriam from 99.9 recalls, "I seem to remember it was a bit of a radical thing to do back then, and it was probably a bit dangerous being so far off the beaten track in an open-top jeep. I definitely felt a bit threatened by some of the characters we encountered. Didn't we take a photo of someone out there who got really agitated about it and started shouting at us?" Yes, and everytime we pulled over and everytime we asked for the directions to Bob Marley's birthplace, it was the same thing: "Nine miles, mahn." We'd reset the odometer every time we'd stop. The gentleman with the

99.9 FM's Miriam Nevill and Brother Jake Edwards at the Ocho Rios, Jamaica, airport after visiting Bob Marley's birthplace, which is a geographical miracle. Nine miles away. From everywhere.

rickety ten-speed bicycle with no tires said, "Nine miles, mahn, nine miles." The man on crutches with one leg and half of one arm cut off, holding a machete? That's right, a machete. The same thing: "Nine miles, mahn." We'd reset our odometer, drive for nine miles, and have to stop and ask somebody else. I thought, this place was a geographical miracle. Nine miles away from everywhere! Again, while it was a sun-drenched day, the music was terrific, the roof was down, the company was hilarious, and we puffed and drank the entire time, we'd still travelled these back roads for miles and miles ... until finally, after what seemed like hours, there it was in the distance. And as we pulled up to the parking lot, the attendant said, "Welcome to the birthplace of Bob Marley, here in Nine Mile, Jamaica." *That* was the name of the town — Nine Mile. OMFG! We had to laugh. Once inside, basically you get a rundown of Bob's life and some history of his family. You take off your shoes and light a candle to walk around his tomb, buy a T-shirt, yada yada yada, and it was back to the resort with much, much different directions from the way in. All along we just had to follow the Rastaman vibrations. Yeah-ya.

TWENTY-EIGHT

THE PRIZEFIGHT WASN'T A "10," BUT BO WAS

(or, as Sugar Ray Leonard goes down and the Caesar's Palace crowd erupts, I look at the line of cocaine on the tank in the media washroom and think ...)

The phone rings, and it's former WBC Light Heavyweight champion Donny "The Golden Boy" Lalonde. The champ is in Toronto for a few days and wants to go out on the town with me and my roommate at the time, former Maple Leaf PA announcer Andy Frost. He says he's bringing a friend, a fellow boxing fan named Tony Hall. Cool. Love seeing the Golden Boy. The bell rings, and there he is in all of his six-foot-two blondness, and he's brought his pally, another famous six-foot-two blond. Tony Hall, you see, turns out to be *Breakfast Club/Weird Science/Sixteen Candles* actor Anthony Michael Hall. An *SNL* cast member at seventeen! Alllrighty then. Off we go. It's a school night, but why be dull? Donny Lalonde and I go back a few years prior. He and Andy are from Winnipeg, and his manager for a time was Q107 Rock Report co-host Steve Warden. Donny had quite a story: how he ended up in Winnipeg at an early age and, according to Boxing.com, "went through the torment of an abusive stepdad who liked to use Donny as his own version of a punching bag," as well as "his tireless crusade against child abuse, working odd jobs at a young age, grade nine education, starting to box on a whim at age of seventeen. He's a survivor, self promoter, with model good looks, articulate and model human being, and yes *always* champion." Yeah, the Light Heavyweight champion of the planet. I used to *dream* about meeting guys like this while reading *Ring* magazine as a kid. To actually befriend a champ, let alone hang out with him, was awe-inspiring. And lucky for me, Donny and I got to be good and fast friends. I tagged along to see Donny win his first title defence on May 29, 1988, when he knocked out former WBA Light Heavyweight champion Leslie Stewart in five rounds. I'm not sure if the term "posse" applied at the time, but believe me, I was part of the champ's "Eddie Murphy entourage" to be sure. By the way, CBS was covering the event, and if you look closely, you can see the ever-opportunistic Johnny G bobbing in the background during the post-match interviews by fellow Canadian Tim Ryan, which you can find on YouTube. I know. What a poser. Come on, you're this far into the book and you haven't figured that out by now?

The most bizarre thing happened to me on that Saturday afternoon at the Hasely Crawford Stadium in Port of Spain, Trinidad and Tobago. True story: I was denied service at the snack/cocktail bar. As perhaps one of a dozen

Caucasians in the soccer stadium that day, I was a victim of blatant racism. I mean, I was just trying to get a cold rum and Diet Coke, but no one, and I mean no one, behind the bar would serve or even acknowledge me. I went up and down the row, belly up to the bar, signalling and waving the local currency in their direction, but to no avail. Perhaps they felt that I was with the "all-white" fan club of Lalonde, who would go on to pummel their local hero. I don't know, but really? Now, let me be clear, this was over a highball, and perhaps my would-be servers were having a bad day, but at that moment I truly understood what being a minority feels like. Maybe if they had pointed me toward the "Whites Only" canteen around the corner, I would have been fine. I never raised a fuss, mind you. I finally had to get a member of the local Trinidadian media to buy me one, "With a slice of lime, please!" but for a good twenty minutes there, I was Vic Morrow in the *Twilight Zone* movie.

After the fight, Donny took us on a cruise ship to Tobago and arranged some prime beachfront hotel property for his peeps for several more days. At the end of it all, we found out that the champ had taken care of every- thing — hotel, cruise, et cetera — from his winnings for the WBC Light Heavyweight title. Sweet. And it got better. Steve managed to have Q107 send us down and cover the "fight of the year" on November 7, 1988. Donny was in line for a huge payday — six million dollars to fight Sugar Ray Leonard at Caesar's Palace in Las Vegas. What a spectacle. Although we didn't get as much face time with Lalonde during the week, there were other things to do, it being Vegas, baby! I soon realized that this was the biggest sporting event I'd ever been to.

There was one night in his hotel room that we had some fun. Rock and roll legend Bob Dylan had just left Donny's room. I brushed by him carrying his guitar in the hallway at Caesar's, thinking, "*There's* some- thing you don't see every day!" A *People* magazine article on Lalonde had come out that week that read, "As far as the boxing sodality is concerned, Lalonde is something of a freak, maybe an embarrassment to the game. He is a long-haired quasi-vegetarian from Canada who lives in Greenwich Village, takes acting lessons, plays Dylan tapes during workouts, reads assorted swamis, and puts his faith in holistic medicine." So Dylan was in town to write a song about him. Hey, if Warren Zevon can pen a tune about Ray "Boom Boom" Mancini (who I also met at the fight), then Dylan can try to inspire the Golden Boy. One night in his hotel room

Donny said, "Hand me the phone, you're calling Bob Dylan." "What?" I said. "Just do it. Call his room, see how he answers the phone." Dylan's hotel room phone rang, and the next thing I heard, in that unmistakable voice, was "Bob Dylan"! Not "Hello" or "Hey" or "Yes," just "Bob Dylan"! Who answers the phone like that? Answer: Bob Dylan. I quickly mumbled, "Sorry, wrong number," and hung up.

It was that kind of a weird weekend, and it was about to get weirder. As if Vegas isn't *meshuga* enough on any given day, it's ten times that when the circus comes to town for a weekend. The city was teeming with big names, and with full passes I was able to fall in with all of them. Kurt Russell and Goldie Hawn hung around. Look, there's Don Rickles! OMG, I'm having drinks with Gene Hackman? Am I trying to convince Don Mattingly to join the Blue Jays? (Yes, and he didn't.) Is that Albert Brooks? I must tell you, I have a list of movies that, if you dislike, you are deemed undatable in my book. Don't worry ladies, it's a short list! One of those films is Brooks's highly underrated film *Defending Your Life*. Please watch it. It is so choice. And sure enough, there was Brooks (and probably his agent) about to order at one of several restuarants in and around Caesar's Palace. "Don't order yet!" I said I as I barged into the conversation. Mr. Brooks looked at me like I had a cabbage for a head. This was before smartphones and quick selfies, so I hurried along with the pleasantries and got an autograph on my fight program. An autograph. How eighties of me. How fifties of me, actually. One of my favourite "sports" is people watching. And looking around one of Vegas's most famous hotels on the night of a big fight? Oh my goodness. Everbody's there. Muhammad Ali strides in. Also Telly Savalas, Sly Stallone, and that no-talent, unfunny comedic hack Whoopi Goldberg as well.

Donny would lose the fight eventually. His size and awkwardness did trouble Leonard in the early going. In the fourth round, while I was taking leave of my ringside seat for a quick "bump" in the washroom, a right hand to the top of Leonard's head dropped him for just the second time in his career. I mean, I'm doing enough coke to make Robin Williams blush, but I'm also an accredited member of the media covering the biggest prizefight of the year. As I do a huge line, I hear the stands of the arena shake above me. I'm thinking, perhaps I can do the rest of the blow post-fight and get back to work. (I didn't end up snorting the rest of that blow until around noon, then had breakfast — that's *breakfast* — at the Las Vegas Denny's at six in *the afternoon*.)

Back to the prizefight. With Donny ahead on some of the judges' scorecards, he stepped up in the ninth and hurt Leonard with a right to the chin. But the Sugar Man fired back and hurt Lalonde with a right. He drove him to the ropes and unleashed a furious assault. Lalonde tried to tie up Leonard but got dropped with a powerful left hook. He rose but was soon down again, and the fight was stopped. Leonard won his fourth and fifth world titles. If Donny had had one more big payday, I'm sure I would have tagged along, but fighting Sugar Ray Leonard at Caesar's Palace? This is as big as it got.

After the fight, once again I was getting up close with *all* of these celebs, and I was just completely gobsmacked. So, I just happened to strike up a conversation with fellow fight fan John Derek post-fight. Look up Svengali in the dictionary and it says "See John Derek." No sign of his stunning wife, *10* actress Bo Derek. Not yet, anyway. I was standing around after the bout taking in all of the post-prizefight interviews from a couple of rows up when I got a tap on the shoulder. The next words I heard were, "Hi, my name is Bo. I saw you talking with my husband, John, earlier. Have you seen him?" Bo Derek, perhaps the most beautiful spectacle on God's green earth that I will ever see, was right there. After a little small talk, she told me that if I *did* see John, to tell him that she'd gone up to the hotel room. I did offer to escort her to the penthouse suite, informing her that "there are ruffians about," but she politely declined. She did sign my program (damn, why didn't I bring a camera?!) and sauntered away as I, of course, watched every step. A *10*? More like a 20.

TWENTY-NINE

CHAMPAGNE SHOWERS AND 'ROID RAGE DREAMS

(or, batting champion Paul Molitor says,
"C'mon, Gallagher, step into the cage.
You need some batting lessons.")

Did you ever hear "that" story about Babe Ruth? It was the early 1920s and a buck naked Babe, the Bambino, sprinted right through a train, racing down the passageway, chased closely by a woman wielding a butcher knife. Oh, and she was naked, too. They ran through the bar car as several reporters watched open-mouthed in silence. They would learn that she was the wife of a Louisiana politician who thought she and Ruth were "exclusive." The writers looked at each other and said, "I didn't see anything. Did you see anything?" That didn't wind up in the papers the next day, or ever. Neither did a Detroit incident in which an irate husband waving a revolver chased a near-naked Babe out of a hotel. Wow.

Imagine that today. Surveillance cameras on trains, in hotel elevators (hello, Ray Rice), and lobbies, and on every street corner? Look, *that* just happened. I'm sure I would have loved to hang around with the Babe. He and I would have gotten along famously. As for some others, I say, hey, raise your hand if you're a dick. Examples?

Jake Edwards and I were broadcasting for a week on Q in Daytona, and I went to a breakfast where Reggie Jackson was speaking to get a few clips for the show. It was Daytona 500 week, and Reggie was known to be into cars and bikes, so I tagged along. I knew that Reggie could get testy with the media, but hand to God, I have never met a bigger doucheweasle than Reginald Martinez Jackson in my life. There were only two members of the media there to interview him afterwards. That's correct, two. It was just myself and a seventy-year-old woman from the local Daytona Beach newspaper. After the kindly old journalist asked her first question, I asked mine — only to have Mr. October put his hand on my microphone and scold me because our journalist friend perhaps hadn't finished her line of questioning. I heard Sparky Anderson of the Reds and Tigers used to do that in scrums, but it had never happed to this reporter, especially when just two of us were standing there. Of course, the entire topic was Reggie. All he wanted to talk about was himself, and I hate, hate, hated those Yankee teams he was on.

Barry Bonds was no walk in the park (as in ballpark) either. Barry was always in a bad mood. I've talked with Muhammad Ali, Pete Rose, Michael Jordan, Cal Ripken Jr., and the like over the years. They were legends of sports and they loved what they did, and gosh darn it, it showed. Gracious. Genuine.

But Barry? I interviewed Bonds before a Jays game at SkyDome, where his Giants were in for a rare interleague game. He was surly with the huge throng of media that had gathered to have an audience with the King, because it was after he'd had a run-in with Roger Clemens during a series at Yankee Stadium the day before. I asked him about it. He retorted, "Why don't you go ask Roger Clemens that! Why don't you ask me something about today's game? Go ask Roger!" Okay, so I turned the questioning toward his feelings about Toronto, and he said, "See, now that's a good question because my wife is from Toronto and I love the city. You see what you did there? Good for you, boy." Boy? I wanted to ask how his shirt size had ballooned from forty-two to fifty-two inches, his shoe size had grown from ten and a half to thirteen, and his hat size had gone from a 7 ⅛ to 7 ¾ because of his human growth hormone (HGH) use, but I wisely didn't. Man, I thought, Barry, a notorious abuser of steroids, and convicted of obstruction of justice for lying to a grand jury about using them probably had more than enough acne on his shoulders to populate a junior high school cafeteria.

It was different between me and another pair of drug-using Blue Jays. Jose Canseco, also convicted, a "Blue Jay for a day" (okay, one year — 1998 — when he hit forty-six home runs and finished only tied for sixth overall in that department!) proclaimed himself the "godfather" of steroids and set about evangelizing their glory to his teammates. One day at his locker he showed me, on camera, all of the stuff he was injecting into himself. At least he admitted to it. And laughed about it.

On the other hand, there was steroid-user Roger Clemens. Probably the greatest pitcher of my generation, he won five Cy Young awards, the last two as a thirty-eight-year-old twenty-game winner with the Yankees in 2001 and a forty-one-year-old eighteen-game winner with the Astros in 2004. He and I hosted a booze-filled night with hundreds of baseball fans at Planet Hollywood at SkyDome and got along famously. When I heard he was one of the Major League Baseball players named in the Mitchell Report in 2007, along with the rest of the usual suspects, I was stunned. But you know what's worse? Some say Roger's legacy has been tainted by steroids even more than Barry Bonds's because of his adamant denials. He once said, "If I had been using steroids, I'd be pulling tractors with my teeth and have a third ear growing out of my forehead." For the record, Clemens was never convicted. Some reporters I've talked to think Clemens belongs in the Hall of Fame, if there is in fact a Hall of

Fame for douchebags somewhere. Again, I liked the guy, but as more rumours of his diva-like behaviour came to light, I had to rethink our "relationship." Jeff Pearlman's book *The Rocket That Fell to Earth* states the following:

> While the Jays struggled in the win column and fans appeared largely indifferent to his presence in town, Clemens did his best to enjoy himself, especially on the Toronto area's many high-end golf courses. Clemens expected every major facility to acknowledge three things: 1. Rogers Clemens is great. 2. Roger Clemens never pays for golf. 3. By "never," Roger Clemens means "never." He was outraged when the National Golf Club in Woodbridge demanded he pay the going rate: $1,000 for his foursome. Over the course of the season, Clemens's golfing addiction became the talk of the Toronto clubhouse. The man who was being paid to lead the Jays on and off the field was often late to the ballpark and absent from team meetings.

Well, he looks good in the photo of him and me on my mantle.

As I've mentioned in this book from time to time, there was a period when the media had close to full access to the biggest names in sports. It was particularly the case for members of the CityTV sports department who weren't looking for the hard-hitting angle of a story. Jim McKenny, Kathryn Humphreys, and myself, among others, had fun, damn it. There was room for the lighter side of sports, and we were the perfect station for it. There were hardly any hard-hitting questions from us for the athletes. We took it easy on them and, as a result, had easy access. Heck, one year at spring training I hid silly trinkets and kinky women's lingerie items in the Toronto Blue Jays lockers so I could play a very David Letterman-esque game of "What's in the bag?" They picked up on the gag and enjoyed taking part. Once, in homage to comic genius Andy Kaufman, I went milk and cookie shopping with Mr. Milk and Cookies and Milquetoast himself, 1993 American League batting champion John Olerud. Olerud had the sweetest swing I've ever seen. And I had seen Pete Rose, Roberto Clemente, Wade Boggs, and Henry Aaron.

In 1995, the mood around baseball was bizarre. The 1994 MLB strike cancelled the entire season (with my Expos at 74–40 in first place and primed to win the World Series!) so, still humbled by the PR disaster of a work stoppage, the Jays and all of the spring training camps were extremely eager to please in order to get the media, and especially the fans, back on side. One day I was getting exclusive one-on-one batting lessons from Hall of Famer Paul Molitor. True story. And later that night I went out with all-world second baseman Robbie Alomar (another Hall member) to "flirt" with women at Tampa/Clearwater/St. Petersburg Beach hotel bars — and I brought the cameras along and filmed that, too! (Strange how he always did better than I did in that category.) Mind you, there was a year when I "befriended" an absolutely stunning waitress from one of the local watering holes close to the Jays' training facility, and we spent a fabulous week together. Several sportswriters were pissed. Hey, they're sportswriters for a reason, right? Leave the skirt chasing to the TV boys. And I had lots of spare time. The CityTV sports reporters had it sussed. Every year for close to fifteen spring trainings it was the same thing. We'd send three reporters down for a week each. I'd usually be the first one, so I could bring whoever I was dating a few days early and sit on the beach soaking up the spring break atmosphere. I'd always get a convertible. Always. The CBC, Global, and CTV boys drove minivans, but I had to go "top down, baby." No diddly, no doubt. But here's the trick. I'd read a stack of baseball preview magazines (I'd been buying Street and Smith's annual baseball almanac since the early seventies — and still do), so I knew the roster by rote and had all the angles planned. Okay, day one and two of spring training we'd bring five or six different sets of clothing. Let's say we start on a Friday. I'd do a story on the Jays' new all-star lefthanded free agent signing and go to the clubhouse and change my shirt and shorts. An hour later, I'd do a bit on the fight for left field now that George Bell had left the team. There's another story "in the can." Lather, rinse, repeat. Heck, sometimes I'd do four stories in a day, and by day two, I had recorded all six for the week! We'd just Purolator the precut tapes out the day before they ran on air. It was all filler/feature stuff.

Now, there was a time in February 1994 when Jays pitchers Dave Stewart and Todd Stottlemyre were charged with battery on a police officer and resisting arrest after an argument over a $3 cover charge at an Ybor City nightclub. The trouble got seriously silly when, Stottlemyre's wife, Sheri, jumped on an officer's back as he attempted to arrest her husband. The two pitchers were charged with battery on a law-enforcement officer and resisting arrest with violence. Okay, *that* time, having a reporter on the scene, we had to go live.

Thank God it wasn't me. Greg Manziuk had to interview the police and Blue Jay reps all day and do a live "hit" off a satellite truck in the parking lot of the Home Shopping Network in Tampa. But, strangely, all during his report he announced that Al Leiter, a different Jays pitcher, had been arrested instead of Stottlemyre as we all screamed, "No, no, no!" at the TV monitors in Toronto. Manziuk, who deserved better from the middle-management types, didn't last at CityTV much longer after that. (Also around that time, Sheri Stottlemyre and half a dozen or so of the Jays' gorgeous blond "cookie cutter" wives came to my back porch to plan out a huge aerobic event at SkyDome that I was emceeing. It was a blistering hot day and I got the wine out for several pours. I let them know that I did have extra bikinis in my walk-in closet if they wanted to slip into my hot tub. They unfortunately passed. What a photo op that would have been!) Okay, so if you're scoring at home (and I certainly hope you are — ba-ding!), you've figured out that all of my ninety-second features from Jays spring training for the week are done and done, and it's only Monday and I've got the next six days to spend in the sun. So while other reporters were standing "live" outside the stadium announcing, "The Blue Jays continue their winning ways down here in Florida with a 3–2 win over the St. Louis Cardinals ... blah, blah, blah," I was on one of the greatest beaches in the USA every day with a cooler full of chardonnay! It was even better when Labatt would send the Q morning team to Florida — everything was on the house.

We got away with an awful lot back then. It was one of "those days," when I was soaking up some serious rays on world-famous Clearwater Beach and was "preparing" to file a Labatt-sponsored "Live from Dunedin" report back to John Derringer as part of our daily 4:20 "sports shorts" feature on Q107. I should have been at the ballpark, but hey, it was ninety-two degrees in the shade. A guy's gotta have priorities and *they must be kept*! You see, all I had to do was call the press box at the park, jot down the score and some highlights, and "Bingo was his name-o." Problem was, the media hotline was busy for half an hour or so and the report was quickly approaching. *Fuck.* It was 4:10, then 4:15, and still busy. Remember, this is a sponsored report, and Labatt is a *huge* client, and I'm down in Florida on their coin. And it's a big coin. So there's *that*. Okay, finally I got through, got the info on the game, and was ready for Freddy. I got the AT&T operator, and she dialed up a collect call to Toronto. It seemed that I missed my time slot, and Derringer was at the end of a commercial break and about to come back on the air to introduce a tune when he saw the hotline blinking. *Great, we're both thinking from several thousand miles apart, we'll sneak in the report just in time.* We were live on the air when John answered, "Hi, Q107?" The operator said, "Yes, we have a collect call from Florida. Will you accept the charges, please?" Now, all this time the operator has been brilliant — getting the numbers and long-distance dialing done as fast as possible, since everybody was a bit frantic, being up against the clock as we were. As the phone was ringing and Derringer was about to pick up, she asked my name. I'd spent the entire day in the sun with a cooler full o' fun, so I was in a playful mood. I responded, "Mr. Chardon. That's Chardon, first name Hugh." You might know where I'm going with this. I know it was so sophomoric. This was grade six "call the local DJ and prank him" silliness. My friends and I were always making prank calls and trying to trick on-air announcers into using fake names. Believe me, I missed out on a lot of concert tickets and LPs by trying to get DJs to "bite." There I was, thirty years later and a grown man, kind of. But I was thinking, even the greenest of operators would pick up on what I was trying to pull off, right? I couldn't possibly dupe this poor young woman into uttering the name "Hugh Chardon," could I? Surely she had heard the names "Ben Dover," "Phil Lacio," "Seymour Butts," "Oliver Clothesoff," and "Amanda Huggenkiss" before. I could have used the all-time classic, "Heywood Jablome."

You know what happens next. Judy, we'll call her, asked Derringer if he would indeed accept a long-distance call from Florida. My unsuspecting friend replied, "Yes, operator. Who is it from?" to which she announced live on the air, "A Mr. Chardon ... a Hugh Chardon." For good measure, John asked her to please repeat that. "A Hugh Chardon ... collect call from Hugh Chardon." The next thing I heard was Derringer's voice asking, "Can you repeat that, just the way you said it?" When she did, I heard the phone hitting the floor and he along with it. The laughter from the other end of the phone was uncontrollable. Judy, now knowing she had been punked, shrieked, "Oh my God!" and hung up. You see, you can't go on the air and say "huge hard-on" or anything of that sort. The key is to have someone else say it. Well, she'd said it, and now it was bouncing off satellites. You've heard or seen radio personalities or local news anchors get a case of the giggles and not be able to recover on air. This was one of those cases. John took a while to get through the now-unimportant pre-season Jays score, because the biggest "score" had taken place thanks to Judy. "A classic" was all we could say after getting our composure back. "An absolute classic." Listeners who heard that day still talk about it. What a stupid way to make a living, huh?

✦✦✦

Personally, I've experienced dozens of memorable almost–"life changing" moments at sporting events over the years: jumping into the ring after world title boxing matches, watching the Vince Lombardi trophy being hoisted a few feet away after Super Bowl games, attending Stanley Cup parades and having Blue Jay Candy Maldonado pour an entire bottle of champagne over my head on live TV after the Jays beat the hated A's in the '92 ALCS. But perhaps my favourite came just a week or so after that. It was on the night of October 24, 1992 — the night the Toronto Blue Jays won their first World Series — and I found myself engulfed by thousands of fans who had poured into the "crossroads of Canada." I had just finished hosting my Saturday night gig at Barracuda nightclub and joined a sea of fans who were stuck dead smack in the middle of Yonge and Bloor. I'll let my friend George Tsiolis pick it up from there:

> It was my U2 "Where the Streets Have No Name" moment. I stood on top of a pickup truck. Using my megaphone, I led the crowd in cheers, chants, and laughter for ninety minutes. Just when I thought the night could not get better, John Gallagher (the Bono of Toronto sports media) hopped onto the truck with me. I instinctively handed him the megaphone and happily became one of the fans as he whipped us up into a frenzy, concluding with a hair-raising *O Canada* that ended in a crescendo of tears and pride. It was well after midnight, and he reminded us the clocks had turned back an hour. The crowd went wild with the knowledge it had just been gifted another hour on a night no one wanted to end. It was the perfect ending to the perfect night. Never to be forgotten.

It was truly a night I will never forget.

THIRTY

JURASSIC PRANK: THE EARLY SALAD YEARS OF THE TORONTO RAPTORS

(or, Charles Oakley on his bobblehead
night at the ACC: "Well, I have a head, so you
never know what could happen.")

There was a lot of electricity in the air and a buzz on the street on November 4, 1993. The city of Toronto got its first professional basketball team since 1946 when the NBA, as part of its expansion into the great white north, awarded its twenty-eighth franchise to a group headed by Toronto business-man John Bitove for a then-record expansion fee of $125 million U.S. The team wouldn't play its first game until 1995, but there was a lot of work to do beforehand. That would include several things, like figuring out where were they going to play and what were they going to be called. Also, among a million other things, what station would get the TV rights and who would be tapped as the official team PA announcer. Those last two, for better or worse, involved me. As the days and months led up to opening night, the team quickly tied all the loose ends together. John Bitove was a terrific guy and we hit it off instantly. One night he took me out for drinks at Gretzky's (he and the Bitove family, along with Wayne, did own the place, after all) and offered me the job of the voice of the Raptors as the official public address announcer. Wow, this was perfect, I thought. I could make a hell of a lot of money, arrange to host live events, make personal appearances on behalf of the team, et cetera. It would be a windfall. All we had to do was come up with a dollar figure. I went to station owner Moses Znaimer, along with on-air types Monica Deol, Denise Donlan, and others, asking what an acceptable figure would be for a gig like that. They suggested somewhere between $500 and a $1,000 a game. That sounded reasonable. I mean, at the time, I'd easily get a grand per public appearance and sometimes up to $10,000! So *how* much were John and his people willing to offer per game? Is everyone sitting comfortably? Okay, then I'll tell you: $50. Yes, in the Raptors' pecuniary fash-ion, they offered up fifty dollars a game. Heck, that hardly pays for parking. I told them a flat no. It was almost an insult. No, wait, it *was* an insult. They did come back with a counter offer. It was $100. Nice try, but again, the answer was no. They tried again, only this time it was $100 per game plus a pair of floor seats. Well, that was all well and good, but what did I need floor seats for? I already had the best seats in the house: front row at the courtside table. I could just picture myself saying into the mic, "Substitution for the Bulls, number 23 Michael Jordan ..." then turning around and saying to my friends behind me, "Isn't this great? Hold on, gotta go." It just wasn't worth it.

The team finally hired Herbie Kuhn to do the job. I believe he worked at a grocery store before becoming the full-time PA announcer for the team. Knock yourself out, kid. Fifty bucks times forty-one home games plus a few pre-season matches equals don't be so patently ridiculous. The same people from basketball operations *did* try to make it up to me a little while afterwards. They needed me to co-host a day-long event at the newly opened Air Canada Centre for fans to come in and check out their perspective season-tickets seats. NBA hall-of-famer and team GM Isiah Thomas would be working along with me. Their offer for the day was $2,500. Now *that* was more like it, eh? The problem was, I had *zero* vacation days left from CityTV and had to take a pass. So they upped the offer to three thousand. Can't do it. Four thousand. I don't have the time. Five and then six thousand. I would have jumped at the chance, but since I worked for the detestable and aforementioned Stephen Hurlbut — I politely declined because I knew he wasn't going to budge. Now, here's where it gets hilarious. Just not on my part. The Raptors higher-ups, who obviously were not going to take no for an answer, went directly to Moses Znaimer to discuss my availability. His answer was this: not only will John host the event, but he will do it — wait for it — for free. True story. The Raptor brass, feeling a tad sheepish, presented me with an expensive limited edition Raptors leather jacket. I wanted to say, "I'll take the $6,000, thank you," but Moses was adamant.

♣♣♣

Covering the Raptors in those early days was interesting to say the least. My first assignment was the NBA draft with long-time CityTV sports anchor, sadly recently departed, John Saunders and the entire City sports team. I showed up at the station with a gorgeous new suit just for the occasion, but Hurlbut demanded that I take the shirt and tie off and put on a Raptors T-shirt. Really? The *Globe and Mail* weighed in with, "He once wore a Raptors shirt while delivering his report and was ridiculed in newspapers for appearing as a fan rather than a reporter." The show turned out to be a bomb, and the Raptors decided to farm out the broadcast to a slicker, more experienced sports production company and not use any City sports reporters on the telecast. Thank goodness. While I would have loved the challenge, it would have meant hours and hours of extra work, plus weekends, for the

Here's six-time NBA champion Michael Jordan just before we teed off. As he told fellow NBA star (and former Raptor) Muggsy Bogues, "Shoot it, you effing midget!"

same pay. I was, however, responsible for a weekly CityTV segment called the "Raptor Rap" (I know, don't ask), a three-minute recap of the "week that was" in Raptor Central. This would be a daunting task, as the Raptors ended their inaugural season with a 21–61 win-loss record, and it seemed everybody in the locker room was in a bad mood. But, I will say, it was seldom dull. There were some highlights — with a chintzy twenty-one wins, they did win their first one. I was among the 33,306 fans there on opening night to witness the Raptors defeat the Nets 94–79. Veteran Alvin Robertson scored the first points in Raptors history, as he hit a three-pointer and ended with a team high thirty points.

Robertson was a beast. You didn't fuck with this guy. The four-time NBA All-Star was once saluted by Michael Jordan as one of the toughest *sumbitches* he ever played against. Opposing players didn't stay too late in the clubs the night before playing Robertson. He was tough and simply wore on his man. Talk about intimidating. To wit: Reggie Miller, hall-of-fame player and smack talker extraordinaire, remembers being pulled aside by a teammate in his rookie year. The veteran player warned Miller not to say anything to Robertson. No boasting, no trash talk, nothing about his mama, nothing. Don't even say hello. Off the court he was even angrier. He was arrested dozens of times and spent months and months in prison stemming from several sexual and assault charges. Let's just say I wisely kept on Alvin's good side during his stint in Toronto. I honestly really liked him. Other Raptors, not so much. Oliver Miller was, simply put, the most out-of-shape and out-of-whack Raptor player — or professional athlete, period — I have encountered in my days covering pro sports. I once made a snide remark (is there any other kind?) on CityTV after Miller landed on the disabled list with a bad knee. I said, "Well, I'm sure his leg would feel better if he'd just shave a hundred pounds or so off his tubby three-hundred-pound frame!" Miller and some other Raptors saw it, and when I approached Damon Stoudamire for an interview shortly after, he yelled out, "Hey, yo O [Oliver], we boycotting Gallagher 'cuz of what he said about choo. We're boycotting this white boy fo' the season, aaayeee?" Oh God. Please no boycott! I have to squeeze a weekly feature out of these guys every week, and if they're not going to talk to me, I'm doomed. It was hard enough having these sometimes moody NBA pros who looked down their noses at Canadian journalists who (they thought) knew little or nothing about basketball (some of us who played varsity b-ball in high school, like myself, did, thank you very much), but to get the silent treatment from them would be a disaster. Let's just say we settled it amicably. The Raptors would release Miller after his weight got out of control. Later, after his NBA days were done, the "Big O" officially became the "Big Inmate" after he was sentenced in Maryland to a year in jail for pistol-whipping his girlfriend's brother, who needed eleven stitches in his head. I mean, everybody I know brings a gun to a family BBQ, right? There were dozens and dozens of other characters who travelled in and out of the Raptors clubhouse over those early lean years. There was a very large and out-of-shape team member who was released during training camp that first year. And when chambermaids went to clean out the hotel room he was staying in during his tryout, they found hundreds of candy bar and fast food wrappers strewn all over the floor.

But then, there were the other-worldly players that come along once every generation, like Vince Carter. The city and country got a rare chance to watch Vince transform into a god-like presence in the NBA. Carter took the basketball world by storm. "Half man, half amazing," indeed. It was in February of 1998 after the utter disaster of the Darrell Walker era, when the Vince Carter Show started. We had come out of the lockout year and the ACC had just opened. That's when the franchise really took off. Vince was so special. Not a great interview, and, like several of his teammates, a tad surly when he wasn't feeling co-operative. But my oh my, what a player. Popular, athletic, talented, and good-looking. Canada couldn't help but rally around him. He attracted the casual fan. He attracted the attention of people who hadn't previously been Raptors fans, or even NBA fans. He was that special. We had seen Vince do his thing on a nightly basis, but it was during the 2000 All-Star slam dunk competition in Oakland that "Vinsanity" began to hit levels of hype and stardom we hadn't yet seen in the Internet era. All of a sudden, in front of the eyes of the basketball world, the Raptors became a "thing," basically thanks to Vince Carter. His series of 360-degree windmill, between-the-legs bounce dunk, and "elbow in the rim/honey dip" dunks gave us the greatest display of dunking anyone had ever seen. It both resurrected the contest and effectively killed it at the same time, because how could anyone match, let alone raise, such a seemingly impossible bar? Even Carter himself could never do that! Carter was easily anointed the champion of the contest, hoisted the trophy, and never returned to compete. You don't repaint a masterpiece.

But the Vince Carter era almost didn't happen. The disaster that was Darrell Walker's tenure as head coach almost killed the franchise before Vinsanity took off and saved the team. Walker's ineptitude almost ran the team into the ground and out of town. Everyone close to the scene knew that very few fans were going to pay top dollar for an NBA basketball team, a franchise well below the Leafs, Jays, and perhaps even the Argos in popularity, that finished with sixteen wins and sixty-six losses. Remember, CityTV was the official broadcaster of the team. I was connected. People told me things. There was so much nastiness going on behind the scenes when Allan Slaight, the former owner of Q107 who, along with son Gary, brought me in from Halifax in 1986, used a shotgun clause to buy out John Bitove. Then GM Isiah Thomas attempted to execute a letter of intent with Slaight to buy the team and force Slaight out. That failed, so he quit. Yowza! Thomas had been the face of the franchise since day one. That look, that smile, that positive attitude. Well, he was going to need that, because the next day he joined the NBA on NBC as the lead game analyst with play-by-play man Bob Costas. So Thomas was out, and the star of the team Damon Stoudamire was sulking. "Mighty Mouse," as Stoudamire was known, immediately sought a trade. Not long after, he was shipped to the Portland Trail Blazers. Looking back, that 1997/98 season was brutal. As mentioned, Darrell Walker was the coach, and he was so far out of his league, and the Association, it was embarrassing. He was totally disengaged; so withdrawn from his surroundings and responsiblities. And a total asshole. My friend Elliotte Friedman spoke about his relationships with the coach on *HNIC* and stated that "Walker hated me, just hated me." TSN's James Duthie said the same thing about Walker, on air. Again, Walker "led" the team to sixteen wins and sixty-six losses. But he took the easy way out. In February, Walker quit as head coach to be replaced by Butch Carter. Question: What coach quits on a team months before the end of the season? You get fired. You don't quit. Name another coach in professional sports who's quit mid-season? Okay, Rocket Richard quit as head coach of the WHA's Quebec Nordiques in 1972. But it was after the first game. He said he missed his family. But when Walker walked out on his players and his organization, he left a big mess behind.

Future superstar and Hall of Famer Tracy McGrady was a disillusioned eighteen-year-old buried deep in the ex-coach's doghouse. Playing little and with his confidence shot, McGrady's fragile psyche took a beating when

Walker publicity questioned his work ethic, claiming the player was "too cool" to work hard. Walker said, "All McGrady wanted to do was play video games." New GM Glen Grunwald said, "I think the whole thing was a disaster, including how he dealt with Tracy." McGrady said that some of Walker's criticisms hit him hard. "The first year I kind of had an 'I don't care attitude' because of the things he was saying, I kind of got down on myself, but then I started to realize once Butch took over I got the opportunity to go out and really gain some confidence and just put those things in my head and just really turned it around." Darrell Walker would never have a head coaching job in the NBA again. Two last-place finishes, a .313 winning percentage, and a 1.000 percentage at being a rude, course, bald-headed dunce will do that to a guy's career.

The thing about Walker is that he wasn't very bright, or at least media savvy. Here's an example: The Raptors were hosting the soon-to-be three-peat NBA champion L.A. Lakers (2000–2002), and Walker decided to put a guy who would last less than a month as a Raptor, seven-foot journeyman centre Benoit Benjamin (fifteen years in the league for nine different teams) up against Shaquille O'Neal. The guy was a big galoot. Benoit played basketball with all the enthusiasm of a man who's been holding his wife's purse at the mall for three hours. I've had kids at Subway make my sandwich with more fire in their belly. What a mismatch this was going to be, I thought, and during the morning shoot around and in front of half a dozen reporters and TV cameras, I asked the coach about his strategy. "So you're rolling the dice tonight with Benjamin against O'Neal. Tell me this. How has Benoit done against Shaq in his career that would lead you to make this decision?" I inquired. Walker was taken aback, like I was second-guessing him. I wasn't. It just seemed like an odd decision not to put in their new golden boy Marcus Camby with his own "Shaq-attack" instead. Walker, obviously flustered, snapped back, "Why don't you ask *him*? Don't ask me, ask *him* how he did against Shaq!" as in "How do I know?" And it dawned on me that he didn't know the answer. He hadn't done any homework on the situation or any advanced scouting. He was just going on a stupid hunch. Or, he was just trying to send a message by sitting Camby, who was selected second overall in the first round of the 1996 NBA draft by the Raptors and would later make the NBA All-Rookie First Team. The same message he would send to Tracy McGrady the next year: "I'm a narrow-minded dickhead and,

Four-time NBA champ Shaquille O'Neal at the 1994 World Basketball Championship in Toronto.

oh yeah, I'm the boss." I followed up. "You don't *know* how Benjamin has done against Shaquille in the past, because you don't know, do you?" Walker just repeated his previous inept answer. "Just ask *him* how he did against Shaquille. Go ahead and ask him!" and stormed off. He wasn't done. While I was actually asking Benjamin, the big centre, about his history with Shaq, Walker busts in and yells, "Ask him ... go ahead and ask him that question you asked me!" "Whoa, whoa, whoa, man!" I shot back. "I know this is your first year as coach, but this is not the way we do things around here. I'm conducting an interview here. You had your turn!" Walker, fuming, barged away past reporters again. Funny thing. Benjamin started the game, was ineffective, and was replaced by Camby, who popped in fifteen, helping the Raptors to a colossal upset of the Lakers 93–92. On a side note, it's amazing what you find out about former Raptors after their playing days are over, even someone as inconsequential as Benoit. His basketball career was, safe to say, uninteresting at best. But the real kicker is that Benjamin turned out to be a dead-beat dad of record proportions, at one time ordered to pay a whopping $517,200 in back child support.

Anyway, back to Walker. He was as disliked a coach as I've ever encountered. I felt like he always tried to find ways to screw me after that. And as head coach, he could. But it was silly junior-high-school "we're not going to let you hang out with the cool kids" stuff. *Mean Girls* mentality. Like the time I was doing a live eye on CityTV from Gretzky's restaurant for a pre-opening game party, and I could see Walker coaxing his star players *not* to go on camera live with me. Ah, excuse me, I'm trying to promote the team and help ticket sales, you moron. Or the time a CityTV cameraman and I went all the way to Buffalo to cover the team's pre-season training camp. Sometimes the team held their camp in Halifax or Vancouver. This time it was Buffalo. The Raptors media relations people posted a daily update on when the team was working out, and that day it was something like ten a.m. to noon. When we arrived, Walker noticed that I was the lone TV crew on hand, so he promptly cancelled practice and announced that they would be going over video tape in a boardroom instead. It was my contention that he did it for the sole purpose of forcing me to head back to Toronto with no practice highlights or footage of any kind. And no story. We had travelled to another country, and this joyless, contentious, insufferable excuse for a man deliberately altered the entire day's schedule out of spite. I had to get something, so my cameraman and I crashed the Raptors' breakfast at the team hotel, interviewed a few players, and gladly chowed down on their huge buffet just to piss him off. I could see him seething, and he even yelled over, telling us that this was a closed team function and that we were not supposed to be there. I sauntered over to his table, smiled, and politely asked if he had any Tabasco sauce for my eggs. Putz.

My favourite moment covering the Raptors came in late summer of 1997, when the team headed down to the Bahamas for an unofficial week of training. The flight left on September first. Diana Spencer had died the night before in a limousine crash in Paris. It was all anyone could talk about as we boarded the plane at stupid o'clock in the morning. The week-long trip was outstanding. Just me, my cameraman Tom Adetuyi, and a reporter from TSN, who, incidentally, fell through a manhole during an early morning jog with me through the streets of Bridgetown. I yelled down to him in the sewage, "I'll pull you up if you put in a good word to convince TSN to give me my own talk show!" He must have. They did the next year!

Now, the NBA players association prohibited teams from training before their camps officially opened, so it was more of a goodwill tour and vacation. Off the record, the team *did* work out, but I was not at the practices and we didn't film anything. Good, another day at the beach or the resort pool for me! The team and my TV crew golfed and attended autograph signings and youth camps for local kids together. We even played beach volleyball and water polo at the pool. I spent most of the time hanging out with Isiah Thomas and sitting by the pool with the players drinking and working on our tans. The best thing was that Walker never, ever came down to socialize. Not once. I could see him in his room high above the grounds looking down at us with his jogging suit on and sunglasses. He was probably pondering his 16–66 season and him quitting the team in February. Again, that season was the low point. Not only did Walker drive them into the ground and lose his only job as NBA coach, but Toronto almost lost the team. Period. I was close to many of the high ups in the Raptors organization, and things weren't going at all well. This was before the Raptors were bought by the Leafs. They had been going on their own, and it looked dubious. It was scary. Low attendance and a weak Canadian dollar weren't helping the Vancouver Grizzlies, whose owners were losing big money. That team was sold and landed in Memphis. The feeling was not good in Raptorsland, but they muddled through.

I got to know big man Marcus Camby quite well in his rookie season. We got along famously in the Caribbean. Sometimes I'd run into him at different nightclubs in Toronto. At six foot eleven, he was hard to miss when he walked into a bar. One late night at a club in the mid-nineties, he walked in and looked rather "disoriented, sporting that glazed-over Expo Ellis Valentine look that I'd seen years before. I stopped him and said hello, and he just floated by like his feet never touched the ground. I knew he was on something. Ask anyone around the league — Camby is a notorious pothead. Allegedly.

Hundreds of Raptors came and went over the years that I covered them. John Salley played just twenty-five games with the team in their first season, but the future actor and talk show host was a hit with everybody. Funny, outgoing, and a great interview, he even took me under his long, outstretched muscular wing a few months later when we met at the House of Blues VIP room in Los Angeles, and he introduced me and my girlfriend around. Funny, he was a big player on the Pistons during their NBA championship teams, got zero playing time in Toronto and got out of his contract, and then won another title with the Chicago Bulls the next year. Then retired. Sweet. Among the players who made my job covering the team a breeze were Morris Peterson, Alvin Williams, Popeye Jones (who my friend John Derringer would hilariously mock on air because of his resemblance to Bubba from *Forrest Gump*), Jerome "Junk Yard Dog" Williams, and Doug Christie — and his wife. They were inseparable, and she supposedly made every decision on his behalf, so you can't have one on your top-ten list without the other. "Whipped" doesn't even begin to describe the relationship between Doug and his wife, Jackie.

Antonio Davis was also a favourite. I had some friends come in from Halifax with their eight-year-old kid and got them courtside seats. I asked Davis if the kid could take one shot during warm-up. He obliged, and the lad, a natural, sunk a three-pointer and posed with me and the always smiling Davis under the basket. But if you ask any fan or media type who their all-time favourite Raptor was, Charles Oakley tops a lot of lists. "Oak" helped the Raptors finally win a playoff series, a huge upset of his former team, the Knicks. The Raps had traded the much younger and more athletic Camby to New York in exchange for the big, grizzled veteran Oakley. Charles brought an incredibly aggressive attitude and a tough, take-no-prisoners mentality to a team that had been all too easy to push around. He was thrilled to be in Toronto (not everyone was) and knew his job. I was pleasantly surprised that he liked it in Toronto because he hated the Raptors' jerseys. According to the website Deadspin, "Remember when the Toronto Raptors entered the NBA wearing their cartoon dinosaur jersey?" (Well, someone thought these were okay. I mean, they were mocked at the time, but not enough. Not enough.) Oakley used some really strong (and homophobic) language to describe the jerseys and he was never one to keep his voice down. Oakley's fellow Knick Anthony Mason said "Dinosaurs, brotha? If I was you, I'd fuckin' kill myself."

Yikes. Now, my favourite Oakley moment was when he whipped a ball at the head of Philadelphia 76ers forward Tyrone Hill during a morning shootaround in April of 2001. He was suspended for one game without pay and fined $10,000. It was the third time that season that Oakley had been involved in an altercation with an opposing player, and the second such incident with Hill. It was weird. The 76ers were preparing to leave the court after the shootaround when the Raptors arrived. That's when I showed up. Oakley walked over to Hill and the two exchanged some nastiness. I couldn't make it out. Then, Oakley threw a ball at Hill from about six feet, hitting him in the head. *Smack!* Wow, I thought, you don't see *that* everyday. The players were kept apart, but Oakley then threw a second ball at Hill from farther away while screaming. He missed. I heard him yell, "I'll do that every time I see you. Where you going to be this summer, n****r? I'll come find you!" I thought the feud might have been over a woman, but I found out later it stemmed from a debt close to $60,000, owed to Oakley. Charles was one of the strangest interviews I've encountered. So, with that, I'll let Oak have the final say on this chapter. Years later, when he was asked, on his bobblehead night at the ACC, whether he ever expected to become a bobblehead, he said, "Well, I have a head, so you never know what could happen." He actually said that. Ah, Oakley. God love you.

THIRTY-ONE

ALL TALK. NO ACTING.

(or, I open my eyes and realize Paris Hilton is sleeping
next to me while rock goddess Joan Jett waits her turn)

Let's just face facts. I'm a terrible actor. On the stage or screen, anyway. Granted, I've always told any and all high school and university students with ambitions of someday making it in this business that if you're not acting when you're on the air, be it radio or TV, you're lying. It's all an act. You're selling *your* product. You're selling *yourself.* But those are just five-minute sportscasts, or twenty-two minutes on your national TV show. And, I reckon it worked. After all, they don't give Foster Hewitt Memorial Awards out to chimpanzees. Maybe they do. The fact that, as of this writing, I have one and Don Cherry doesn't is beyond belief. But when it comes to the big screen, it just hasn't worked out. And I'm being kind. I was up for a screen roll portraying the ringside announcer for *Phantom Punch*, starring Ving Rhames as former heavyweight champion Sonny Liston. I knew every minute of that second Ali-Liston fight, the history behind it, every jab, every shuffle. I nailed the audition with an ad lib that blew eveybody away. "Jersey Walcott has stopped the fight! He has *stopped the fight!*" Didn't get it. I also didn't see it, as it went straight to DVD. *Total Recall* with Colin Farrell? No. *Snowcake* starring Sigourney Weaver and the late Alan Rickman? They passed. A sportscaster in the race car film *Driven* with Sly Stallone, shot at the Molson Indy? Perfect, right? Wrong.

So, one day my agent sent me in to audition for a horror movie, one of dozens shot in a regular week up here in Hollywood North. The script called for somebody portraying a futuristic "Entertainment Tonight" type with flashy clothes and big blue hair. Okay, then. Now, usually the casting director would sit behind a desk and go over the lines with you. On this occasion it was just me in an empty room and someone from the casting agency, who had *no* involvement in picking the actors for the film, behind the camera. They wanted "over the top"? I gave them over the top. When I asked who was in this low-budget B-movie, the gentleman replied, "Paris Hilton!" "Well, good luck with that," I yelled back, à la Jerry Seinfeld. I guess that did bring me good luck, because I got it. My first major movie role. Toronto radio veteran Humble Howard Glassman and I were cast in, get this title, *Repo! The Genetic Opera*, directed by Darren Lynn Bousman, who was responsible for the *Saw* horror movie series. *Repo* is a horror musical about organ recipients who face a visit from the repo man if they fall behind on the payments.

Besides Paris Hilton, the movie starred Paul Sorvino, Sarah Brightman, Joan Jett, and, for anyone who's a fan of *Little Britain*, veteran English actor Anthony Head, who played the prime minister. He was also Rupert Giles in *Buffy the Vampire Slayer*. All we talked about between takes was *Little Britain*, one of my top-ten all-time fave TV shows. Hanging around backstage with these folks was an absolute hoot. It's all about hurrying up and waiting, and, in my case, standing in front of a green screen. But when you spend hours discussing Paul Sorvino's role as Paulie in *Goodfellas* with Robert DeNiro and Joe Pesci, well, I could think of worse ways to spend a cold afternoon on a sound stage in Toronto. Truth be known, all Paul wanted to talk about was his then-new line of Italian sausages that he was pitching to ShopRite, a New Jersey–based retailer-owned chain. He wrote down the website where I could order them, and right out of *Goodfellas* said, "And if you don't buy my sausages, I gotta turn my back on you," and walked away, leaving the make-up room roaring with laughter. It was an eclectic cast to say the least. Sarah Brightman, who played Blind Mag, was once married to Andrew Lloyd Webber. There was a lively chat. Also, how many people do you know who bought the first two Runaways LPs in the mid-1970s? Joan Jett was impressed.

Then there was Paris. Ahhh, Paris Hilton, who at the time was at the top of her fame game, famous just for being famous. Nice gig if you can get it. The local crew working on the film told me that our little Hollywood starlet had some late, late nights while filming and that "marijuana cigarettes" (as I jokingly like to call them) were her substance of choice. Everybody knew that she was in the city filming, so this quickly came to be known as the "Paris Hilton movie" shooting around town. I, well, "met" her once on set. With the hustle and bustle of five a.m. wake-up and make-up calls, there were a lot of comings and goings in the early hours. And yes, one morning after getting my ghoulish and futuristic make-up on, that I am almost *positive* Stanley Tucci's make-up artists "borrowed" for the big-budget *Hunger Games* trilogy (the comparison is uncanny), I look over and see "our" Paris, our star, fast asleep in the make-up chair right next to me. I mean, right out. Again, I'm thinking, this is something that you don't see everyday, huh? Joan Jett and I exchanged winks. Upon its release, the film received dozens of negative reviews and a 35 percent approval rating on Rotten Tomatoes. One reviewer wrote, "I don't know if words can describe just how awful and disgusting and insulting this movie was to watch." It was a box office bomb, earning $146,000 in North America. But it wasn't until that year's Razzie awards, celebrating the absolute worst in cinema, when I yelled "All right!" The film was up for an award. I mean, if you're not going to have a part in *Citizen Kane*, *Gone with the Wind*, and the greatest films of all time, then why not be in one of the worst? I was. With three nominations, Paris Hilton tied the record for most Razzies in *my* film debut. Bonus! It's been said of Hilton, "She is the twenty-first-century Zsa Zsa Gabor. She is famous for who she hangs out with. She's not famous for any talent she has yet exhibited." Of course, she won the Razzie. I loved it. And this, too: the movie has gained serious cult movie status over the years since its release in 2008. In fact, it was rated as the twenty-second greatest cult film of all time by *Rolling Stone* magazine. The winner was a film I have seen over two hundred times — the low-budget 1975 classic *Rocky Horror Picture Show*. Could any other movie possibly have won this poll? Like *Repo*, *Rocky Horror* tanked when it came out, but within months a fiercely devoted cult started seeing it over and over, dressing up like the characters and singing along to the songs. The tradition continues today. Just like *Repo*. Mmm, maybe I'll be part of a Fan Expo autograph session soon. Hey, a paying gig is a paying gig.

Even the big name films I'm in sadly tank. In the 2016 gun-control big budget film *Miss Sloan*, filmed in Toronto, I played a New York–area Rush Limbaugh–type radio host. In the credits, I was listed between *ET Canada*'s Rick Campanelli and the wonderful Christine Baranski. The movie tumbled, then collapsed at the box office in its first weekend, taking in only $1.9 million. *Forbes* summed it up by saying the movie "bombed" and that it had been expanded "with tragic results." What did they expect? People want to be entertained at the theatre, not preached to. The fact was, I couldn't even save a big budget film with Oscar winners from tanking. Mind you, it was a pleasure to sit around the set with actors such as Jessica Chastain, along with Michael Stuhlbarg, Sam Waterston, and John Lithgow. And the film's director, John Madden, and I hit it off from the get-go at the audition.

I once went for a TV audition to portray an after-dinner speaker at a golf tournament. Strangely, when you walk into these "cattle calls," you see every single sportscaster, past and present, sitting in the waiting room. Yes, a dozen sportscasters, plus half the cast of Second City's comedy troupe. So, for this one, the script *actually* read, "Looking for male 35–55, veteran sportscaster — think Jim Van Horne or John Gallagher–type." John Gallagher–type? I *am* John Gallagher. Still didn't get it. No word of a lie. What an actor, eh?

I posted that story on Facebook and received quite a response. Some examples: From Steve Anthony — "Exact same thing, Johnson. Auditioned for something that was described as a 'Steve Anthony–type.' I didn't get it either." Then there was *the* quintessential North American voiceover veteran Earl Mann. Remember those epic NFL films on VHS and DVD with slow-motion montages of game highlights, while that perfect voice offered insightful commentary? That was my friend Earl Mann. He wrote, "The exact same thing happened to me, John. Last year I received an audition from my agent at Wm. Morris telling me that the client 'wanted the v/o to sound like Earl Mann.' Rather smuggly I layed down a few reads and my producer pressed 'send' … Needless to say they booked someone else as the announcer. Maybe I just didn't sound enough like *me*!"

THIRTY-TWO

(NOT SUCH A) ROCK 'N' ROLL SUICIDE

(or, the only thing worse than not having a father was having mine)

Mmm, I think somebody might have daddy issues, and I think that someone might be me. Hey, remember the TV sitcom *The Courtship of Eddie's Father?* I know that catchy theme is probably still bouncing in your head: "People let me tell you 'bout my best friend / He's a one-boy cuddly toy / My up my down my pride and joy …" Bill Bixby was not my father. I repeat. *Not* my father. Nor was my dad the typical father you'd see in other sixties television shows like *My Three Sons, Family Affair,* or *The Andy Griffith Show.*

My father grew up in rural New Brunswick during a very rough time for many families all around the world. It was after WWI and the Great Depression. He came from a large family of seven kids (my mom was from a family of eight). His dad died when he was eight, and his mother ruled the home with an iron fist. He grew up in an era when force and mental discipline were de rigueur, and in his way of thinking, that was the way to bring up a family. Perhaps he could not make the switch to a more gentle way of managing his family and showing that there were other forms of discipline that are less harmful. His house, his rules.

I see Facebook posts on Father's Day from friends who celebrate and honour the passing of their dads over and over. "Miss you, Dad," and "There's not a day goes by that I don't think about you." Touching, and all

Your author, just after losing in the Gerber baby food label auditions in the early sixties.

of them true, I'm sure. But one year, little Mr. Daddy Issues came up with this brilliant Father's Day eulogy: "Francis James Gallagher — 1927–1974. At least the beatings stopped." A few of my brothers and sisters (there are six of us) were mortified and told me so, but it still doesn't take away the fact that it happened. And it damaged me as a child. It made for a fearful childhood, and I'm here to tell you that children shouldn't be living with fear.

I look back, and I think I should have been quite content. I was generally a happy kid growing up in the Toronto suburb of Etobicoke and later in the quaint little town of Montreal West. My friends talked about candy, cartoon characters, baseball cards, and Raquel Welch's breasts. Our family enjoyed an upper-middle-class lifestyle. I played Little League and vacationed every summer on the grand banks of Grand Lake in New Brunswick.

On a side note: One of the fondest, and scariest, moments from my childhood was when I went fishing for pike at this fruitful and fantastic pond near the cottage at six a.m. I was by myself, or at least I thought I was, when a five-hundred-pound eight-point bull moose that was out foraging for the day appeared out of the bush and right over my left shoulder. I just froze until he pulled some weeds up from the pond and, chewing on them, snorted at me and sauntered away. It wasn't until his frost-filled breath hit me like the waft of a wave. Bam. Worse then Howard Cosell's. It would have made a memorable selfie.

The Gallaghers took long family car and train rides all across North America. We were the first family on the block to get a colour TV. We had two cars. We went to the best private Catholic schools. So why, then, did I try to commit suicide at the ripe old age of nine? Difficult to comprehend, to be sure. I will say this. A good majority of my memories with my father were warm and sunsplashed, as evident in the 8mm films that he took over the years. Well, it looked like I was having fun anyway. Some of those moments are burned in my brain. Some examples? Again, these are not Brian Keith, Fred MacMurray, or even Herman Munster moments, but I'll take 'em. It was the mid-sixties, and we'd taken a family trip to Lake Louise. We were staying at my dad's co-worker's house, and he and I got up to fetch a glass of water from the kitchen at the same time (it's two a.m.). He says, "Hey, I'm hungry, son. How about you and I go get a hamburger?" Still in my pajamas, we went to one of those twenty-four-hour A&W drive-in joints. It's still the single best hamburger I've had in my life.

Dad wasn't a very affectionate man. You've heard the Carly Simon song that starts with, "My father sits at night with no lights on. His cigarette glows in the dark. The living room is still; I walk by, no remark." Well, that was *totally* Frank Gallagher. Dead on. It was hard to steal a kiss or get a hug anywhere near that five o'clock shadow, since you had to maneuver around his ever-present cigarette and highball. All you got was the smell of Brill Cream and cigarette smoke. But when he did show you a little love, you didn't forget it. I do fondly remember him tucking me in and kissing me on the forehead one night. I lied there for about an hour, trying desperately not to ruin the creases of the sheets that he'd pulled up to my chin. In 1967, he took the entire family to view the Disney classic *Jungle Book*. With people lined up around block to see the big-ticket blockbuster, F.J. instead took us to see the crime-filled movie that caused major controversy by redefining violence in cinema. The film was *Bonnie and Clyde*. Oh yeah, I was five. I distinctly remember Dad asking the manager, "Are there any knifings is this film?" When the answer was none, he put his money down. No knife fights, just dozens of people shot in cold blood. That will make a difference, huh? Maybe Dad was trying to set me on a different career path.

Thankfully, a lot of fond recollections with F.J. came down to sports. Frank Gallagher fun fact: As the story goes, when on leave in Manhattan while serving in the navy, he got drunk and busted out the "D" in the front window of the world-famous Dempsey's restaurant, yelling for Jack, the former heavyweight champion, to come out and fight him. He never did. Good thing, too. One of my favourite memories was of him taking me to the Sportsman Show at the CNE or to watch drag racers "Big Daddy" Don Garlits and Don Prudhomme from *Wide World of Sports* at the Cayuga raceway one "Sunday! Sunday! Sunday!" afternoon. Just him and I. Years later I would learn that former NHL star defenceman and my good friend Marty McSorley grew up in Cayuga and hocked hot dogs and soft drinks at the drag strip as a summer job. He said there was a good chance he served me up some fries that day.

I remember playing Little League and telling my coach that "We'd be a way better team if *my* dad was in charge!" Kind of one of those "my dad can beat your dad" acclamations. And he even coached us for a few weeks before we headed out for our annual summer vacation in New Brunswick. Everyone talks about going on family trips back then without seatbelts; well, we packed eight family members into our trusty AMC Rambler, with us lying in the back on cushions and pillows. Seatbelts? Please. And Dad drank the entire time. He always had a cooler filled with beer and a trusty stubby between his legs on those long trips. Then he'd make these left-handed Kareem Abdul Jabbar hook shots with the empties over the roof of the car, and the Gallagher kids would cheer when they'd smash on a rock. Can you imagine?

Do you remember Daniel Stern's character Phil in the film *City Slickers*? He told Billy Crystal about the troubled relationship he had with his father and said, "When I was in my teens and my dad and I couldn't communicate about anything at all, we could still talk about baseball." And that was us. Those trips to Jarry Park in Montreal were the best. He would always leave in the eighth inning to beat traffic, which drove me crazy, but still. It made me feel normal. But I learned at a very young age that I was not normal, and I'm here to tell you that anyone about to act on a suicide at nine is decidedly not normal.

How did I get to that point in my young life? Where do I start? Well, being the quintessential middle child of the six Gallagher kids didn't help. I know that's a mathematical impossibility, but I was in every way, shape, and form "Malcolm in the Middle." It's true what they say about middle children like me. It's a pretty easy term to grasp. There's no need for explanation. A middle child is simply the kid in the middle of their siblings according to age. You could have two siblings or twelve siblings; either way, you can't avoid the math. Sometimes it can be really difficult to feel like you belong in your family, especially when your older brother (Steve) is just like your father and your younger sister (Jackie) is just like your mother. So who am I supposed to be like? Where am I supposed to fit in? What is my role in this family? What am I to do when I am just in the middle and sometimes overlooked? Feelings and questions like these can often make a kid feel like a curse, and they sure did in my case. It always seemed like I was targeted. I looked it up and it's true, all of it. A survey of 1,000 parents and 1,000 middle children was commissioned by TheBabyWebsite.com. They found that the middle child in a family does get less attention than their older and younger siblings. A third of mothers and fathers who have middle children admitted that he or she gets left out. Four out of ten children said they had to fight for attention, and one in three felt there was no real role for them in the family.

Okay, so how did all of this lead to me lying under my bed with a butcher knife pointed at my chest? It has to go back to my father. I know, I'd like to spare you the psycho-babble father-and-son bullshit, but I can't. My father was a rare man. A veteran of World War II who lied about his age and joined the navy at the age of sixteen, he returned from the war broken yet proud. But he never talked about it. Ever. Family, friends, and people close to him during his short lifetime tell me that he was wound up pretty tight. Was the war to blame? Did he suffer from post-traumatic stress disorder? Well, he wouldn't be alone. Heck, even the great actor Jimmy Stewart suffered extreme PTSD after being a fighter pilot in World War II, and acted out his mental distress during *It's a Wonderful Life*. That was just a film. No one wants to see that scenario play out in real life, especially as you hide behind your mother trying to avoid another thrashing from Dad's trusty belt. Sure, spatulas and wooden spoons, and later his canes, were used for beatings, but the belt was his go-to weapon. As I stood and braced myself for a whipping, it seemed like the belt was coming out of the loops of his pants in slow motion. Sticks, or switches as he called them, were also handy. One time at our cottage in New Brunswick, and I'm not making this up, he told me to pick out a switch and whittle all the leaves and stems off it so he could thrash me with it later. Some kids and cousins would see me and ask, "Wow, what are you doing? That looks like fun." If they only knew.

Charming, I know, but it gets worse. On the surface my father seemed like a regular, God-fearing, and at times, convivial family man. A hard-working, award-winning salesman for Liberty Mutual Insurance. But underneath he was a deeply, deeply troubled man. My mother would tell me that we were too much alike. Sure, I was admittedly a yappy little fellow at times, but other kids like me are clumsy, laugh too loud, yawn at their homework, and roll their eyes, too. And I'm pretty sure that, looking back, I obviously suffered from mild symptoms of ADHD. I remember coming home with Cs and Ds, with the odd B, with Father telling me, and I'll never forget this, that I must "apply myself." Whatever *that* meant. Oh yeah, I was seven. I wasn't a terrible student. Just below average. Well below. I never flunked a grade, but I always had major difficulty concentrating on a single issue in class. I was easily distracted, had difficulty paying attention, and would daydream all the time. I remember sitting in a math class one day studying a subject that I hated and secretly knew that I would have no use for in the future. It was a glorious sunny first-day-of-spring afternoon at Montreal West High School. I was sitting by a window that overlooked the huge baseball diamond, with kids playing a pickup game below me, and wanting, no needing, so badly to get down there and join them. It drove me insane. Yes, I've been diagnosed with SAD. No one looks forward to spring more than people with seasonal affective disorder, who grow depressed in the waning light of winter. I mean, on my fourteenth birthday I asked for and received a sun lamp, for goodness sakes. So ADHD and SAD meets PTSD. Nice combination. That was no excuse for the mental and physical abuse I endured during our time together, but my father's punishments were so unusual. So twisted. I will give him points for originality. One of his favourites was to tell me to go upstairs, take off all of my clothes, stand in the middle of my bedroom, and wait until he'd come up to give me a spanking. So I'd do exactly what he told me to, sometimes waiting for hours. I mean, who thinks this shit up? Did he have his own special handbook on childrearing? Some kids get sent to their room without dessert. I got that. Spankings? My father once pulled down my pajama bottoms and spanked my bare bottom in front of a dozen or so co-workers and their wives at a cocktail party he and Mother were hosting at the house. I was absolutely humiliated. As I cried and ran upstairs, my father laughed along with everybody else and poured another round of martinis from the bar. What was the crime? Who knows.

This is so silly, but true: Dad *did* always warn us to stay away from "scary" comics and magazines because they would, of course, give us nightmares. Naturally, one time, being the little shit that I was, I stuffed several *Monsters of Filmland* and *Twilight Zone* (still the best TV show of all time) magazines into a big pile, surrounded by Archie, Batman, and Superman comic books. I got them out of the store, but somehow he caught me with them. I got spanked, and then he ripped them up. This was years before Joan Crawford did this to her daughter in the film *Mommie Dearest,* but sausages for Sunday brunch sometimes meant a long day inside on sunny afternoons. If I was served sausages and didn't eat them — which I never did, and still don't — I would be forced by my father to sit at the dinner table all day, "until you've finished your sausages," while the five other

Gallagher kids jumped through sprinklers and hula hoops. They'd be called in for dinner at five — it was always five o'clock sharp — and I'd still be sitting there with the cold sausages from six hours before staring up at me from my plate. It happened so often that my poor mother stopped serving sausages to save me the ongoing weekly anguish. At those times I'd wish we had a family dog to feed them to. It's funny, if we asked for something big, like a puppy, Dad's reply was always, "Sure, two of them." Mind you, after years of begging to get a dog — I mean a real dog, like a Labrador — Dad brought one home. It was a pure white miniature toy poodle named Emperor Napoleon Bonaparte III, complete with the Town-and-Country clip job, that I got to proudly parade around the block. Fuck it. The little fellow was high maintenance and high strung, but it was still a dog. We quickly named it Snowball.

Was that another test? More mind games? I think he was just getting warmed up. To wit: In 1967, the Beatles (the Fab Four) and the Monkees (the Prefab Four), along with every other "mop-topped" hippy band, were "all that" with their paisley shirts, striped pants, and long hair. I returned home from the barber one day to find out that, in my father's opinion, our neighbourhood coiffeur hadn't taken enough off. Not nearly enough. So Pops takes me, by the ear if I recall, into the car and back to finish the job. Out comes the barber with his electric hair clippers, and he proceeds to shave my hair down to the scalp. That was worse than any spanking I would endure. In fact, I would have preferred a spanking. For the entire "summer of love," I looked like Sergeant Carter's kid from *Gomer Pyle U.S.M.C.* The next day in school, I wanted to die. You could hear the laughter over my new 'do throughout the hallways. I'm not kidding. Yes, the brush cuts, sometimes crew cuts, would continue as long as F.J. was the head of the house. While my brother, his friends, and all of mine got to grow their hair long — sometimes really long — throughout the swingin' sixties, I would, unfortunately, be known as "peach fuzz."

This is a good one — tragic, but true. It's 1969. Now, for months and months I wanted a tape recorder as a gift. I ask you, what future Foster Hewitt award–winning sportscaster didn't want one of those bad boys to tape sporting events off of TV and radio and to tote around the neighbourhood and to Expos and Canadiens games to work on his chops? Christmas came. Nothing. My birthday in April? Nada. What kind of a hint did they want? Fast-forward to late June and my younger sister Jackie's birthday party, with dozens of friends and family gathered around. I think you know what's coming. When she tore the wrapping off her new deluxe Panasonic tape recorder with all the bells and whistles, Jackie looked up dumbfounded and said, "What? This is what John wanted!" We all turned to Frances J., with his cigarette and stubby bottle of Cinci beer. He wore a strange smirk on his face. Then he started laughing. God bless Jackie, who followed Dad's big surprise with a "This better not be my big gift!" comment.

There were other not-so-pleasant surprises. My father cancelled a birthday party, that all of my friends were invited to, at the Royal Ontario Museum (I had a huge thing for dinosaurs) at the last minute. On another memorable birthday, when given the chance to either go to Montreal to take in the opening-day Expos game at Jarry Park or attend the Jimmy Ellis versus George Chuvalo heavyweight fight live at Maple Leaf Gardens, I chose the big fight. Wrong choice. Dad told me that the fight was sold out, so I was SOL. I called the Gardens. Only 6,000 tickets of the 18,000 had been sold. It gets better. Instead of watching a real, live prizefight involving a man who would become a dear friend years later (Chuvalo), I got a pair of North Star running shoes. (North Stars were a Canadian Sears brand that were made to look like Adidas, but they were banned from the gymnasium at schools because they left long blue skid marks on the floor.) Happy birthday. Screw the Expos opener. I got stuck with running shoes I wasn't allowed to run in. Another thing that got me. My brother Steve was always allowed to bring his friends on vacations, fishing excursions, and trips to other cities. Not me, or even my two older sisters, who had seniority, for goodness sakes. My mother and the rest of the family, including myself, could never, ever figure that out. Steve even got an extremely expensive "Little Indian" mini bike for his birthday that year. Are you fucking kidding me? None of this was even close to being fair. There was picking your favourites, but this was beyond comprehension.

It would soon all almost come to an abrupt and tumultous end. The year 1970 was when I attempted to take my own life. During the Christmas before, I'd endured perhaps one of the most terrifying moments a young boy could and should ever experience. It was Christmas Eve and being, of course, excited, I couldn't sleep, so I tiptoed down the hall and noticed that my little sister Judy was looking out the window for eight tiny reindeer to land on the Gallaghers' roof. I suggested we head downstairs to see if the "fat man in red" had already been there. Big mistake. Instead of being as careful as mice in the dark, one of us inadvertently nudged a record player — a gift for my older sister — off a chair, and it came crashing to the floor. As I hurried upstairs to slide under the covers, trying to be inconspicuous and go unnoticed, the door flew open from my parents' room and out came my father hunting for bear. F.J. often had spastic attacks of rage when he was drunk and angry. And as this was Christmas Eve, with lots of drinking, and a son who had the audacity to ruin the big surprise for the rest of the kids, he was both. I'll never forget the closed-fist pounding and punches I received that night. He left me bruised and twitching in my bed. You'd think someone, my mother or even my brother, who was sleeping in the next bed, would have helped me or pulled him off. Looking up at him, I didn't see the man who was supposed to protect me from the monsters in my dreams and under my bed. I saw the monster.

The next day in church I was a complete mess, ashen white, shaking, and completely zoned out. Noticing this, my mother took me to the car in the middle of the service and sat with me for a few minutes. *Well, this Christmas is completely ruined*, I thought, trembling and sobbing. So, like many times before, I lost myself in the world of Mattel's Major Matt Mason, comic-book superheroes, good memories, and hoped that someday I wouldn't have to deal with my father anymore. So I tried to run away. Not to join the circus, but just to get out of that environment. Looking back, it was a silly idea. Obviously. I had a stick with a pillow case tied up at the end filled with items that were sure to last weeks and months: a loaf of bread, peanut butter, a butter knife, and, being a huge fan of Hot Wheels, drag racing and funny cars and my favourite collection of hot rod magazines. Mind you, I only got as far as the Richview Plaza strip mall (off Eglinton in Etobicoke) up the street, a mere ten minutes away. When the word got out that I had run away, from neighbourhood kids (snitches!) who told my parents, my father picked me up at the mall. There was an eerie silence on the quick drive back home. And instead of getting another beating to teach me a lesson, which I surely expected, I got sent to my room without supper while I heard my father and my brother Steve laugh about the contents of my "getaway goody bag" from the living room downstairs.

Running away is always a cry for help, and if it's ever happened to anyone in your family or friends' families, you know that there must be some underlying issues. Instead of Mom or Dad or even my older brothers and sisters asking me if they could do anything or helping to try to get some lines of communication opened, I just got sent to my room. Steve was twelve, Karen thirteen, and Joanne fifteen, so did they give a fiddler's fuck? It seemed no one cared or even understood what their desperate child and brother was experiencing in this world. So much for having "helicopter parents," eh? I mean, gee, how about a hug? I'm trying hard not to come off looking like a wuss in this chapter, but it was a troubling time, and I know it's happened to kids for centuries. You read about Charlize Theron, Christina Aguilera, Halle Berry, Rihanna, Tina Turner, Steve McQueen, Oprah Winfrey, Bill Clinton, and Michael and the entire Jackson family, who were all abused by their parents. They had it much worse, I'm sure.

One of the most famous abusers, besides Joan Crawford, was Bing Crosby. His eldest son Gary wrote a tell-all entitled *Going My Way*. In it, we learned that Bing was very much to blame for all the deep problems his four sons suffered. It was Bing's strict upbringing and lack of love and affection that affected the four Crosby sons for the rest of their lives. In fact, Gary's three younger brothers all committed suicide. I guess there, too, was where I was at the crossroads of my young life. That was the next step, I suppose. Ending it all. Months later, the Gallagher family was experiencing the most beautiful vacation, at Bluewater Beach on Georgian Bay in the summer of 1970. Every recollection I have of that glorious summer was out of a movie. *The Summer of '42*. The opening scene in *Grease*. The sand dunes from *Jaws*, only without the police finding a dead body on the shore. (Or would that also play out? Oooh, the suspense.) Around that time Dad was in a foul mood because my two older sisters had run the battery dead in the family Mustang while trying to get a clear signal from 1050 CHUM back in Toronto. It didn't end well for them. All we heard was bloodcurdling screams as they took the brunt of yet another F.J. tirade. I'm thinking, well, Christmas was a washout, my birthday was complete suckage, and here goes summer vacation. I wanted out of this family and this dysfunctional household. I was just sick of the fact that my parents treated me as if I was not their son.

I think the majority of us have seen the coming-of-age film *Stand By Me* by this point. Well, it wasn't until years and years later, when I saw the film, that I realized that the lead character was actually me. Young Gordie Lachance was, in some aspects, John Gallagher. Wil Wheaton played Gordie, who broke down in front of his best friend Chris Chambers, played by River Phoenix, when describing his own family crisis.

> Gordie: I'm no good. My dad said it. I'm no good.
> Chris: He doesn't know you.
> Gordie: He hates me.
> Chris: He doesn't hate you.
> Gordie: He hates me!
> Chris: No! He just doesn't know you.

We've all had childhood friends that, at the time, were very important to us but that we've since lost track of. The final scene from the film still resonates with me to this day. "It happens sometimes. Friends come in and out of our lives like busboys in a restaurant." If that line doesn't get you thinking, then the last line in the movie will: "I never had any friends later on like the ones I had when I was twelve [or in my case, nine]. Jesus, does anyone?" I had one that summer. Jody was a good-looking older kid who was staying with his family at a nearby cottage. He looked like one of the blond "surfer dude" Van Patten brothers from Hollywood. We hit it off immediately. Like the River Phoenix character, my friend would turn out to be a fiercely loyal, caring, and intelligent kid. He was from a normal family. I read a book by author Laura Bogart titled *Don't You Know That I Love You?* In it, she described her father as "a sad, sick man; a man who'd been broken by the yoke of his past." She wrote, "The thing about growing up in a family like this is, since it's your family, you don't know any better until you are around healthy families, and the horrible imprint left on you, that you don't even know is there, is pulling you around to all kinds of dysfunction." I find it odd now to actually break down and cry in front of a friend, telling him "that my parents don't love me." That just wasn't done. It just wasn't cool. I told Jody of my plan to kill myself. He kept telling me to talk to my parents and tell them about my dire situation. Suicide? "Don't do it," he kept telling me. "Don't do it." I could sense he could see the pain, the film of grief filling in my eyes. He told me my situation must be confronted and resolved. I couldn't do it. Then Jody said something to me that I remember to this day. It wasn't touching or moving or poignant or anything. I mean, the kid was probably twelve or thirteen, but he seemd to know his subject matter very, very well. He just said, "Johnny boy, when they find you, you're not exactly going to smell like perfume from Paris." Man, he nailed that one, huh?

I would cry myself to sleep at night a lot that summer. I was just terribly sad. If I recall, there was nothing that my father did to me that night to set me off, when the moment came to actually "do" it. But in the middle of the night, I half-instinctively went to the kitchen and took one of my mother's longest butcher knives, crawled under my bed, and pointed it toward my chest. I lay there crying for some time. But when I thought so intensely about ending it all, I never thought about the screaming and the blood that was to immediately ensue. Keep in mind, I'm nine, but I never thought of wanting my parents, even though I hated them and knew they hated me, to have to live with the heartbreak of a son committing suicide. Especially my mom. And what about my five soon-to-be-remaining siblings? What would be the subject of their "What I did on my summer vacation" essay in September? Years of endless pointing and whispering, "Their brother commited suicide." Most of all, I didn't want Mom and Dad and my brother and sisters attending my funeral.

I cried and cried some more. And, ultimately, I think I just went to sleep after that.

My father died a few years later in 1974 from cancer. At six foot two, my dad weighed less than ninety pounds when he passed. I got the phone call from Montreal just after Christmas. I was standing in the exact room where he was born, a short forty-seven years before, in Minto, New Brunswick. My parents had sent me and my little nine-year-old sister out east after Christmas, sensing he was in his final days. Telling young Judy that she was now without a father was not the highlight of the trip. I distinctly remember my wonderful aunt Caroline holding her annual Christmas party, which just so happened to be on the night he died. She and my father were the two youngest of the eight. Nat, one of my uncles, without an ounce of compassion, asked me, "So, John, do you think it's going to be an open casket or a closed casket?" I'm thinking, *Really? You ask a grieving little kid that on the day his father died?* I spent the rest of the night crying under the dozens of winter coats the guests had thrown on a bed. It all happened so quickly, my father dying.

My "Irish twin" sister Jackie told me years later that he probably died of embarrassment. He was too embarrassed to have the cancerous lump on his testicle checked, and it spread everywhere. My father used to partake in a strange ritual where he, my brother, and I used to shower together. Not all of the time, mind you, but still. After he did have one of his testicles removed, well, there it was in the shower one night, looking me right in the eye. Looking back, I should have acted like an MLB umpire and yelled out "Ball one!" Come on, I think we all need a little levity at this point, don't you think?

The timing was also bad for the entire family. In the fall of 1973, he had informed us that we were selling the house and moving to San Francisco, California, because he had been offered a huge promotion from Liberty Mutual and jumped at the chance. San Francisco? Wow, I loved Montreal, but that was one of the greatest cities on the planet.

Why would I ever get married when I have this young lady? With Mary Stella Gallagher, apparently just before I headed off with the Rat Pack in 1995.

I often wondered how much our lives would have changed had he not gotten sick and we had moved there.

As for my wonderful mother, Mary, I always tell her that I've never got married because "I have you, Mother." She was much more than just a shield I hid behind on the days my father wanted to "make a point."

And admittedly, in later years growing up as a teen, I was quite a handful. Despite having success in sports, drama, and public speaking, I was a terrible student. Brutal. In fact, I made Ferris Bueller look like class valedictorian. Before graduation, with the class ring ordered and the colour photo sent out to all the relatives, I decided to go to Daytona Beach for spring break with some friends in 1979. Only problem is that I fell madly in lust with a gorgeous blonde who was in from Georgia Tech. I ended up spending the next month or so doing odd jobs and staying in her off-campus apartment in Atlanta. When I came home later that summer, my mother had one word for me: "Out!" Mind you, less than a year after being expelled, I miraculously (okay, it some some talent and good timing) landed the job as morning show co-host and six o'clock sportscaster at CHSJ in Saint John, and she and I held each other and cried in her living room. I'll never forget that. Tears of joy. And when you were in those arms, it was the safest place to be in the world.

And she turned out to be the most rocking mom in the neighbourhood. At least in Rothesay, New Brunswick. Mary Gallagher was a cool "new wave" mom. To wit: She would invite all the members of my hockey team to watch World Series and Stanley Cup games and such in the basement, which had a big TV and a fridge full of beer, saying, "If you're going to drink, why do it in the dugout of the baseball diamond when you can do it here and watch the game?"

But she could also be "unpredictable," and not in a good way. I brought home a "dime bag" of some fine blond Kashmir hashish that I purchased in Montreal prior to the Frampton/J. Geils concert on the day Elvis Presley died in August '77. After a week of frantically searching through all of the socks that I had stuffed this primo hash into a week before (a week that included conversations with siblings who promised they would pummel me if they caught me lighting up), I finally confronted Mommie Dearest, who told me that she had indeed found said stash (I mean, who cleans *clean* socks?) and took the little baggie to the police! She said, "They're not going to arrest you, they just want to talk." To which I, pissed off that my little blond bundle was gone forever, queried, "Why would you do that?" Mom replied, "I read it in the *Reader's Digest*. That's what they suggested I do, and I did. Err, was that wrong?" I would've preferred if she'd said, "It was the final thought from Huggy Bear on this week's *Barretta* episode!" Epilogue: No "talk," hence no charges, no harm, no foul. Just some very happy and high policeman in Rothesay, N.B.

I have always wondered how she kept her sanity with six kids and a husband who wasn't the easiest man to live with when he was alive. She kept the family sane in sickness and in health. Even after Dad's death and managing the move to the Maritimes, I never once saw Mom wring her hands in worry or fear. She soldiered on. My sister Jackie remembers, "I loved that she would rather be baking than cleaning her house. An apple pie trumped dust bunnies! Mom always cared about what her kids were up to and loves to hear the stories we share. Mom has never been a complainer, even in 1995, when her whole body was attacked by arthritis and not one part of her body was spared by pain. She soldiered on. Now at ninety-two, I am amazed at her strength and amazing attitude. Losing the use of her legs after a recent stroke has not stopped her. There is no time for self-pity and she enjoys her life. There are bingo games to win and singalongs to attend." Keep your chin up, she says, and soldier on.

In the years leading up to his death, and with the inevitable a matter of months away, I tried to spend as much time with my father as possible. I mean, hello, I'm going through puberty over here! Got a question or two for the old man! I became his personal orderly, wheeling him to and from his cobalt treatments at different hospitals around Montreal. I remember one day I arrived at his room at the Reddy Memorial Hospital, near the Forum, and he had the biggest smile on his face. A reporter from TV station CFCF had been to my class that day to do a story on sex education and I had been interviewed. I remember it like it was yesterday. While being filmed, I asked my sex-ed teacher, "What happens if you have to urinate when you're having sex and instead of sperm pee comes out?" A fair enough question from a twelve-year-old, right? Well, after the cameras had left, my teacher scolded me for a being a showoff and asking such a question. Hey, I made the cut, didn't I? My dad saw it from his sick bed and thought it was hilarious. He beamed. And, hey, not a bad way to kickstart my TV career, huh?

A few months later, a strange thing happened. On what would be his farewell tour back to New Brunswick in the late summer of 1974, Dad took me aside and told me something that I'll never forget. With mere months to go, my father was getting his "house" in order, and he went to financial advisor, who wanted a description of all of the Gallagher kids. A few days later, in his final report, the man told my father that I would be the rock of the family, the "go-to guy" sort to speak within the family and moving forward during the coming years. My dad told the man, and me that day, "No, you mean Steven, not John." "No," the man said, "I've analyzed everything you've given me. I've talked with other relatives and friends about your kids. This is my final report: it's John." Well, I didn't know how to take it at the time, but that didn't stop my father from giving me one final thrashing later that "holiday." With his cane. Can you believe it? I don't even remember what I said this time, but he began beating me with his cane at an empty cottage. Less than three months before his final breath, and he's getting his last licks in. I distinctly remember him hitting me quite dispassionately. Never raising his voice. Always even-tempered. He never blew the old cool.

And I could have taken him out. Again, he was a ninety-pound weak-ling! I even grabbed him and hugged him and said something along the lines of, "You *can't*! I'm the chosen one!" It didn't work. But when he died, the beatings stopped. I would ask my dear mother, Mary, about all of the abuse. She told me, "I think he enjoyed it." Strangely, I became somewhat obsessed with my father in adulthood. I started collecting his sales trophies, awards, and photos, and I even got ahold of his favourite ashtray. I'd even fly into his hometown of Minto to visit with his remaining siblings and talk for hours about what he was like growing up. Sure, admittedly I was chasing a ghost, but I needed some closure.

One night years ago, when my TSN show was doing well, I was drink-ing with my brother Steve. He was in one of those Guinness-aided, "You're the only brother I'm ever going to have" moods. He started to cry when I asked him how Dad would feel about *The Gallagher Show* being the number-one talk show in the country (there wasn't much to choose from at the time. Michael Landsberg? Mike Bullard? Dini Petty?) on TSN. (Steve and his wife Joanie's three kids cried when Steve came home from work the day my show was cancelled. I heard they ran to his car as he was getting out and demanded that he call the network to try to reverse the decision.) Steve told me how much my father was so proudly Irish and he out and out loved the Gallagher name. And sports. And here I was, Steve told me, with my own national TV show on The Sports Network, called *Gallagher*. He said he'd be over the moon. Kind of like that day in his hospital bed when he saw me on TV and beamed at me and gave me a little wink as if to say, just like Phil in *City Slickers*, "You know? I mean, my dad's not the warmest of men. But he winked. And I remember thinking, I'm grown up. You know, I'm not a goofball anymore. I made it. I felt like a man. That was the best day of my life."

And it would certainly have been for me. But if you had to sum up my short but turbulent time with my father, it was if we were like strangers who knew each other very, very well.

Thank God for rock and roll and David Bowie. You know, when I was going through a tough time trying to "find myself" as a tween, Bowie was there for me and millions of others just like me. And for that, I am forever grateful. As it all hit the fan in the same year that my father, Frank James Gallagher, left this mortal coil, I turned to the words of rock's greatest gift, David Bowie, who seemed to have pointed right at me in row D of the fabled Forum in Montreal, and sang "Rock 'n' Roll Suicide" just to me. The message was you're not alone.

So, what have we learned here? To stay in school, go to university, make something out of your life, get married, raise kids, and so on and so forth? Or take the road "less travelled." Drop out of high school and chase skirt all over Florida during spring break. Then be hosting the CBC six o'clock sportscast just a few months later. Sure, a little talent and some big connections will get you places in life but that was ridiculous. Then, I'm starting in goal alongside my heroes on Team Canada '72, sparring with Muhammad Ali, lighting David Bowie's cigarette while Howard Cosell lights mine, playing in front of 20,000 fans *against* the Harlem Globetrotters, making half a million dollars a year, hosting my own national TV show, covering every sporting event I've ever wanted to, and travelling the world while dating the most beautiful women in the country? And along the way hobnobbing with names like Sugar Ray,

Aykroyd, Belushi, Will Ferrell, Colin Farrell, Kevin Spacey, Robert Plant, Pete Rose, Billy Martin, Michael Jordan, Wayne Gretzky, and Grandpa Munster, and speaking "double dutch" with a *real* double duchess, Princess Di. Can you repeat that? What was that middle part again?

There's a brilliant line in the film *Broadcast News* where William Hurt's character asks Albert Brooks's character, "What do you do when your real life exceeds your dreams?" Brooks replies, "Keep it to yourself."

Oops. Too late.

It's true. Sometimes you can be walking around lucky and not even know it.

ACKNOWLEDGEMENTS

Firstly, let me say *this* about *that*: This entire not-so-dangerous undertaking has been an absolute pleasure from start to finish. And in this first — and hopefully not last — foray into writing a book, the members of Team Gallagher, as I call them, have been the most talented, patient, and understanding group of literary professionals that I've had the pleasure to work with. It's been like going on a rock music tour with the best roadies and lighting and sound technicians.

I am a voracious reader, so writing this book and going through the process with a wonderful literary agent and publisher has been nothing short of fascinating. When I was growing up, sportswriters had as much influence on me as DJs Ralph Lockwood and Duke Roberts, and TV types Dick Irvin Jr., Danny Gallivan, Dick Enberg, and Howard Cosell. (Heck, I even got Howard Cosell's book *Cosell* for Christmas in 1974, when I was knee high to Yvan Cournoyer.) *Sports Illustrated*'s Frank Deford, Rick Reilly, the *Detroit Free Press*'s Mitch Albom, Jim Murray of the *Los Angeles Times*, and Dick Young, who uttered, "This is one of the few businesses where you can laugh while you work," were gods, as were the Canadian writers I was lucky enough to meet including Red Fisher (who actually sat down and wrote a pen to paper thank you note after being on TSN's *Gallagher* show), and the dearly departed Trent Frayne, Ted Blackman, Earl McRae, John Robertson, Jim Hunt, and Milt Dunnell. Back in the seventies, when *Montreal Gazette* veteran writer Tim Burke came to our house to do a story on my boxing brother, Steve, I tried to convince him to stuff me into his suitcase before he left for Expos spring training the next morning. Sadly, I didn't fit.

Big thanks to Dundurn managing editor Kathryn Lane, whose time and space were intruded upon, lo these many months, while helping me write this book. Thanks to Scott Fraser who unravelled storylines during long conversations and nights out. He's also the man whose task it was to chop seventy-five thousand words from the manuscript to get *Big League Babble On* down to the size you're holding in your hands now.

Publisher Kirk Howard, who has been at Dundurn since day one, has stood by this project from the get-go. You have impeccable taste, good sir. Editor Jenny Govier, who I could always make laugh during our conversations, was a big help, as was Jaclyn Hodsdon, my publicist. Laura Boyle designed the cover, which just jumps off the shelf. (People have told me they'd buy the book for the front cover alone!) Courtney Horner designed the interior, which rocks. Also, thanks be to Margaret Bryant, Sheila Douglas, and Lorena Gonzalez Guillen.

Props to Haskell Nussbaum, Sam Hiyate, and Cassandra Rodgers at the Rights Factory for shopping around this long-winded, self-obsessed, name-dropping tell-all and getting it picked up. They, along with friends and fellow authors, sent a lot of good karma my way despite the fact there wasn't a sniff of evidence that I could write at all. Thank you to award-winning author Perry Lefko for his not-so-subtle critiques that always forced me to up my game. The *Globe and Mail* once asked me years ago in an interview, "What do you most value in your friends?" My answer: "They take my calls." While I was writing this book, Perry always answered.

I've been lucky enough to be hired by some of the true giants of the media in Canada, including Moses Znaimer, who hired me three times (!) and has been a mentor for decades, the wonderful Waters family at CHUM/ CITY, and Gary Slaight and his father Allan, just to name a few.

To all of my best friends, and mostly to my girlfriends and ex-lovers (many show up on these pages but some don't, like my BFF Joanne Ball), for lighting the candles and popping the corks, for their late-night silliness and love, and for their funny dances. And thanks to my beautiful chocolate Labs, Reuben Kincaid, Richard Dreyfuss, and the insanely lovable Nicely Nicely Johnson, for watching over all of us.

A shout-out to brother Steve; sisters Karen, Jackie, and Judy, and Jo Ann (who left us just recently but lives in spirit through her son Dominic); and ex-brother-in-law Danny for their contributions and long memories. I thank them here because they may not be speaking to me after depicting our father, Frank, as the monster he may or may not have been. I love you, Dad. I just wish we had had more time together. I know you would have been proud.

Most importantly, to my mother, Mary (you know, "when I find myself in times of trouble"), thanks for all the love and hugs. I'll tell you, when you are in those arms it's the safest place to be in the world.

When I started on this project, one of my concerns was that delving into the past would be a painful reminder of how awfully old I had gotten. You know what? Reliving that glorious age of TV and radio sports along with all of the terrific on-air co-workers and cohorts, Hollywood celebs, and girlfriends helped me feel young again. Mind you, I lie about my age, so even younger than that.

Finally, to everyone who was along for the ride and supported me through it all, I am personally coming to your house to bake you my famous five-cheese lasagna. Congratulations! Hugs and knishes.

📚 dundurn.com   📷 dundurnpress

🐦 @dundurnpress   📌 dundurnpress

📘 dundurnpress   ✉ info@dundurn.com

FIND US ON NETGALLEY & GOODREADS TOO!

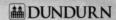

🏛 DUNDURN